HONOURABLY WOUNDED

Honourably Wounded

Stress among Christian Workers

MARJORY F. FOYLE

MONARCH
BOOKS
Oxford, UK, and Grand Rapids, Michigan, USA

First published in the UK in 1987 by Monarch Books
(a publishing imprint of Lion Hudson plc),
Wilkinson House, Jordan Hill Road, Oxford OX2 8DR.
Tel: +44 (0)1865 302750 Fax: +44 (0)1865 302757
Email: monarch@lionhudson.com
www.lionhudson.com

Revised edition 2001. Reprinted 2009.

ISBN 978-1-85424-543-4 (UK)
ISBN 978-0-8254-6333-4 (USA)

Distributed by:
UK: Marston Book Services Ltd, PO Box 269,
Abingdon, Oxon OX14 4YN;
USA: Kregel Publications, PO Box 2607
Grand Rapids, Michigan 49501.

This book has been printed on paper and board independently
certified as having come from sustainable forests.

British Library Cataloguing Data
A catalogue record for this book is available
from the British Library.

Printed and bound in England by CPI Cox & Wyman.

*This book is dedicated to my family
who have supported me
through fifty years of expatriate service.*

Acknowledgements

I wish to express my gratitude to the editor and staff of Monarch Books, to the many people worldwide who have given their time to discuss personnel problems with me, and to the personnel themselves who have talked with me, answered my many questions, filled in questionnaires, and provided hospitality and care during my overseas work. My prayer is that this book will support them in their work, and help them to maintain their health and well-being in difficult circumstances.

I am also deeply indebted to the Panahpur Trust for travel and research grants which have enabled me to do the work God entrusted to me, and to those who have read chapters of the book in manuscript and made many helpful suggestions.

Contents

Introductory Notes

Examples used in this book do not describe any one person. Details have been altered, identities disguised, and problems of several people combined into one story to preserve confidentiality. They should not, therefore, be identified by any one individual as their personal story.

In preparing the second edition, **terminology** has been a problem. The use of the terms 'old and new sending countries' are based on a recent research project on missionary attrition, 'old sending countries' indicating those with a longer history of modern missions, and 'new sending countries' those with a younger history (Taylor, 1997). The same division has been utilised throughout this book.

The second problem has been what to call the people I am writing about. Due to the changing face of missions, use of the word 'missionary' is becoming rare in many old sending countries. As Bryan Knell wrote, 'the word missionary has passed its sell-by date and is now more unhelpful than helpful', but so far nothing acceptable to everybody has been found to replace it. This current uncertainty has led to a plethora of different terminology. During my travels in 41 different countries to consult with mission personnel, I have found that in most of the new sending countries and many of the old sending countries the term 'missionary' is still used. In other countries such as the UK, the word 'mission partner' is more common, signifying the co-operative relationship between the sending agency and the host country. However, to make things even more confusing, in one very large organisation the overseas national host is called 'the partner', and those who go are the 'personnel'. Other agencies use the rather clumsy term 'church-related volunteer expatriates', or simply 'expatriate' or 'personnel' or 'cross-cultural worker'. This last term is perhaps the most useful, for it indicates not only those who go overseas to serve the Lord but also the many others who remain within their own countries to serve people from other cultures, although they may move interstate.

Because of this confusion I have decided to use the term 'missionary', but must be forgiven for using the other terms on occasions. In the context in which I am writing they all mean the same thing: Christian people sponsored by their home churches to serve God cross-culturally, whether or not this involves crossing national boundaries. In addition I shall use the term 'sending agency' to indicate the old 'missionary society', this being common practice in many countries.

The final semantic problem concerns the absence of a **common pronoun** for both sexes in the English language. Therefore, unless I am dealing specifically with male or female problems, 'him' also means 'her', and vice versa.

References. There are many ways of inserting references, but in this book I have decided to use one of the standard methods. They will be inserted in alphabetical order at the back of the book, and will be indicated in the text by a name and date in brackets. As an example, if I write 'it has been found that missionaries have fun' (Foyle, 1999), it means 'look me up at the back of the book, note the date, and find out where I wrote about it!'

Statistical significance. Many people, and I am one of them, thoroughly dislike statistical terms, so by way of introduction, whenever the term 'significant' is used it merely means important, more likely to be true than not.

Introduction

This book deals with some of the stresses experienced by mobile Christian workers serving cross-culturally. Included within this major category are three groups of people. The first is those who feel God has called them to serve as expatriates, which involves crossing national boundaries into a totally new pattern of life. The second group includes those who remain within their own countries but cross State boundaries, which often involves adapting to a new language and unfamiliar local culture despite being of the same nationality. In the third group are those who remain more or less within their familiar environment, but because they work mainly with immigrants and their descendants, they have to familiarise themselves with the customs and background cultures of the people they serve. In addition, past experience has shown that some who are not working cross-culturally and are not actually involved in mission have found areas of the book relevant to their needs. My basic prayer as I write is that anyone who reads this book will find it helpful.

I have aimed at keeping the book both descriptive and practical in approach — without this balance it would be unproductive and possibly threatening. It is not intended to be a textbook, hence such advice as is given is aimed at practical self-help rather than a detailed technical description of how to do things like selecting missionaries. I have tried to maintain the original easily readable approach so that it does not become boring. Some areas are inevitably a bit complicated, but if the reader perseveres, hopefully the writing will become a little more exciting after a few pages.

The publishers have asked me to provide a little **autobiographical information** to complete the introduction. I became a Christian as a medical student in 1942. Initially my conversion was a somewhat emotional affair, but in God's goodness the next day the Travelling Secretary of the (then) IVF came to our city and took me out to tea. We sat for four hours while she taught me that there was more to it than emotion, and that biblical understanding was also involved. Naturally, we kept one eye on the waitress and ordered more tea whenever she looked unhappy. I went back to the same city recently, went to the same seat in the same café, ordered tea and sat thanking God for all he had done for me during the past 50 years.

Shortly after this famous tea, I was reading a book about Dame Mary Scharleib, a renowned British woman doctor who was concerned at the needs of Indian women prevented for religious reasons from being treated by male doctors. This was her motivation for graduating as a doctor, and as I read it I realised that this was to be my own future life. Accordingly, after graduation as a doctor and gaining experience in UK hospitals plus two years Bible training, I joined what is now called Interserve and went to India. There I worked for five years in women's hospitals, five in the exciting newly opened work in Nepal, and a further five back in the same hospital in India until it closed down. During this last period I had a time of illness for which I am deeply grateful. What I learnt during that time set me on a new pattern of personal development that is still continuing. I began to understand that dedication and commitment to God, while essential if we want to go on with God, do not mean wholesale denial of the real person within, but provide us with freedom to expand, develop, and enjoy the good things God has created.

When I had recovered I was unexpectedly offered the opportunity to do postgraduate training in psychiatry. I felt this was the right move, and so from 1965–1969 did my resident training and the requisite studies in the UK, and obtained my qualification. By that time I was 48 years old, but felt God was calling me to return to India to work as a psychiatrist at Nur Manzil Psychiatric Centre, Lucknow, founded by Dr E Stanley Jones. I joined the staff in 1969 on the strict understanding that I would never be asked to become Director. In God's humorous wisdom, I became Director in 1972, and remained in that position for nearly ten years. Interestingly, nothing is ever wasted. What I had found so difficult in an administrative and clinical leadership position in the women's hospital now became very useful in my new job, and where I had failed the first time I could now do better because of what I had learned first time round. I still made lots of mistakes, but kept my sense of humour and coped.

In 1981, when I became an old age pensioner (60 years old!), I retired from Nur Manzil, but was sure God had another task for me. He presented this to me as a sort of blue print one evening in New Delhi. I was to start travelling, to give lectures in simple psychiatry to rural mission hospitals, and to start caring for the needs of national and expatriate personnel. I expected this programme to last for a year, but instead it has continued for nearly twenty. In these years I have concentrated predominantly on the mental health needs of expatriate personnel through visiting, lecturing, writing the first edition of *Honourably Wounded*, and helping to open Interhealth, a London-based clinic for expatriate volunteers.

Over the past six years I have been able to return to academic work. I discovered in professional literature that there are other groups such as business companies, the armed forces and secular volunteer agencies that are also concerned with expatriate mental health, and are facing the same issues as the Christian groups. Some of the papers indicated to me that we in mission have knowledge that needs to be shared, and the best way to do this was by careful and sensitive writing for professional journals. I also felt it was important that Christian workers continue to ensure that their work and knowledge is sound by submitting it to peer approval. With this in mind I combined travelling with a long-standing research programme, and so far have published one paper in a professional journal and successfully completed a doctoral thesis on Expatriate Mental Health for the University of London, material from which will be incorporated in this book. Please be reassured that in preparation of such publications I have been careful to write about principles of expatriate care rather than particular circumstances, so that sensitive issues and personal confidentiality have been protected.

Finally, when I was asked to prepare a revised second edition of *Honourably Wounded*, I realised that God was again calling me to travel so that I could modernise my knowledge. I have spent the last twelve months visiting major mission-related conferences in nine countries, at which I met personnel and leaders from many different countries and was able to sit quietly and talk with them about current personnel and leadership problems.

If I could try to work out what has been the most meaningful thing I have learnt, I would settle for the fact that the promises of God are personal for each individual. I now understand that if God promises to provide for our physical, mental, spiritual and any other needs, he will keep his word. We may not always like the way he meets the need, but he will certainly do so. As I get older and maybe a bit senile, I pray that God will constantly remind me of his promises and faithfulness until I go on to the next bit, the heavenly experience.

CHAPTER

1

The Changing Face of Missions

Someone has said that 'change is now the only constant'. It is therefore important to look at this as a preliminary to the rest of the book. Following my recent travels I feel there are four major changes in mission that need to be considered: the impact of generational psychology on selection, care and administration of personnel; changes related to duration of service; the growing importance of holistic member-care world wide, and change in the social backgrounds of new personnel. Some of these will be outlined briefly at this point, and the remainder in the relevant chapters.

Generational psychology

Generational psychology tries to explain the differences between generations partly as the result of global mega-events such as the World Wars, the Vietnam war, and the collapse of communism. Sine (1991) described three successive generations by the terms booster, baby boomers and buster, each of them having different characteristics. This work has been excellently outlined by Donovan and Myors in *Too Valuable to Lose* (Taylor, ed., 1997). In a nutshell, the boosters form the traditional school of expatriates, hard working, conscientious, strong in institutional loyalty and led by strong, rather authoritarian figures. These provided the 'model of missionary service still followed by traditional missionary societies today'. The next generation, the baby boomers, were the idealistic, questioning protesters, with a strong feeling of personal responsibility and respect for all who do their own thing. The most modern of this group were the busters, who because they came

17

from a fragmented society tended to look to each other for relationships, to try to live broadly balanced lives, and to reject pressure to follow an established pattern just because it had always been done that way.

Tony Horsfall (personal communication) reminds us that generational study is not an exact science, and it has certainly proved difficult to discover whether these categories were based solely on research in the US or were internationally valid. I have, however, found the same concepts present in all four continents in which I have travelled, although their terminology and cultural expression may be different. These new concepts have profoundly influenced selection and management of mission partners and have been found useful to agencies in their efforts to select and nurture new personnel in cross-cultural ministry.

Together with the work on generational psychology based on mega-events, it has become apparent that there is also a change in how people think, their general philosophy of life. This has led to the creation of terms such as generation X, modernism and post-modernism. Just to make things more complicated, there is now a post-post modernist group emerging, and a generation Y that is characterised by a more optimistic outlook than generation X. This has been attributed to the new millennium, a time of hope and of change. (To avoid confusion I shall use only the term generation X, or GenX in this book, the other groups being too long to insert every time!). To put things shortly, the philosophy has changed from acceptance to rejection of authority, from a scientific approach to a search for reality through music and poetry, and in the West a marked increase in tribalistic thinking and a search for community and relationships. The need for relationship and community is related to the fractured social backgrounds of many nations, but this fracturing has had some positive spin-offs. Many of the new generation are remarkable people. They are survivors, many of whom became converted to community before coming to Christ. They have learned to be flexible, and to cope with change usually through the strength of their community. This one sees in the streets of London, where the homeless often form a spontaneous community whose membership fluctuates but which endures through change.

It is important also to remember that the new generation is preoccupied with 'stories'. Individual stories are more important than the meta-narrative, the overall big story. Every life has a personal story which needs to be fulfilled, and this idea partially explains the response of the young when they are asked to do something — 'it's not my scene, man'; it is not part of their story, so they don't feel the need to get involved. The outcome is that the current story is more important than history, and what is being experienced is more important than revealed truth. This of course has a profound influence on teaching the history of the Bible as a background to the story of our salvation. It has necessitated a totally new approach to teaching the integrity and authority of the Bible, and it demands almost a quantum leap for generation X to adjust to the possibility of a reliable body of truth, to a mega-story from God, and not just to the events in an individual life-story.

The end result is a series of significant differences between this generation and the older ones. The older generation responded to a task, the new responds to a relationship. They will ask themselves how they feel about it — do they feel they are simply being used to accomplish a task or will relationships be helped? The older has difficulty moving internationally, the new accomplishes this with ease, but due to their mobile habits have more difficulty staying in one place than the older group. The older generation did not make frequent job changes, the new one does, often going through six to seven jobs in their early working years. In the sphere of missions, this tendency is revealed in the growth of short-term appointments and loss of long-term workers, the new generation operating on job changes, moving on, and developing through freedom to change. This is in line with their motivation for short-term, cross-cultural work. They want to do something practical and to accomplish something during their time overseas, and they want it to be church-related. They want to 'rethink the Church into the missional community, not an institution' (personal communication) and are little interested in the old-style mission institutions unless they are a part of the local church outreach. This of course is related to the 'instant generation', which is accustomed to speedy results to their demands. Which McDonalds they hang out in depends on how quick the service is, and how undemanding the place is.

Generationally it is harder for them to operate on the old concept of constantly sowing seed and perhaps never seeing a result. Hence the enormous growth in both secular and Christian organisations of short-term, work-oriented projects which enable the young to see what they have done. Their usual motivation is to empower and support nationals rather than to sit in a job slot, and seeing the completion of the project they came to help in is what satisfies them. A letter from a generation Xer in November 1999, quoted by Tiplady (2000), is revealing:

> Today's world is a temporary place. There is hardly a job that comes with long-term security these days, but mission agencies still talk in terms of long-term and short-term, with short-term as somehow lesser. But people live in an environment in which they are expected to move on after a time, otherwise they are seen as no longer fresh, in touch, cutting edge. It is seen as a necessary movement in order to gain more experience, to be more employable, more relevant to the work... There is a view that says those interested in mission today are not as committed as previous generations because they will not offer their lives in long-term service. I believe this to be incorrect, and see many who are committed to living one day at a time for God, reflecting the temporariness of life and its situations. This could actually be seen as a healthier more honest commitment.

There are many refreshing aspects to this generational change, and the expressions of faith used by the young are delightful. I was recently at a rather solemn conference where a young music group led the singing. One day the leader was asked to pray before the talk began and he said 'Thanks God, we've had a good sing, now help us as we hear all the other stuff.' I don't know what the eminent speaker thought of the reduction of his paper to 'other stuff', but the audience was delighted with this fresh approach. There is a sincerity and genuineness about the new generations that gives confidence to those they work with, even though some of their trends are decidedly startling. At a recent graduation ceremony at London University I was astounded to see young people going on stage to receive their degrees wearing academic gowns, dirty jeans and T-shirts, and dirty thonged beach sandals or huge macho boots with no socks. Then I remembered it takes all sorts to make a world!

How then do we react to all this confusing theory and wholesale changes in the familiar set-up? Under no circumstances should modernisation programmes be seen as a negation of all that has been achieved by the older generations. Modernisation is essential to meet modern needs, but must incorporate all generations of missionaries. It is indeed wonderful to see the old and new generations working together in many countries, and establishing new methods of working to fulfill the task the Lord has given them. These include new strategies for reaching the younger generation with the gospel and then mobilising them for cross-cultural service, as well as the modernisation of methods, principles and practices, and overseas care of personnel.

In practical terms it has been found better to recruit teams, or to train for working in teams. 'Beware of the post-modernist loner' is an important truth to remember, for they are acting against their own generational culture. Some of the younger generation have remarkable entrepreneurial skills which need to be harnessed for use in fulfilling the missionary commission. Principles of agency practice have had to be adapted to suit the short-term service pattern on which the new generation tends to operate. This has resulted in the closure of some long-established institutions overseas which for various valid reasons had not been nationalised. Instead, expatriate personnel are increasingly being utilised for tasks seen by the national church as important, such as sustainable development programmes based on local needs. Training and teaching has a high priority, skilled expatriate personnel offering their skills to the church for a short-term appointment in many differing fields. Short-termers often have a remarkable gift for working with the local church in evangelistic, practical and spiritual growth projects and are often much loved by the time they move on.

Catering for the needs of the younger generation does not imply that they do not need to learn discipline and endurance, faith, and tolerance of frustration. They do, but it needs to be taught in a different way, through stories, role play, discussion and multimedia-derived academic knowledge. These then may become the introduction to the practise of personal devotions and Bible study which are so important during cross-cultural ministry.

Change in duration of service

As explained above, the well-understood 'long term' and 'short term' have undergone a radical change, and there has been a huge swing to shorter periods. Average terms now range from experience groups (one to two weeks), short term (two weeks to two years), and long term (two to six years), these often being people who have paid off their study debts and have had some work experience. There are still some who become long long term. An interesting group is the 'creative access group', also called 'the finishers'. These are people aged about 40 who leave their employment early to spend the rest of their working lives in overseas service. There are others who after retirement at 55-60 spend a few years serving cross-culturally, their success depending on the degree of adaptability and humility they display. 'If they think they have all the answers this disempowers and upsets the local nationals,' a prominent leader said to me, but the overall impression is that they do very well indeed.

It is interesting that the post-modernistic generation has been described as finding it easier to transfer to longer-term service because they are more adventurous. Longer-term personnel are still very much valued, the duration of their service providing them with a unique opportunity to acquire language fluency and cultural understanding, these being so valuable in cross-cultural work that missions are now having to rethink how best they can give short-termers some opportunity to acquire at least a little of both.

Change in personnel care

This will be outlined throughout the book, but here it should be mentioned that the importance of holistic personnel care has become widely recognised and developed. Through the initiative of the World Evangelical Fellowship, Global Connections, Lausanne movement and similar organisations, the formation of member-care groups world wide has re-emphasised the importance of caring for personnel, and resulted in such care being set up in the very early stages of missionary development in the new sending countries.

Perhaps the most important issue in personnel care remains the question of accountability. To whom are missionaries accountable, the church or the sending agency or both? Many young people prefer to be sent overseas by their own local church. The difficulties as well as strengths of this will be discussed later on, but the immediate question is who is in charge of them overseas, the local bishop or church pastor, or the overseas mission leader? Who is responsible for setting up the care they may need overseas, the local church authorities or the sending agency? In some areas of Canada, for example, the pattern is changing, with churches demanding 100% accountability, and being responsible for multicultural team training within the church and provision of pastoral care. At a recent conference someone said 'mission agencies need to be re-invented', thus adding to the general sense of change that is in the air. These important questions remains open for discussion, and the new century may well see a massive shift in emphasis. My own view is that partnership is the key, a unity of purpose between the individual, their church, the sending agency and the skill and expertise of both national hosts overseas and designated overseas agency leadership. This is fraught with dangers, but if it works is magnificent.

CHAPTER
2

Understanding Stress

Cross-cultural partnership is an enriching experience. This is why so many partners at the end of their service say they are glad they did it, and have no regrets.

It is, however, true that on the usual stress scales such as the Holmes Rahe, partners habitually operate at well over the danger level, and yet manage to do this and survive. Dodds and Schafer (1995) found in one survey that cross-cultural workers experience about 600 points of stress each year, well over the accepted norm. Survival may well be related to the fact that many training colleges spend much time talking to candidates about stress and how to handle it. While this excellent policy needs to be maintained, a few are in danger of over-emphasising stress and minimising the positives of cross-cultural partnership. This can result in a negative conditioning which causes personnel to go to their location expecting the worst, not the best. Equal emphasis should therefore be placed on the possible gains, such as the enlarging experience of serving God in the place he has chosen, learning to live with him and others through good times and bad, developing unusual professional skills, learning about community, and the marvellous experience of living in, and integrating with, a totally new culture. This will keep stress-management training in a healthy perspective.

I have often been asked why a book about cross-cultural stress is necessary, since everyone has to cope with many changes when transferred to a new job in a different area of their own countries. Moving cross-culturally, especially when expatriation is involved, adds an extra dimension which demands a massive adjustment. Every aspect of personal and family life is affected. Language, food, climate, housekeeping, job patterns, local politics, geography and history, the impact of the move on children, separation from parents, siblings, friends and church, are all exchanged for a new situation which has to be organised and assimilated before people can begin to feel at home. It is the totality of the impact of the unfamiliar that some people find stress-inducing. We can thank God that it is inaccurate to say that all cross-cultural workers feel stressed all the time. Most of them cope amazingly well once the first few weeks are over, experiencing no more than the usual stress of starting any new job combined with a Christian ministry.

The reality of partner stress opens up a spiritual problem. There has always been a vocal minority that claims Christians should not feel stressed. In the old days to acknowledge that you felt anxious, depressed or stressed-out indicated spiritual backsliding, failure in your devotional life or your Christian service. As a result, many people kept quiet about it and just tried to cope. There is little evidence in Scripture for this belief. Both Jesus and Paul were careful to make stress positive as well as negative. Jesus warned us that 'in this world you will have trouble', also translated as 'tribulation' or 'pressure' (John 16:33), but went on to say that we should take heart because he had overcome this on our behalf. In other words, we shall experience pressure but it will not destroy us, he will bring us through. Paul indicates that coping with stress is a recurrent problem for Christians when he says that despite his own period of discouragement and despair, God 'has delivered us from such a deadly peril, and he will deliver us. On him we have set our hope that he will continue to deliver us, as you help us by your prayers' (2 Corinthians 1:10–11). What he means is that we may be stressed out, almost to the point of despair, but God will deliver us, even if we have to wait for it, and even if the problems return again for a time. This deliverance does not always mean resolution of the problem, but release from the paralysing feeling that we can't cope any more.

When we are stressed-out we feel almost ashamed to call it suffering, it seems so petty, but as we experience acute homesickness overseas, or get more and more stressed by a work and domestic overload in a very difficult expatriate situation, God in his love understands that some of us really suffer, despite others apparently taking it all in their stride. I suppose I was homesick for the whole of my 30 years overseas, despite the many positives, and I certainly suffered from occupational overload. This finally helped me to learn something very important. Paul wrote in Philippians 1:29, 'It has been *granted* to you on behalf of Christ not only to believe on him, but also to suffer for him.' When we feel stressed and battered by our service for God it does not feel like a privilege and we may not understand it to be so for many years. In the end, however, we see that carrying this suffering for a period of time has done something positive in God's kingdom. What has been achieved varies, but usually includes an element of personal growth and enhancement of the ministry God has given us in this world. So let us take heart, for 'we are hard pressed on every side, but not crushed; perplexed, but not in despair; persecuted, but not abandoned', the purpose being that Jesus' life may be revealed in our mortal bodies (2 Corinthians 4:8–9,11).

In order to help us handle stress we need to understand what it is, how it develops, why we react as we do, and how we can learn to cope better.

Definitions of stress

The word stress was first used in the 14th century to indicate hardship or adversity, but by the 20th century it had become an important engineering term connected with the strength of structures like bridges. My architect brother tells me their security was ensured by making them capable of withstanding 5 times the expected load! In modern times it has become attached to human problems, and at present there are at least 9 different models of human stress. In my opinion the easiest and most useful definition comes from Donovan who wrote 'Stress is the normal protective response of the body to a perceived significant threat to the status quo' (1991).

Components of stress

Three different things are important in considering stress. The first is **the event itself**. This is usually something external to the individual, and out of personal control, both factors determining whether or not it will be stressful. It is important to remember that events which we can control may make us feel very anxious, but they are not as stressful as when we can do nothing about the situation. This is the common experience of expatriates in some violent countries. They live with the normal concern about the possibility of being attacked, but it becomes stressful only when it actually occurs, for there is nothing practical that can be done to control things when the gun is actually pointing at you! Similarly, lack of control is a major feature in the stress experienced when our aircraft is grounded for emergency repairs, and we are due to speak at a meeting soon after we were originally scheduled to arrive. It is also a feature in the stress experienced by being transferred to a new location without being consulted, the denial of personal control creating much stress to the person concerned.

The second component of stress is **appraisal of the event** as potentially harmful to us or not. As Gish wrote, 'Stress depends in part on whether an individual appraises a given situation as benign, neutral or stressful. Even appraising a situation as stressful does not necessarily result in distress for those who view it as a challenge. However, if the person sees harm, loss or threat in the stress, the result is often very different' (1983).

An important ingredient of appraisal is our *personal filter* (Donovan 1991). This has many components such as family background and genetic influence, culture, personality, age, physical health, past experience and personal values, but a most important part is the question section. The filter will ask,

'What is the significance of this for me?' and, 'What will I need to do?' Filters are unique, hence we need to remember that individuals react differently. This is why someone involved in an early-life car accident will experience much more stress during a later-life narrow escape from an accident than others without the same history.

Possibly the best example of an event and it's appraisal is the experience of people living in mountainous areas. I recently discussed this with someone from Switzerland. She told me that on occasions they see a mass of snow collecting high up in the mountain, and before the authorities can get up there to deal with it, the snow begins to fall creating a dangerous avalanche. If it looks likely to land on their house, the mind appraises the avalanche as potentially dangerous to both life and property, and because there is nothing they can do to stop it the lack of personal control might create acute stress. However, at this stage of appraisal the filter lets off an alarm bleep which moves us on to the third component of stress, the **coping methods** employed to deal with the situation.

Two common coping methods are used. The first is *problem solving*, the method we may utilise when we see the snow start to fall. We yell to everyone in the house to get out, grab the baby and run. The problem is solved, we are breathless but not severely distressed. Should the situation be totally out of our control, however, severe stress can develop. Suppose we were on the other side of the river when the avalanche began, with no mobile phone, and could only watch helplessly as the snow slid down. Our inability to do anything to control the situation would certainly make it maxi-stressful.

A second example will explain what happens when we can take action to avoid the problem. I was walking along a narrow path in a river gorge in Nepal. Suddenly a stone dropped at my feet, and I did not think anything of it until the man behind me gave me a big push and yelled in Nepali, 'Run!' I joined all the other runners, and just after we got away the whole hillside came down. I never felt at all stressed by the event and did not fear going through the gorge again, because action had been taken, personal control utilised, and safety ensured.

It is interesting that subsequent problem-solving may preserve us from persistent damaging stress, although will not remove grief. This was the experience of an Eastern colleague who was caught up in a very violent situation. He himself managed to hide behind a pillar where he was safe, but he witnessed all his staff and patients being murdered and everything he had worked for destroyed. In the aftermath he managed to cope by problem-solving, which is not the same as pointless hyperactivity to blot out the memories. He rebuilt a small patient service in the damaged hospital, gradually got a staff together, and by working together to solve the huge problems they all survived as individuals, despite the psychological scars they would carry for life.

The second method of coping is *palliation*, which indicates the things we do to make the current stress bearable. Withdrawal into helplessness is a great danger to us all, and we need actively to search for ways of palliation to enable us to preserve our psychological integrity. Good methods include talking it over, taking advice, taking active steps to handle what is possible, leaning hard on God and waiting patiently for him to act, finding something that you enjoy doing and if possible taking short breaks from the situation. Bad methods are what has been called 'the ostrich principle' (pretending the situation will go away if we don't look at it), or taking drugs or too much alcohol, or taking it out on everyone else by quarrelling and being difficult.

Sometimes we may develop stress-related symptoms such as anxiety. These indicate that our coping methods are beginning to fail, but we should not automatically blame ourselves. Some things are so traumatic or so long standing that at times the only possible coping strategy is to do nothing but wait and see how it works out, and this creates much distress. During my professional career overseas I was once falsely accused of making a serious mistake in my work, as have other missionaries.

In reality, what had happened was unavoidable, but as director of the unit I was targeted and accused of an ever-increasing list of things, none of which I had done. In situations like this one has no personal control, and can only get good advice, tell the truth, read the Psalms and ride out the storm trusting in God to bring it to a safe end. By the end my coping methods were beginning to fail, but I survived with only a few symptoms which healed up as time went by. No human is superhuman, and inevitably long-drawn-out stressful events will take their toll. We can only aim at limiting the personal damage as much as possible. It is comforting to know that we tend to improve as we get older. Recently I was stranded with a colleague in an airport overseas and we did not know either where we were supposed to go or how to get anywhere so late at night. To my surprise my friend told me later that I had handled it better than he did. Progress at last!

Stress reactions

Hans Seyle (1974) described three reactions to stress. They are automatic, instinctive and usually occur without our noticing them very much. I have found it helpful in understanding stress to spread these reactions out and examine them so that we can learn from them what is normal and what is not, and how we can cope better.

Stage 1: Fright, the alarm reaction

This is one of the most useful reactions in the body. A sudden emergency occurs, and the body instinctively prepares for action by pouring out hormones and chemicals into the blood stream. Physically we are aware of this by rising pulse, cold skin, cold sweat, deeper breathing, apprehension and tension. As an example, I was once being driven to a conference centre to give lectures, and we had to go up a mountain. The snow had fallen unexpectedly and there were no snow tyres on the car. Towards the end of the journey there was a hair-raising last bend on which we got stuck, so the driver had to slither about and reverse round it, right on the edge of a steep drop. Stage 1 reaction worked overtime, I was sweating, cold, apprehensive, breathing deeply, and my pulse rate rose to something phenomenal. But this does not indicate abnormality. It shows that the body was prepared for action, to jump out of the car if it began to go over the edge.

We need to thank God for this reaction. Christians do not always understand this. Recently a missionary was sitting in the church vestry waiting to take part in a large service. She was feeling nervous, and told the pastor so. In a rather severe tone he said, 'But it's all of God, isn't it?' Of course it is, but God will use normal human reactions to help us perform better in difficult tasks, and one of these is the stress alarm reaction. This enables mothers to leap up from their chairs to rescue toddlers getting into dangerous situations, and then to sink back breathless waiting for the pulse to calm down. While waiting to take an oral exam we experience alarm reactions such as sweating and rapid pulse, and we should welcome them as a mechanism inbuilt into our bodies to help us perform better. Where it goes wrong is if people misunderstand the normality of the reaction, and say that because they get nervous beforehand they are failing to trust God. There is no point in telling yourself that if you trusted more you would not have these reactions. If you did not have them you would be either dead or a vegetable, for they are a God-given mechanism to prepare us to handle danger and difficulty.

Over-strong alarm reactions are related to personality type, but they can also can occur in periods where there is much environmental insecurity. In the expatriate situation during periods of political turmoil, a tree branch banging on the front door will alarm us because we interpret it as the rebels coming into our house. Poor support systems, or a threat to the family may also precipitate over-strong reactions. These need to be recognised for what they are, understandable hyper-arousal to prepare us to deal with possible difficult situations. They should not, however, be allowed to continue. If we are constantly being over-alarmed we should get out of the situation for a time, get rested, and then decide what to do.

Stage 2: Fight or flight, possible coping methods

Sometimes we get into situations where the stress goes on for a long time. We have had the initial helpful fright reaction, which we have dealt with, and sometimes that is the end of the matter. At other times, however, the stress extends for a longer period. The example used in the original description was two dogs facing each other. Both experience fright, with hackles rising and tails swishing, and they are growling fiercely as they face each other. Then for some reason the situation terminates in one of two ways, they either leap on each other and fight it out, or one shows healthy flight by turning tail and running away.

In long-continued stressful situations humans also have the same reactions, but in these circumstances we do not usually act instinctively, we make a choice. Either we decide to stay on and fight the stress (healthy fight), or we feel God wants us to leave the situation (healthy flight). As an example, a group of people were working in a location with severe interpersonal problems in the staff, difficulty with the administration, and a somewhat hostile national group in the area. Several workers developed symptoms of distress, they were taken out and new people sent in, with similar results. Finally a consensus of opinion decided to pull everyone out, to let the location lie fallow for a time and then see if it could be reopened under a better system. This was sensible management of a difficult and prolonged high-stress situation, based on patience, prayer, a sense of guidance by the Holy Spirit, discussion and personnel agreement.

If we decide God wants us to stay on and fight it out, certain things happen to us. Because we have made a decision our emotion is reduced and the turmoil in our minds gets less. We learn a huge amount through the experience, and find it exceedingly useful to us in future. However, we often feel very fatigued, and it is wise to cater for this. We need to build into our schedule rest periods, regular breaks, and the use of personal treats, things we love to do but tend to ration for various reasons. However, this is not the time to indulge in things that endanger our health such as eating too many chocolate bars. I love chocolate, and while writing my thesis began to eat too much of it and began to gain weight. So I went back to restrictions, one small chocolate bar every Sunday with an occasional lapse if someone was unkind enough to give me a box.

During healthy fight we need to ask God for ordinary human courage, because staying to fight things out is often very difficult. I once met a highly trained professional woman whose husband was offered a job in a strictly Muslim country. There would be no role for her other than the traditional hidden wife, and it demanded careful thought. They decided to go, and she summoned up all her courage and wisdom to make her life bearable. She accepted as her role 'the woman in the back of the house', supported her husband, got to know her women neighbours, developed a formidable grasp of the language, kept her mind alert by correspondence courses, and finally became a valuable resource person on the needs of Islamic women. Her courageous decision paid off. Nowadays of course she could also use the Internet, a God-given way of keeping the mind going.

Healthy flight is a different matter. Usually we begin to think we should leave because of a growing conviction in our mind that this is right. But we should never act on this alone. We need to discuss it with reliable people, and to take our time making the decision if external circumstances permit. It may be sensible to take a short break from the work before making the final decision. Most importantly, we should never decide when we are emotionally upset. I have known young language students go to their leaders in floods of tears within a week of arrival saying, 'I need to go home immediately, I should not have come here.' To leave at this time would have been an emotional not a rational decision, and it is better to urge the distressed person to wait, take a little break, think and pray carefully about it and talk things over with friends and leaders. All of these may help them to settle down and decide to stay.

In a few cases returning home may be the right course of action. It is of course imperative that local and home-based leaders be consulted as soon as possible. One of the things they will need to do is assess the general and mental health of the person concerned, the best pointers being evidence of ability to think about the decision rationally, to weigh up the pros and cons, and to postpone action until the matter is clarified. This was a situation that faced a young man who went to a rather remote location. Shortly after arrival he became concerned about a matter he had left unfinished in his home country, and was convinced that he should return and settle this before starting a career overseas. This was highly unusual, but his leadership handled it most wisely, talking and praying with him and finally allowing him to return home after only one month in the host country. On his return home he settled the complicated unfinished personal business that had troubled him, although it took three years to do so, and ultimately returned to his original location where he made a fine contribution. It is noteworthy that his agency and church supported and encouraged him throughout the whole difficult period, and he returned overseas a stronger and wiser person.

Common problems during stage 2 stress
The first of these is the many **questions** that come into our minds such as, 'Does God care, and if so why doesn't he do something?' These sort of questions may be worse if we are from an insecure background and have had poor parental care. We thought we had found a true carer when we believed in Jesus, but now he doesn't seem to be doing anything at all to help us. We should never be ashamed of our questions and doubts, and never think we can hide them from God who knows all about them anyway. In these circumstances it is a great relief to learn to talk with him freely and openly about

everything, and to ask him to help us understand what is going on. One of the most helpful verses in this situation is Hebrews 10:36 — 'You need to persevere [have patience and endurance] so that when you have done the will of God you will receive what he has promised.' Another good one is James 1:4 which says, 'Perseverance must finish its work so that you may be mature and complete, not lacking anything.'

It is during this sort of experience that we really grow in confidence in God and his promises to us, but we also find it much harder to pray and to do regular Bible study. I have found a little book from Scripture Gift Mission called *Words of Comfort* most helpful. The short verse and prayer given for each day provide enough spiritual food to carry on till the worst is over.

The second problem that arises is **anger**. We should never wallow in self-condemnation if we have an occasional spiritual temper-tantrum and accuse God of not caring for us and not bothering to help us out of the situation. This is just a human being blowing a gasket and God fully understands our humanity. What is more important is understanding the truth about the more prolonged anger that is such a common component of stress.

There are two kinds of anger, creative and destructive, and Dr Dwight Carlson (1981) has explained these very clearly. He points out that the person most often angry in the Old Testament was God himself, 375 times in fact. He explains, and I agree, that anger is a neutral force that can be picked up and used constructively as creative anger, or used destructively to the detriment of those around us. Our Lord used creative anger during the cleansing of the temple, and much missionary and social enterprise was founded because of anger at injustice and ignorance.

Our difficulty is knowing whether our anger is creative or destructive. Generally speaking, creative anger has three important characteristics: appropriate emotions, realistic assessment of the situation, and wise decision-making. Destructive anger is the exact opposite, consisting of inappropriate emotions, unrealistic assessment of the situation, and poor decision-making. These need to be discussed so that we can learn more about our anger and become more able to keep it constructive — a lifelong task, let me add hastily!

Appropriate emotion implies control both in quality and quantity. The Gospels never indicate that after the cleansing of the temple Jesus continued to rage round inappropriately. He was seized with constructive anger, used it to do what had to be done and that was the end of it. Conversely, destructive anger produces emotional outbursts at the wrong time and in the wrong quantity. As someone said of a notoriously angry person, 'He should have given a mild reproof instead of which there was an atomic explosion.'

Certain things can trigger off destructive anger. One is fatigue. After a very arduous tour, a missionary went to the capital city of the country where she worked to take up residence for a year. She expected to find that a small suite of rooms had been prepared for her, and discovered the room was there but there was no water and no hope of any for some time. She was very tired and felt full of anger and resentment, which she handled by bursting into tears and crying for most of the morning, anger and weeping being part of the same package in women. Nothing much was achieved by such a reaction, but finally she calmed down, sorted out in her own mind why she felt so upset about an unavoidable circumstance, and was then able to organise a workable plan for going to her new home. The problem is that realistic assessment of the situation is difficult when destructive anger blows up. In reality the authorities had done everything they could to make the new home habitable, but the landlord and workmen had let them down, and they themselves were stuck in conference and could not leave.

Destructive anger also makes wise decision-making more difficult. In my hospital work I learned never to make important decisions when angry or emotionally upset, finding it better to let the emotions settle before deciding what to do. Some time ago a missionary going home on leave discussed his problems with me. He was angry about a lot of things, including his own inadequacies and could say little that was good about his term of service. After hearing the story and observing him carefully, I advised him to shelve it for the moment, to go home, sleep, eat, rest and enjoy whatever he liked to do for relaxation. Then he should take the problems out again and look at them. I told him to write to me at that time if there was anything I could do to help. When I heard from him he was much better, could see things in perspective, and found very little to be angry about.

In summary, when angry, wait. Constructive anger is retained during delay, destructive anger is not. Help the anger to settle down by going away from the scene if possible, and do something energetic which gets rid of anger. In India, if I was fed up with a committee wrangle I used to leave the room and go to the toilet, where I washed my hands VIGOROUSLY, calmed down, and then sailed back into the room smiling sweetly and saying, 'Where were we?' When you have cooled down, try to find the facts which may put a totally different slant on the situation. If there is much destructive anger floating around, postpone any action or decisions, for it is easy to make a mistake. Simply ask to have a little time to think it all over. Incidentally, this principle applies when helping people with their problems. There may be much obvious anger and emotion, and it is better to wait till this has all settled down before trying to get at the truth. This prevents misinterpretation of the situation and produces decisions based on reality rather than expressed emotion.

Stage 3. Unhealthy flight

The term unhealthy flight indicates flight into illness — the stress has become more than the person can cope with, and symptoms develop. Prolonged stress may interfere with the immune system so that the over-stressed fall prey to repeated recognisable physical illnesses, or to physical symptoms for which no other cause can be found than the stress they have endured.

In the psychological area, a whole group of illnesses called adjustment disorders has been separated out, indicating that they are the result of either prolonged or cataclysmic stress. The commonest of these is depression. Expatriates with adjustment disorders do not usually have anything in their personal or family histories that would indicate a liability to develop depression. The illness usually develops because they have experienced prolonged stress, and it has all got too much for them.

As an example I have permission to quote a true story, with some of the details disguised to prevent identification. A young man told me he had been appointed to a new job by his mission, but had not been consulted about it and felt from the beginning that the appointment was a mistake. Basically, he was being asked to leave a job he loved and to take on a work that he personally felt was no longer viable and should be closed down, but the leadership wanted to give it new management and try to keep it going. For various reasons he did not feel he should refuse the job, partly because there was quite a strong code of discipline and acceptance of decisions within the mission culture, although he did make vigorous protests. Initially he appeared to adapt quite well, and began to reorganise the work and to plan for its future, but inwardly he remained desperately unhappy. The old job he had loved was still asking to have him back, but his leadership was making no plans to enable him to do that. To try to make himself feel better he kept himself hyper-busy, and made frequent rededications of himself to God in an effort to make the present situation feel right, but nothing worked. For three years he managed, but then his coping mechanisms broke down. He began experiencing old problems from his earlier life that he thought were settled, he developed multiple physical illnesses, and finally became seriously depressed. In other words he was battered by what we would today call a 'triple whammy', the unwelcome job, the mental re-emergence of old personal problems and a depressive illness. Finally he had to go off work for many months but thanks to excellent treatment was able to get back to work in another area, and ultimately to enter a new life with many exciting challenges. In later years he often said that the depressive illness was the best thing that ever happened to him, for he had been able to take stock of himself, to deal with his past, and to find a new freedom to live for God and enjoy it at the same time!

This example raises the question, 'Why do breakdowns occur?' It is important that we do not read into this that everyone who is over-stressed will break down, or that those who do break down are weaker than others. That is not true. I believe there are two major reasons for breakdown. One is that partners are engaged in a spiritual battle against evil of many forms. Just as in human warfare there will be casualties, so it is in spiritual warfare, and God's servants can be wounded in mind, body or in their private lives. The tragedy is that for many years psychological casualties were not recognised as such and the victims feared (sometimes mistakenly, thank God) that when they went back home to their own church and family they would be considered failed missionaries, or 'returned empties' as someone said to me very bitterly. These days this attitude is very rare, those returning home with psychological damage usually being recognised as the 'honourably wounded', hence the title of this book. Of course it is not only those with psychological problems that are so named, casualties can occur for other reasons, but what should be understood is that there is no dishonour in this. People who break down physically or mentally, or have to return home early for other painful reasons which are usually beyond their control, often feel really guilty about it. They failed to do what the church had sent them to do. Let them take heart. They are God's honourably wounded, and when I lecture on this in the home countries I tell the church to polish the organ and get out the trumpets to welcome them home with love and honour!

The second reason for breakdown is related to overload in the personality structure, which will be discussed later on. In brief, certain personality-related factors are liable to blow up in the expatriate situation, and to make stage 3 stress more likely. Overloading with old broken relationships, or old negative emotions such as unresolved jealousy, bitterness and hatred may make it more difficult for people to cope with an overload of stress in the cross-cultural situation.

Perhaps the biggest question of all when considering break-down is 'Where is the power of God in this situation?' Paul said in Philippians 4:13, 'I can do everything through him who gives me strength', and in Ephesians 3:20 that God 'is able to do immeasurably more than all we ask or imagine, according to his power that is at work within us'. Why then the wounds, the breakdown, the hurt? I believe the answer lies in the story told by the recovered young man mentioned earlier which other people have also experienced. He, and many others, have real-ised that God wants the very best for us. He sees our old wounds and scars, when we ourselves are not always fully aware of the damaging impact they have had on us. He longs for us to be free, to be rid of the damage of the past and to begin to live in joy, in the excitement of being committed to his world, his service and his love. If we were healed instantly we would learn nothing and this would hamper our ministry to others. For this reason therefore I believe that God may allow us to be broken up. Jeremiah 18:4 tells us that when the vessel the potter made was marred, it was squashed down and remade into something beautiful. This is what can happen to us in a breakdown, or a long-drawn-out problem or other pain-ful experience. It gives us a chance to get good help, to look at ourselves, and to look to God to remake us even if it demands a bit of squashing down of the old. When the new begins to emerge, which is less fettered, less bound up by past or present trauma, then something wonderful has begun to happen. In my own experience I have had to learn some important les-sons, and even at the age of 79 God is still teaching me vital things. Some squashing down of the marred vessel has been involved which I have learnt to value, for it has proved to be the pathway to a very exciting life with God, despite the associated stress!

The final question is why some people are left with residual difficulties after a breakdown or other serious illness. No quick answer can be given to this enormous problem, but a global concept does help us. Suffering and anguish are part of this present world and will remain so until the Lord's return. Why certain people have residual disabilities or chronic untreatable illnesses I do not know, but I am able to hold onto the certainty that the God of love does know. Perhaps the biggest work those with residual difficulties have to do is to keep themselves without bitterness which, as Paul suggests in Hebrews 12:15, impacts adversely on many others. No one who suffers constantly can be without these feelings from time to time, but it is the retention of them as a fixed way of life that is so dangerous to our mental health. This will be discussed later, but here it should be said that it helps to accept the fact, often against serious odds, that God has no favourites, that he is lovingly concerned about us, and that he is in charge of us no matter what happens. It is right that people should protest against their disabilities, fight to overcome them, periodically shout and scream about them, but underlying all this must be the basic knowledge that ultimately God is in charge of us and he can be trusted to know what he is doing. I once heard an alternative free translation of 1 Peter 5:7 which is very helpful: 'Cast all your anxieties and cares on him because it matters to him about you' — and this is the only thing that can sustain us as we struggle with residual difficulties after a prolonged period of stress and depression.

Knowing when you are over-stressed

We need to understand what sort of symptoms should alert us to see the doctor. Remember that all of us have these from time to time, but if you have too many of them for too long you should have a check-up. I am indebted to my colleague Dr Ruth Fowke for this helpful list.

Physical effects
Tired all the time
Headaches
Backache
Constipation or diarrhoea
Sweating
Dry mouth
Palpitations
Tight chest
Nausea and vomiting
Sleeplessness
Appetite poor or increased

Mental effects
Feelings of failure
Fearfulness
Obsessional
Totally useless
All failure due to me
Poor concentration
Thought blocks, poor memory
Difficulty in prayer and Bible
    study
Loss of interest in usual pursuits

Emotional effects
Unusually high or low
Agitated or too calm
Irritability or hostility
Feeling constantly guilty
Feeling frustrated
Feeling anxious or apathetic
Feeling threatened
Feeling useless
Loss of sense of humour

Effects on behaviour
Over or under-eating
Too much alcohol or smoking
Argumentative or aggressive
Driving too fast
Not bothering about others
Loss of interest in sex
Over-demanding of affection
Over-demanding of reassurance
Excessive rituals

Practical suggestions for handling stress

(See also Chapter 6, Interpersonal relationships.)

- Recognise and welcome stage 1 stress reactions, you are being prepared for action.
- Determine to deal with negative emotions like bitterness and jealousy very quickly.
- Take sensible steps to handle prolonged stress. It is only the minority that learn through the breakdown path.
  1. Take more frequent breaks from work, obtaining permission from your leader to do so.
  2. Develop mental escape routes on the job. Something like birdwatching really takes your mind off things, since as you walk around your work you can do it in any odd moment.
  3. Keep adult 'toys', whatever you find relaxing, and use them as often as you can. I recommend binoculars and badminton!
- Reduce anger by keeping a 'displacement object' (not a human being or the cat). This is something that you can hit, bang, slap or kick such as paint on a canvas, a tennis ball, a football, or baking bread.
- Talk to God frequently about the problem. He knows anyway but it does help to verbalise it.
- Try to make decisions about the problems involved in stress. Even if they apparently cannot be resolved, it helps to think of a decision-making process anyway.
- Never think you are backsliding because you are in a period of heavy stress and may be too tired to pray. When you are tired your head feels as if it is stuffed with cotton wool, and long periods of prayer and Bible study are very difficult. God knows that and loves to see you use rapid aids like a few verses from a booklet or New Testament kept in your pocket, cassettes and CDs and a sermon tape as you wander round the job or home. These are often enough to keep you going when strength is limited and you are very hard pressed. Get on the e-mail to your church and say, 'HELP, give me a little encouragement.'

- If coping with prolonged stress, keep a stress diary. For four weeks write down every day the things that make you feel stressed, who else was involved, what actually happened and how you felt and behaved. After four weeks look through it and try to identify recurrent things that make you feel stressed. In this way you recognise trends and needs in your own personality structure. Talk to God and others about these, and maybe you can link them up with areas in your past that need to be strengthened. Recognising that you are always stressed about the same things is very helpful, for you can look back and think about them, where they came from, and discuss with friends how to control them. It also helps you to learn to laugh at yourself, and to joke with your friends about your 'habitual panics'.
- Never forget to look after every aspect of your make-up during stressful times. The body, mind and spirit must all be cherished and cared for. Later reference will be made to this, but perhaps the best thing at this stage is the comment that any form of overload needs to be rectified as wisely as possible, while taking care not to push the load onto someone else. Projects may need to be put in cold storage for a time, family plans altered, short breaks taken, anything at all that may relieve the current prolonged stress situation even temporarily.

The relationship between depression and stress during overseas service

The remaining chapters of this book will examine various stressors which impact on people during cross-cultural ministry. People worry about stress, thinking an overload will inevitably make them depressed to the point of illness. By way of introduction to the subsequent chapters we need therefore to discuss this fear and to get things into perspective, although they will be discussed more widely in Chapters 3 and 13. I must apologise to non-medicals for the next few paragraphs, but I hope they will find them comprehensible and interesting. As mentioned in the Introductory Notes (p 12), when I use the word **'significant'** I am indicating that the finding is important and should be taken seriously. It means there is a strong probability that the research on which the comment is based is right and not just a chance finding.

Whenever home-office staff hear that one of their missionaries is depressed they immediately blame themselves. They think that at the time of selection they should have been able to predict the possibility of the person becoming depressed overseas and taken steps to prevent it. This is actually not true, because not all kinds of depressive illnesses are the same and so prediction of possible future health risks may not always be possible.

There are two major diagnostic categories of depression, which will be explained more fully in Chapter 13. In brief, one kind of depression is called **'mood-disorders'**, and research showed that people who develop this kind of depression are significantly more likely to have had a previous attack of depression and to have a family history of mental health problems (Foyle, 1999). This kind of depression is not caused by stress, although it may act as the precipitant. It must however be strongly emphasised that those with past personal and/or family histories of mental ill health will *not* inevitably become depressed overseas. In reality, many with this kind of history are strong people, the survivors, but it is helpful to selectors to discuss the history with them and make sensible decisions. Candidates themselves welcome this, feeling really relieved that at last they have been able to talk over such deeply personal matters with trained staff and be better able to cope with their backgrounds.

The second category is called **'adjustment disorders'** which were found to be significantly related to current overseas stress but not to a past personal or family history of mental health problems (Foyle, 1999). There is no reliable way that the possibility of developing adjustment disorders overseas can be predicted, although for a long time people have been trying to discover what makes some more vulnerable to stress than others. Since 1957 they have blamed it unhelpfully on 'the unknown X factor'! We do know, however, that two important personality factors increase vulnerability to stress reactions. One is personality traits that make it difficult for people to control what is happening to them (Lazarus, 1993). These kinds of people never stand up for themselves, but constantly endure being pushed about, resenting it, but doing nothing about it. The other is the Type A personality structures, people who are very time-conscious, hard-driving, over-confident and hyper-ambitious (Rees, Cooper, 1991).

Although this lack of clear understanding about causes of vulnerability to stress makes it hard to predict who will be at risk of developing adjustment disorders overseas, it does indicate the need to try to reduce avoidable stress, and to train people how to manage the unavoidable.

CHAPTER
3

Dealing with Depression and Discouragement

Many partners overseas, in common with those who remain in the Lord's service in their home countries, feel depressed from time to time. What they mean by 'feeling depressed' is that they feel sad, despondent, doubt if it is worth continuing with the work, and generally out of sorts. This of course is common to all human beings, and I understand that animals would tell us they sometimes feel depressed if we could speak their language. In India we had a little dog, and if he did anything he knew was wrong we would come into the room and find him standing in a corner, which he had been trained to do if he had been a bad dog! He looked at us very mournfully until he was welcomed back into the fold with pats and sweet words.

This sort of reaction and its accompanying behaviour are very common, are in no way abnormal, and should not be regarded as a spiritual lapse. The tragedy is that some people still think that if we are Christians we should always be happy, basing this on texts such as 'Rejoice in the Lord always. I will say it again: Rejoice' (Philippians 4:4), 'always' being the difficult word when we feel depressed. The last thing we feel we can do at such times is to rejoice in the Lord, i.e. with that visible joy that the text seems to require.

There is no evidence in the Lord's life that Christians should always be demonstrably joyful. He himself experienced great grief and heaviness of spirit when he was in the Garden of Gethsemane, this being translated as depressed in the Amplified New Testament (Mark 14:33). He groaned and wept over Jerusalem and over Lazarus' death, and we read several times that both Jesus and the apostles wept and groaned and felt heaviness of heart. Therefore our periods of depression are not intrinsically wrong, but they do need to be understood so that we know when feeling depressed has become abnormal, and what we should do about it.

In this chapter we shall look at depression under three headings, depression as a mood, the depressive personality, and depression as an illness.

Depression as a mood

This is a normal human reaction and does not indicate there is something wrong with your psyche or your soul! It is characterised by feeling a bit down, not so energetic as usual, general fed-upness, and often by being a bit irritable. Such moods tend to come and go, and are often relieved by doing something different such as having a treat, going round the shops, kicking a football around for a bit, or generally doing something that gives us a rest-break. I usually commute down the road to a shop called Marks and Spencers. I just wander round and look at the lovely clothes that I can't afford, or try on a pair of shoes I don't intend to buy, and end up in the coffee shop reading the paper and relaxing. Then I can go out all cheerful and able to face the world again. I regard this type of depression as a normal reaction to living in a stressful world, and is just the body's way of saying take a break for a bit. One thing to avoid is taking it out on our nearest and dearest, who certainly don't want to have to cope with us when they also may be feeling a bit down.

Common precipitants of depressed mood

There are certain things that may precipitate depressed mood, and understanding these helps us to cope with it.

The menstrual cycle

Every woman, and possibly her family, knows that just before the monthly period she may be somewhat edgy and irritable. This is not the same as the illness PMT (pre-menstrual tension) in which the malaise is more serious, does not usually resolve spontaneously, and often needs medical help. What I am talking about is the 'monthly blues'. Recently I was travelling and as I was feeling tired put on the TV in my hotel room. There was a programme called *Roseanne*, which I had never seen before or since! Roseanne was a fat and cheerful lady, but in the episode I watched she was definitely not nice to live with, and her kids said to each other, 'Watch out, she's got PMT!' She hadn't, but that's what they called it, and it explained beautifully the impact of the menstrual cycle on a household. New husbands need to be aware of this problem. They have had a lovely wedding, and everything is sweetness and light. At the end of the honeymoon they go home and start life together, and one day he finds his lovely bride has changed. She becomes generally a bit fed up and fractious, is not too nice to live with, and he doesn't know what he has done wrong. But in a few days her period begins and she reverts to her usual sweet self.

Women need to be sensible about the impact of the pre-menstrual week on others. It does not necessarily mean that life for those who live with them will inevitably be difficult, for usually it passes over without causing too much trouble. We need, however, to beware of always blaming our hormones for behaving badly. Instead, we should look around our lives to see if any adjustments need to be made which, in turn, will help us handle the pre-menstrual week. It is also important to remember that should the condition progress from being manageable to out of control, it would be wise to see a doctor for advice and treatment.

Childbirth

What a lot of confusion and pain the 'baby blues' cause! Usually everyone is overjoyed at the birth of a new child, but they go to the ward to visit and find the mother in floods of tears. 'I've got the best baby I could ever have hoped for and I feel so miserable' is the only explanation she can give. Baby blues are common, transient and normal, indicating the mother's physical and emotional adjustment to the post-delivery situation. They are not the same as post-natal depression which will be discussed later, but require a little time and patience while everything settles down again in the mother's body and mind. Before I became a psychiatrist I was in obstetrics and gynaecology, and formed the view then that animals can teach us something about the post-natal period. Mother foxes hole up with their young for some time, allowing no one to enter their den. In humans I believe that a short period of pure family time with the new baby is very valuable, keeps down the impact of returning to the hustle and bustle of ordinary life too soon after the birth, and enhances family bonding. A time of peace after delivery is probably now an old-fashioned dream, but however we manage the post-natal period, we need just to sit out the baby blues, understand they do not mean we do not love the baby, and receive as much loving support as possible from our family and friends.

Certain illnesses

Viral infections like dengue fever, hepatitis and flu are often followed by a period of feeling depressed. This does not usually reach a clinical level, but can take some time to get over, so it is wise to take adequate time off before returning to work. This will not prevent the depressed feelings, but will reduce the time they take to clear up. To quote Dr Ted Lankester writing on hepatitis (1999), 'Those who fail to rest or who return to work (or looking after children) too quickly risk a longer illness or a relapse.' Do not, therefore, allow your conscientious attitude to your work and home deprive you of the rest you need.

Loss of any kind

When we lose something that is important to us, although it may be unimportant to others, we can experience a depressed mood which is called mourning, grieving or bereavement reaction. This is not abnormal, it is the healthy way in which people come to terms with losing something valuable. Christians do not always understand this, feeling we should be rejoicing that our loved one has gone to be with God, but that would deny our need to mourn and so achieve a healthy re-integration of our lives after the loss.

Mourning reactions can occur after any loss, the key precipitant being the importance of what has gone. For example, old ladies who lose their handbags can become really distressed, for in some communities the handbag becomes a microcosm of daily life, and therefore very important to those whose quota of time is running out. Incidentally, two famous ladies in the UK, now becoming a little elderly, have equally famous handbags: Queen Elizabeth uses her handbag to indicate the start or end of an audience, and former prime minister Margaret Thatcher used hers so powerfully that a bit of slang crept into the language — to 'handbag' someone, i.e. to express displeasure. More seriously, the severest mourning process follows the loss by death or separation of a person of importance to us. It is also a component of culture shock where we deal with all we have lost by leaving home through a modified mourning process.

The healthy mourning process is usually described in several stages. These are not clear cut, some may be entirely missed out and there is often much overlap, but usually a little of each is present. Final resolution may be accomplished quickly or take a longer period of time. The mourning process will be described in terms of loss of a person by death.

Stage 1: The stage of numbness. The bereaved person cannot believe that the death has happened, and will often say, 'I can't believe it, its not true.' I call this 'God's anaesthesia'. After a death there is often a lot to do, and if the mind was actively grieving then it would be very hard to deal with other things. Hence God puts the grief to sleep for a time, but this passes and the next stage begins.

Stage 2: Recapitulation. The mind constantly goes over the event, often itemising the details very clearly. In India one sees this at hospitals when a death has occurred. The women sit crying and recounting over and over again exactly how the death occurred in the minutest detail. This may continue for many hours, and is a cultural way in which they come to terms with their loss.

Stage 3: Anger. This is another tool the mind uses to cope with bereavement. Knowing that we Christians are warned, 'In your anger do not sin' (Ephesians 4:26), I have thought carefully about it. I think that the anger we feel during bereavement is a sort of existential anger, an anger that sin and death are still a part of our lives which we will have to endure until Christ comes again. The anger may include criticism of God because he allows suffering and death to remain, but in my opinion this is not a sinful anger. It is not permanent, it is a passing phase during which we are trying to make sense of things, and God understands that. Real trouble arises when people never get over a death and because they remain stuck at the anger stage never progress to the mature resolution of the problem.

Stage 4: Resolution. This may take some time, but finally peace is restored. The loss is incorporated into our lives as something important in our personal story to which we have adjusted as far as possible. The memory of the loss never goes, but the severe pain is resolved and people 'begin to make a life' as a bereaved person said to me recently.

It is important to remember that all these reactions occur to a differing extent after any important loss. We shall think of them again in Chapter 4 under culture shock, but here it should be mentioned that we experience some of these reactions when we move to another country if in the process it involves losing our homes, friends, church, job and familiar culture. So do not be alarmed if you feel a bit angry from time to time, especially when you are new — it is a normal stage and will pass. It is very helpful to talk over your mourning reactions with a trained person or understanding friend, and constantly to remind ourselves that God is planning for us in love. 'I know the plans I have for you says the Lord, plans for your welfare and not for harm, to give you a future with hope' (Jeremiah 29:11, RSV).

Adequate involvement in our ministry

In Chapter 2 we touched on spiritual understanding of the reasons why we experience suffering and difficulty during missionary service. This needs some amplification. If we are truly involved in God's work we really care about what we are doing for him. Hence we may experience sorrow as we see the needs of the people around us, and we long to help. We begin to share some of God's burden for the world which may lead us into a form of depressed mood that is not always recognised as such. It is normal, and indicates that we are involved in the kingdom ministry. Jesus demonstrated the pain of such involvement as he wept over Jerusalem, and over Lazarus' death.

The Scriptures reveal what is going on. When Jesus suffered, being tempted, the Greek word *pascho* is used (Hebrews 2:18). In 2 Thessalonians 1:5, when Paul is writing of the fact that believers are suffering for the kingdom of God, he uses the same word, *pascho*. But the principle behind it is explained in Philippians 1:29 — 'God has graciously granted you the privilege not only of believing in Christ but of suffering for him as well' (RSV). The same word *pascho* is used again, indicating that we are experiencing a little of the same sort of suffering Christ experienced on earth. This is nothing to do with salvation, for only Jesus could experience that form of suffering as he died for us on the cross, but the use of the word indicates that our *pascho* experiences have plenty to do with the spread of his kingdom on earth.

If we have committed ourselves to sharing in the kingdom ministry under his direction, and experience something of this kind of suffering, it usually takes the form of a depressed mood. If this persists we need to check round our daily lives to make sure there is no imbalance that is prolonging the mood abnormally. But having done that, we should continue to bear the burden, to pray or to do whatever he directs, until the time comes for us to move on and that particular burden is relieved or passes to someone else.

During these periods of depressed mood or exceptionally stressful load-bearing, we should take care of ourselves. Take time off, relax with other things, and above all remember that these pressures usually have a time span attached — they will end some time. When things are difficult I have found it helpful to divide the time into short periods, and then take a short break. In one place where my work load was very heavy I mentally divided it into seven-day periods, going down town with a friend every Saturday to eat fish and chips and ice-cream. So I thought of it as 'working from fish and chips to fish and chips', and survived! This did not detract from my involvement, I was totally committed, but it made it bearable.

The depressive personality

Everyone has different traits in their personalities which give us individuality and make us more interesting people. It is true that certain traits can become more dominant when we are under stress, and may cause trouble to ourselves and others, but usually they are just part of what I call our 'quirky individuality'.

As an example, an overload of obsessional traits can cause trouble in the home if the personality traits of the others living there are predominantly slapdash, happy go lucky, and couldn't-care-less! If the obsessional members of the family become over-stressed they can blow up and demand a little more order, which then upsets the more slap-happy members who like things the way they are!

Those with depressive personality traits tend to be pessimistic, to expect things to go wrong, and to be more anxious than others. Usually it causes the owner and friends little trouble, but may, for example, blow up if there are problems when travelling and so impact on the more phlegmatic members of the family who just sit it all out without much bother.

In reality, there are good things about depressive personality traits. Provided the owners do not become hyper-preoccupied with their own affairs, those with depressive traits tend to be sensitive to the unspoken needs of others, and very sympathetic towards those who find life a struggle. In addition, they have increased opportunities to be thankful — more was expected to go wrong than actually did go wrong, hence there is more to be thankful for! In addition, because people with depressive personality traits usually have more cares than others, they learn a great deal about casting all their cares onto God — there are more to cast!

Another good thing about this type of personality is that it acts as a healthy check on the more exuberant. I do not know if you have ever sat on a planning committee with someone of a rather manic personality structure, full of plans and creativity but with little practical understanding of the grass-roots implications of what they are suggesting. The depressive personality structure will be able to look at realities and to check the unrealistic exuberance, so that a middle course can be followed. This holds true in relationships like marriage, where if a man who is depressive marries a very optimistic woman they will probably balance each other out, if they have the patience to listen and understand.

Rather than belittling ourselves because of our depressive personality traits we need to accept them from God, and to rededicate them to him. There is nothing he cannot redeem and use for our good and his glory, and it is amazing how he can refine what is excessive and make our personality traits very useful in his kingdom ministry, even the depressive ones.

Practical advice on handling a depressive personality structure

- **Accept it from God** and ask him to purify and strengthen it for use as he wishes.
- **Never allow it to make others uncomfortable.** People with depressive traits tend to over-share their problems with people, and it can get wearisome. Share conclusions, rather than giving a blow-by-blow account of what may seem to others a trivial matter.
- **Watch for trigger factors.** Certain things tend to trigger off over-reactions in those with depressive traits.
    1. *Feelings of rejection.* These often stem from painful childhood events, such as being made to feel inferior at home or school. As a result anything in adult life perceived as a rejection tends to trigger off the depressive traits. Finding out if rejection was intended is helpful, because usually it was not and had only been perceived in that way. I had such an experience recently when I thought I had accidentally hurt someone's feelings, and that she had been avoiding me. A few days later I met her unexpectedly and asked her about it, and in reality it was the opposite of what I had thought. She had been delighted with our whole conversation. This strengthened my belief that if you think you have been rejected why not try to find the facts? That way we learn the truth about events.
    2. *Feelings of failure.* The problem with people with depressive traits is that they globalise. Usually when something goes wrong, instead of looking at that one event they globalise it and say, 'I've made a mess of everything.' This is a long-standing habit, and people need to remind themselves not to do it by sticking the words 'don't globalise' on the bathroom mirror. This reminds them to take one event as it stands, one area of failure, rather than globalising it into total failure.

In the context of failure Easter Saturday is very important. I recently asked a big conference how many had ever heard a sermon on Easter Saturday, and only one person put up his hand. We can imagine the scene. The disciples were in shock, grieving for a dead Lord, and feeling everything had gone wrong. Peter must have been devastated, feeling that his betrayal had spoiled everything, and that there would be no future place for him among the disciples. We sometimes feel like that when things go wrong and we wonder if we are to blame, adding on globalisation to make ourselves feel even worse.

In reality, where was Jesus? I am no theologian, but I have never believed that Jesus lay in the tomb until Easter Sunday morning. According to Bible scholars, 1 Peter 3:18–20 indicates that between Good Friday and Easter Sunday (our time) Jesus was busy proclaiming good news to the spirits in prison who disobeyed at the time of Noah's flood. I am not intending to be irreverent but I cannot help imagining what the Lord was feeling like between Good Friday and Easter Sunday. I am sure he was longing to rise again visibly. It reminds me of parents of a child whose only request for Christmas was a bicycle. The parents had not much money but in the July sales they bought the bicycle and hid it. The child got more and more despondent as Christmas approached and there was absolutely no sign of the bike anywhere. But the parents were counting the hours, longing for Christmas morning when their darling son would be made so happy. What joy for all of them when the great day came. So it must have been for Jesus, counting in our time the hours of ministry to the spirits and eagerly waiting for Sunday when joy would replace grief.

I believe that when things go wrong for us we need to remember it is only Easter Saturday. In God's time there will be a solution, there will be a restoration of joy, even though we need to wait for it and to live through the darkness of our individual Easter Saturdays. As surely as Easter Sunday came for the grieving disciples, so God's time will come for us in our difficult situation, and even though we may remain scarred, we shall experience a new and joyful Easter Day. As I have grown older I have come to understand that God's time may not always be during our lifetime, but at some time, in his own good time, there will be a solution for those already with God in heaven and for those who were involved in the problem and are still on earth.

Depression as an illness

Many of us live and work in isolated places, with little or no access to doctors or anyone with specialised knowledge. We can therefore get very worried about ourselves, our families and colleagues if we feel someone is unwell. This is especially true of depressive illness, and I have seen too many national workers and missionaries who were really neglected because no one recognised they were suffering from treatable depression. The purpose of this final section is to look at this problem and to do what I can to explain how to recognise depression (the illness) so that you can advise someone to go for proper care. It is always dangerous to do this, since it is so easy to imagine you have the illness being discussed. This problem is, of course, shared by medical students who think they have every illness they learn about. Even qualified doctors have the same difficulty, and in fact there is a noted male obstetrician who went into the speciality because obstetric problems were the only illnesses he couldn't get! Despite this danger, however, I feel it is better to give some diagnostic pointers rather than to leave isolated workers untreated.

People often ask what causes depression, and the right answer is that we do not always know. We do know that some people with depression have a chemical imbalance in the brain, often with a genetic basis. This does *not* mean that if you have depression in the family you will automatically get it; it only means there is a slight bias towards it. Some of the other causes are stress overload, prolonged bereavement reactions, or an underlying physical problem. Some cases, but not all, have difficult childhood backgrounds that may reduce their cope-ability in adult life, and possibly lead to a depressive episode. It is also known that a depressive illness may be the first indication of a developing cancer or other physical problem. Many people think that depressive illnesses are based solely on spiritual failures, although in my experience the depression usually comes first and then the patient develops spiritual problems as a result of the illness. Therefore, to ensure that all possible causes are adequately investigated it is very important that anyone with depression receives a careful physical, psychological and spiritual assessment.

To help isolated people diagnose depression, a useful chart has been produced based on the grouping of depression in the International Classification of Disease-10 (1992). Please read it sensibly and do not start thinking you have all the symptoms, but it may help you as you care for others. In addition, the book *Where there is no Doctor* (Werner, 1991) is being extended by adding a second volume called *Where there is no Psychiatrist*, and we hope this will provide additional help to those without adequate medical facilities.

Introduction to the chart

The chart is divided into mild, moderate and two kinds of severe depression. After looking at how long the illness has lasted (duration), it then ascertains how well the person is functioning. It then examines symptoms in three groups, and I have added on sections on spiritual problems and advice.

The **first group of symptoms** contains three items (1–3), and the columns indicate the number of symptoms required to diagnose mild, moderate or severe depression, e.g. for mild and moderate depression only two out of the three would be required, whereas for severe all three would be present.

The **second group** contains seven symptoms (a–g), with the numbers indicated in the other columns as in the first group. Here, for example, mild depressive diagnosis would require only two of the symptoms to be present, moderate three to four, and severe four.

The **third group** of symptoms is headed 'others' to indicate other symptoms that assist in making the diagnosis. Two of the words used require definition: *Delusions* means firmly believing things that are not true and are out of touch with reality. *Hallucinations* means hearing, seeing or tasting things that are not there. Do not worry, these are rare under your circumstances.

Types of depressive illness and how to diagnose them

Symptoms	Mild	Moderate	Severe (1)	Severe (2)
Duration	two weeks	two weeks	two weeks	two weeks
Function level	Moderate	Poor	Almost nil	Almost nil
1. Depressed mood 2. Loss of interest and energy 3. Unusual tiredness	two of 1–3	two of 1–3	three of 1–3	three of 1–3
a. Reduced concentration b. Reduced self-esteem and confidence c. Ideas of guilt and worthlessness d. Pessimism about future e. Ideas of self-harm or suicide f. Disturbed sleep g. Reduced appetite	two of a–g	three or four of a–g	four of a–g	four of a–g
Others		Somatic (bodily) complaints	Slowed down or restless	Slowed down or restless Delusions or hallucinations
Spiritual problems	Possible	Common	Common	Common
Advice	See doctor	See doctor	See doctor. Tell family this is urgent.	See doctor. Tell family this is urgent.

Cultural additions

The way depression may present varies from continent to continent, and sometimes from village to village. Broadly speaking the Western presentation is much the same apart from cultural expressions. For example in one district of the UK people use the expression, 'I'm not being mardy' to explain they are not putting it on, pretending. Asians and Africans have cultural ways of describing depressive symptoms which we need to remember if trying to help colleagues from these areas. The secret is, if you do not understand the term they use, ask them to explain what they mean. Two papers were published in Pakistan (Ahmad, Arif and Zuberi, 1981,1982) which noted that the commonest presentation of depression and anxiety in rural clinics was complaints of giddiness, headache at the top of the head, palpitations and weakness, and unless the right questions were asked about sleep, energy and appetite and possibly some of the others on the chart, the actual diagnosis of depression was missed. In Nepal I noted that the local colloquial expression which often indicated depression was 'worms are eating me', plus the headache on top of the head. In the West, Christians often present to the pastor with spiritual problems when actually there is an underlying depression that needs attention, and in many countries depressed Christians present for spiritual help because they and their families think they are demon possessed. Hence if we are trying to help people we need to remember to ask the questions contained in the chart plus the cultural additions if we begin to wonder whether they are becoming clinically depressed.

Practical advice

Having a depressive illness does not mean automatically leaving the working location. Schubert, an authority on care of missionaries, believes as I do that simple cases of depression are best treated overseas. 'These illnesses respond well to counselling and medication, and clients can usually return to productive work wiser and more insightful. In addition, these people are saved the disgrace of returning to their own constituency in a depressed condition' (1993). However, any persons in the four categories described in the chart should see a doctor or trained mental-health worker. If there is no doctor, and you have had some medical training you can treat mild cases yourself, but be prepared to send them to a doctor if they do not improve. The sheet anchors are examination to exclude physical illness, antidepressants, care of food and fluids, security through the presence of a caring person, regular talking sessions to see how things are, and when better going on holiday with a close friend. Remember a holiday without proper treatment will do no good if they are in any of the categories in the chart. The person who is unwell needs to be assured that friends will continue to pray, and must understand that it may be difficult to pray much for themselves until the depression begins to ease up. Explain that this is normal, and that as they get better their prayer life will return and be even better than before.

Where there is evidence that people are getting depressed, in some cases the illness may be prevented. This is especially true where there is no previous history of depression, and their symptoms are related to current stress. With the agreement of management, suggest they go away with a friend or family to a place they will enjoy, and there take the opportunity to unwind, talk to someone, have a good medical check-up, and see how things go. Make no demands on them during this time, but remember that supportive spiritual care is as important as the other forms of care. They should not be allowed back to work without a medical clearance. If, however, they refuse to go away for a period of rest and you are worried about them, communicate with the responsible executive in your area. The person may be annoyed with you, but when they are better they will be grateful. I recently met someone I had not seen for a long time who said he was most grateful to me for sending him off on short leave when he was in danger of becoming over-stressed and depressed. He got better and has never looked back.

Unless you have a proper hospital or a good local doctor with mental health training, *never* treat locally people who express suicidal thoughts or have delusions or hallucinations, i.e. those in the severe category. Make sure they are escorted by reliable people to the nearest treatment centre.

Summary of common treatments of depressive illness

You can only treat very mild cases of depression on your location unless there is a good doctor nearby. However, depressed missionaries are often reluctant to go for adequate treatment because they do not know what it will entail. This section outlines briefly the different forms of treatment, and may help you reassure them and finally persuade them to accept help. In addition you may be helping them while they get over the illness, and need to know some of the ordinary things you can do.

1. Medicines. These can be prescribed only by a properly trained person. Patients need to understand that they are not habit-forming 'drugs', but together with talking and care are curative of the illness.

2. General care. Decisions need to be made about where they are to be treated, who will look after them, whether they can work, what arrangements can be made for their safety.

3. Opportunity to talk:
- Simple talk may be enough, concentrating on the here and now.
- More prolonged discussion sessions especially for serious stress-related depressions and those related to a depressive personality structure. Prolonged sessions require trained personnel, so going to a nearby treatment centre would be the best plan.
- Talking in groups may help.
- Remember, concentration is poor, use short sentences.

4. Simple work. When they are well enough.

5. Care of the body:
- Good medical examination.
- Treat associated physical illnesses.
- Food and fluids.
- Exercise when well enough.

6. Spiritual care.
- As part of the illness, God seems very far away to the depressed person. This is a clear-cut symptom, just as having a sore throat is a part of influenza. This can be explained to the person, a reminder given that God has promised never to leave us or forsake us, and a promise given to continue to pray for them. If you pray with them at their request, use short sentences due to their poor concentration, and keep the prayer short. Later you can reassure them that in the end they will find it has been a valuable experience — they won't believe you but it should be said anyway.
- Remember that the guilt they express may not be true guilt. Generally speaking, advise them not to act on it at present but to wait till they are less depressed and then sort it all out. Usually the false guilt disappears as the depression improves, and real guilt can then be dealt with. As an example, one person thought she had made a sexual approach to someone in her family during her childhood, and wanted to write to him to put the matter right. She was dissuaded from this by her doctor who advised her to wait till she was better, and in the end it proved to be only a fantasy and not true at all. Much damage could have been done if she had been allowed to proceed with her original plan.

7. Dealing with shame. This is a big problem during depression. Africans and Asians tend to feel more shame than guilt, i.e. they have let their tribe or community down by getting depressed. Western people struggle with this too, but more in terms of what the church or mission will think rather than the wider community. I have found the best way to deal with this is by trying to enlist the support of a vital member of their community. Once he/she is on their side, patients feel more assured that the community will understand, which in turn reduces shame. The biggest problem in this area comes from churches or missions which believe that all psychological symptoms are based on sin. In the early days of my work with missionaries, I occasionally experienced such hostility from mission leaders when I was trying to explain that one of their personnel had a depressive illness that I sometimes wondered if they thought I had two horns and a tail! Thankfully this attitude is now very rare.

8. Loving care. In general, be guided by what the person wishes in terms of support and spiritual care. Stand by, be there, provide food, fluids and general sympathy, read and pray with them if they wish, but most of all just *be* there. Take care of your own health at the same time since it can be quite draining to support a depressed person. If it gets beyond you then ensure your management knows what is going on, and ask for help such as taking the person out of the location for a time.

4

Adjustment and Culture Shock

The term 'acculturation' is being used increasingly in literature on expatriates, and indicates the whole process of adjustment overseas, coping with culture shock, and generally settling down in the new culture. Several terms are currently used for the act of taking up residence beyond your own cultural boundary such as 'transitional experiences', 'sojourner adjustment', and 'stages of adjustment'. Reactions to the event are termed 'culture shock', 'adjustment stress', 'culture fatigue', or 'cultural bereavement', so we have a wide choice in terminology and it is all very confusing. I have utilised the term 'adjustment' for the process of adjusting to a new culture, mainly because it is so much easier to pronounce than acculturation, and 'culture shock' for the adverse reactions that may be experienced.

In 1955 Lysgaard described the process of adjustment as a U curve, initial optimism being succeeded by a trough of difficulty which gradually worked its way up to satisfactory adaptation to the new scene. Torbion noted (1982) that the lowest point of the trough took about a year to reach, with satisfactory adjustment taking one to two years, and super-adjustment being achieved after fifteen years! However this is based on work with business expatriates and may not be relevant to missionaries who seem to accomplish it more quickly than this.

After a lot of argument the process of adjustment was redefined by Adler (1975), and this has been the most frequently quoted work. He described it as a four-stage operation: *contact* phase of excitement and euphoria, *disintegration* accompanied by confusion, *autonomy* indicating gradual understanding of the new culture, and finally *independence* which cherishes cultural differences while displaying increasingly trusting and creative behaviour. I think most cross-cultural workers would accept these as valid experience.

In cases of depression overseas, difficulties in adapting to the new culture were found to be significantly related to the development of the adjustment disorder type of illness, as described in Chapter 3. The major problems were vague and non-specific, people saying it was just difficult. Local customs came next followed by environmental adjustment. In another study of missionaries, a significant relationship was found between adjustment difficulties and developing psychological symptoms overseas, the main problems again being non-specific (Foyle, 1999). I think it is the vagueness that is so trying, people finding it hard to adjust but even harder to define exactly what the difficulty is.

Most people have adjustment problems but not everyone suffers from culture shock. Mumford (1998) writing on the measurement of culture shock quoted Taft (1995) who outlined six different aspects of it:

- Strain due to the effort required to make the necessary psychological adaptations.
- A sense of loss and feelings of deprivation in regard to friends, status, profession and possessions.
- Being rejected by and/or rejecting members of the new culture.
- Confusion in role, role expectations, values, feelings and self-identity.
- Surprise, anxiety, even disgust and indignation after becoming aware of cultural differences.
- Feelings of impotence due to not being able to cope with the new environment.

The best concept however is the one described in Chapter 3 which identifies culture shock as predominately mourning for what has been lost, and I think this sums it up very well.

Some of the causes of culture shock

The first one is that theoretical work has become practical. All you heard about during orientation is now before your eyes and that makes it stark reality. Any medical student understands this. They read about operations and see them on the TV in soap operas, but the day they stand in the operating theatre to see their first one is a totally different experience. The blood mentioned in the textbook flows out as the incision is made, and it is such a shock that wise nurses often stand behind new students to catch them as they faint. The same applies to a certain extent to culture shock. People are habituated to the sight of poverty, disease, refugee camps and murders on the TV news, but in reality nothing prepares them for actually being there. I once had to remove a friend from a place we stayed in during our travels in Asia because she could not cope with the squalor, and kept saying 'why don't they do something about it, why leave it like that?' I had immunised myself against reacting so strongly by staying there for many years, and had forgotten the impact it could have on new folk.

The second cause is the loss of familiar cues. Sexual cues are mentioned in the chapter on singleness (Chapter 8), but there are many other cues we do not realise we utilise. I was taught in my childhood that to be polite one ate things like bread with one's left hand, and I never gave it another thought until I arrived in India and discovered one had to eat with the right hand, the left being reserved for 'dirty purposes'. To eat with the wrong hand in some circles was the cue that indicated you were of poor social status. Similarly, dealing with officials overseas may be a minefield of cues which if you do not understand keeps you hanging around their offices for a very long time. To the locals, aspects of their behaviour would indicate that if a bribe was forthcoming the work would be done speedily, but of course most foreigners do not recognise these cues and would not bribe anyway! I made a serious mistake in my last week in India. There was an official in a department who had been very helpful to me and we had got on well. I wanted to say thank you before I left so bought the traditional box of sweets and gave it to him in the office. To my surprise he hastily pushed it into a drawer and banged it shut. Later I asked someone why, and he explained that what I had intended as a polite 'thank-you' gesture would be interpreted by everyone else in the office as proof he had accepted a bribe from me.

The third cause of culture shock stems from the vast amount we have to learn about the fables, myths, fairy stories, legendary heroes, and the religious content of the people we serve. We do not realise the huge amount we automatically learn about our own culture. In the UK we know about Robin Hood, Cinderella, fairyland and the elves, and many other things, and have little idea how we actually got this information. When we become expatriates we are faced with the memory bank of another culture. We have to learn what they mean when they use one of their cultural sayings, or use a mythical character to explain something. There has been a long-running TV series on the Hindu god-kings, which most of us would know little about, but Hindu children have incorporated this knowledge in their memory banks from very early years.

If we do not attempt to learn at least part of the memory bank of our host culture we lose a lot of understanding of what makes our new community tick, and may get into real professional difficulties. To give a practical example. We used to have smallpox epidemics in India, and would organise mass vaccination programmes. In some village areas we noticed that there was some hesitancy and discussion before people would be vaccinated, and thought this indicated they did not trust us. I then learned that the Hindi name for smallpox was 'chhoti mata', small mother, and she was a powerful goddess. The villagers therefore had to discuss what sort of sacrifices they could make to prevent smallpox without displeasing the 'mother'. As another example, I was puzzled why large numbers of women would come to the hospital at certain seasons of the year with their chests badly bruised. I thought their husbands had been beating them but was surprised it all happened at once. Finally a nurse explained to me about the festival of Muharram, where women beat their breasts to mourn for the death of Hussein/ Hussain, and the harder they beat the more devoted they are.

The attitude to evil and good differs from culture to culture. In the UK these days the average person would personify Satan, the prince of darkness, by drawing a figure with two horns and a tail. There is little sense of dread or awe apart from those who practise satanic worship. For example, some years ago there was a shop window near our church displaying slim and beautiful model figures dressed in revealing costumes, horns and tails. The caption was 'Have a hell of a Christmas', the whole conveying a sense of mockery not fear. (Needless to say, a lot of church members went in to explain that the two were incompatible since we were celebrating the birth of the one who came to destroy the power of hell, and to date the shop never repeated this sort of window again.) There is much the same thing in Kathmandu, where there is a huge angry-looking idol that we would find a bit terrifying, yet little children play around it quite happily. In most countries, however, as well as the more joking representations, there is a dread of satanic influence and possession by demons, and a constant stream of propitiatory sacrifices to ensure people are not harmed by him or his forces. The expression of the principle of good also varies enormously. I suppose in the average UK school good would be expressed by an angel with wings and a halo, and to believers would be mentally represented by Christ himself. In India it would be expressed by the monkey god Hanuman rushing to rescue the god Ram's wife, who had been kidnapped and taken to Sri Lanka.

I came to realise quite late in my time overseas that one unconsciously absorbs a lot of understanding of the basic cultural thought patterns in the host country. I feel it is important to do so. We never accept what is contrary to our Christian faith, but understanding how the new culture expresses certain basic things in life, such as the existence of good and evil, is very helpful to the development of the right kind of integration with the people we have come to serve. In the early days overseas all these adjustments may be very tiring, so take it all very slowly!

It must be noted that generation X may prove not to be so liable as other people to culture shock when going overseas but this is not yet certain. They usually have prior experience of overseas countries from holidays or brief excursions, but whether that will be enough to prevent them reacting to the culture when they stay longer remains to be seen. Many of them have said that going for a holiday is OK, but if you go for a longer time and do not have a return ticket then the whole flavour of being overseas is different and may prove more traumatic, and some have had re-entry shock on returning to their own country after only a few weeks away.

Language study

This section relates more to the longer-term missionary than the very short-term, although all benefit from a having a few words of the local language. Stress over learning the language is not in itself a form of culture shock but since both types of stress are happening at the same time language stress can make culture shock worse.

It was noted in the business world that a policy which enabled expatriate employees to become familiar with the language would be an effective way of reducing stress (University College, 1991). Another paper from the same expatriate sector said that the importance of language training is being increasingly recognised by British multinationals (Scullion, 1992), although the Americans had previously found that two-thirds of multinational companies did not feel a knowledge of the language was necessary for conducting business (Baker, 1984). In a study of many large business companies, one participant wrote:

In one area in the health care sector... they consider language training to be very important. You cannot operate overseas at a senior level without at least a business level understanding of the language. You must be able to communicate with the whole of the workforce and with customers (UMIST, 1995).

Most missionaries serving more than a very short term are required to learn the local language, this usually being combined with cultural orientation. Several strong points have emerged over the past ten years. The first is that language methods have become more linked with individual choice than in earlier years. Some, because of their personality structures, feel they do best in a classroom and private teacher set-up, but others do better using the LAMP method devised by Brewster (1976) where they learn a bit and go out and use it, although there is much more to it than that! In many language schools the principle of living with a local family for a period of mentoring and cross-cultural experience is adopted for all students, not just the LAMP method users. People who are shy and sensitive find this difficult but if placed together with a more confident person it usually works out well.

Another major difficulty is language learning for those whose mother tongue is not English. Different approaches to resolving this problem have been made. For example, if the national language overseas is French, then usually English-speaking expatriates go to a French-speaking country for a time before proceeding overseas. When the only language schools overseas will use English as the teaching medium, non-English speaking candidates are advised to try to improve their English during Bible college and orientation periods. Sometimes language learning is accomplished through other national languages, which may be facilitated by use of language-learning cassettes from the home countries. This pattern, however, may create later difficulties if the *lingua franca* of their location is English. At the moment English remains the most common language medium for learning other languages, although in parts of Africa it is French. With the growth of Spanish as a major world language this may change, but all we can do at present is to follow the trends and change what appears to be necessary when the time comes.

My recent research into a group of serving personnel has shown that the overall pattern of language learning has been well devised and implemented. Some did experience severe stress, but this was not significantly related to the development of psychological symptoms. Such complaints as were made concerned inadequate arrangements, poor tuition, and an inflexible tuition pattern, but on the whole the current systems appear to be very suitable.

It is after leaving language school that the major problems begin. In some countries the nationals automatically assume that they will not understand what the expatriate is saying, so however good his or her language may be the usual response to a sentence in fluent Hindi is 'no speak English'. Or else the expatriate sees an apparently attentive audience and thinks he or she is explaining something quite well, only to be asked at the end 'Why is your skin so white? Did your mother wash you in milk?' This is very disconcerting but never mind, just keep on laughing at yourself, go on trying, and accept that the nationals may politely wait till you have gone and then have a good laugh at something you have said. I made a very bad mistake once when going into a national monument, and used a very rude word indeed due to a mispronunciation. As I went in I heard the gatemen laughing, realised what I had said and blushed absolutely scarlet. When I went out an hour later I scurried past them with my head down. However, the local people really appreciate it when you try to say something in their language and this makes the struggle worth while.

Interpersonal relationships can be affected by language study. One marital partner may be much better at the language than another, and where management demands passing language exams as a condition of remaining in longer-term service, this can cause real difficulty. It becomes extra stressful when the partner good at language was born in the country and can not only remember some of the language but also knows a lot more about the culture than the other partner.

It is axiomatic that language students need support, and many agencies now have special national or expatriate personnel allocated to help the students. It is equally important to make it enjoyable. Of course it is a grind, but it can also be made fun. This is one of the strengths of the language school pattern, for in their free time the students can go down town and enjoy the sights as well as practising language.

Components of culture shock

General symptoms occur such as loss of interest, homesickness, occasional disturbed sleep, loss of appetite and poor concentration. Fatigue is the major development. After an initial period of excitement and interest in the new surroundings, people often begin to feel very fatigued by the effort of absorbing such a lot of new things.

Social and professional anxieties are a common component. Socially there is uncertainty about how to behave, what to wear, and how to entertain others. Housekeeping may be a nightmare until local methods are understood. Professionally, despite the kindness of the host people, there is often apprehension at starting the new job and fears of being unable to cope in such a totally new environment. Some of the working customs are culturally so strange they take a lot of getting used to. As a doctor I was trained to respond to an emergency at once, even if I had just started to eat. In India however nothing was allowed to interrupt the meal, and sometimes a nurse who had come to call you would be found sitting outside waiting till you had finished, while a woman was bleeding heavily in the labour ward.

Guilt is an important component of culture shock. Most people are conditioned by TV and newspapers to the problems of the developing world, but as was written earlier in this chapter, when you get there the reality hits you. At this point an imbalance can develop, guilt at what you own and where you live making you feel prematurely responsible to try to do something to help. What is not always understood is that local government and aid programmes may already be addressing the problem with great energy. I feel it would be most helpful if as a part of arrival orientation a talk on current local projects was given, so that new arrivals learn what has already been accomplished and what is on plan, and can quickly gain a clear picture of the situation. This would reduce the guilt that sometimes leads people to write things about their new country which are not actually true, or to attempt to raise immediate funds for a project that may already be part of a local plan.

Some people handle guilt by the mental mechanism of denial. After the first shock they simply blot it out because they cannot cope with the volume of need. After my long service in India I found I had stopped reacting to things that shocked newcomers, such as the crowds of homeless refugees existing on station platforms. I knew all these huge problems were there, but just concentrated on the little bit I had been given to do. If I had not blocked them off from entering fully into my conscious mind, I doubt if someone of my personality structure could have worked so long in Asia.

Anger is another component of culture shock, anger at politicians or mission leaders or United Nations staff for apparently doing nothing to relieve the situation. This is not the whole truth, most of them are doing as much as they can, but the problem may be so vast that they have to be selective about the help they give, and to be content to do their job as well as possible despite the large amount they have to ignore.

Anger is an important topic for it can be creative as well as destructive. Missionaries can get angry when they see so much injustice and need in the world, especially when it is associated with corruption. This becomes destructive when they get a bit depressed by the situation and begin to blame themselves and others for apparently doing so little. In this connection I found a very helpful passage in Zechariah 4:10. The background is that the temple was in ruins and had to be rebuilt, which was a mammoth task. God sent Zechariah to stand in the ruins with a plumb-line in his hand to indicate that God would enable them to accomplish the rebuilding. (For those who do not know what a plumb-line is, it is a piece of string with a lump of lead hanging down to show builders their line is straight.) I have often wondered if he did not feel a bit foolish, but he obeyed God and stood there with a very small thing which indicated the great thing God was going to do. Verse 10 shows the attitude we should have to even the smallest bit of service for God: 'Who despises the day of small things? People will rejoice when they see the plumb-line in the hand of Zerubbabel.' The same passage teaches us that God works not by human might and power but by his Spirit (v. 6), and therefore our service will be accompanied by the presence of the power of God, although this may take years to be revealed. Spiritual revivals have come about because three old ladies decided to pray together every day that God would work in their community. Culturally compatible Christian hospitals have been built in very needy areas where the work started in only two rooms, and the first people who worked there had to be content with adding their drop and never saw the final dream come true. I know of an area where several generations of women worked steadily for about 70 years, and twenty years after they had all gone it began to produce God's fruit. Never feel you are not doing enough, never despise the day of small things, for you never know what God will ultimately make of anything we do for him at his command.

Prevention of culture shock

This may not be 100% possible, but a few things may help to reduce it. The first is mentoring on arrival. The lack of an overseas mentor has been commented on unfavourably in my research programme. Missionaries have said that initially it is better to use an expatriate, but as soon as possible a national should be introduced. This support may be enough to help the new person adjust with little trouble, and continue to do well due to ongoing mentoring

Another useful aid is a post-arrival orientation course. On the post-arrival orientation section of the research questionnaire I used, several missionaries wrote 'WHAT orientation', and expressed their dismay at finding that nothing at all had been arranged for their introduction to a totally new country. They just seemed to have to muddle along and learn everything by themselves. I personally feel that even if only one or two people are involved, a few days spent explaining the local area and including practical as well as spiritual, historical, political and geographical information would be time well spent.

The creative use of mental mechanisms described in Chapter 6 can prevent serious culture shock from developing. For example, new people may find themselves having uncharacteristic outbursts of temper, a regression to the age of temper tantrums. I worked briefly in Bangla Desh and found some of the restrictions on women rather irksome. I had friends who were members of an American club and they used to ask me over periodically. Being trained in healthy regression, I ran inside the door, played ball with the kids, jumped in and out of the swimming pool, hit a tennis ball against a wall, and generally behaved as if I was six not sixty. This enabled me to cope with the outside problems, and is strongly recommended if you are fortunate enough to live in a place that can provide temporary respite.

Practical suggestions for coping with culture shock

Children's problems with culture shock, have been described in Chapter 4 but the following advice is also relevant to them.

- Recognise your symptoms for what they are. Fatigue and loss of energy in the adjustment stage are an indication of culture shock, not of breakdown. At intervals withdraw briefly from your new culture if you can.
- Be kind to yourself as you settle down. If you develop mild culture shock, restrict your access to the new country for a time. As Dye wrote (1974), 'since involvement is a key factor in culture stress, escape is the effective remedy'. Stay at home or nearby, play music from home and read a familiar book. As you improve, go out to a neutral place such as a local beauty spot or a park and gradually reintegrate with the local community.
- When things calm down, slowly re-expose yourself to the local area, keeping the duration of exposure below anxiety level. Gradually increase the time until you are back to normal.
- Concentrate on finding good things in the new country, and look for a local interest as fast as you can.
- Reduce other tensions in your life. If you are married, both of you may be experiencing culture shock and it is easy to have a row, and the same applies to singles sharing a flat. Use a displacement object rather than taking things out on your spouse or living companion.
- Drop anything you can to reduce current overload during a period of culture shock.
- Never decide to return home during a period of culture shock. Discuss it with a friend or local counsellor, wait and see how you feel after a few weeks, and make a slow decision about what to do.
- Lean hard on comforting verses of Scripture and on local national and expatriate friends. You may not be able to pray much if you are stressed, but that makes no difference to God's care of you.

Severe or prolonged culture shock

Occasionally initial stress can lead onto illness which requires skilled help. In Chapter 3, I outlined the symptoms and signs of a depressive illness, and if you are not getting over your shock and develop some of these symptoms you should see a doctor quickly. Additional ones that indicate you need medical help are total withdrawal from the new community with inability to return to it, and acute homesickness that does not improve.

CHAPTER

5

Occupational Stress

In a list of stressors which cause trouble to missionaries, occupational stress emerged as the major one in mission, general aid programmes and in the business world (Foyle, 1999). In mission there appears to have been a change, occupational stress coming higher in the list than in previous papers by Gish (1933) and Carter (1999) where interpersonal relationships were the major stressors.

A few important points have emerged from my thesis on Expatriate Mental Health which may help agencies and personnel as they seek to decrease the impact of occupational stress on the health and well-being of their personnel. The first point is that although 80% of people with depression complained of occupational stress, which appears to be an alarming figure, this must be counterbalanced by the encouraging fact that there are more people complaining of occupational stress without being depressed by it than in the depressed group. In other words coping strategies have been well learned, and we should continue to make such training an integral part of preparation.

The second important point is that candidates complaining of occupational stress at the time of their selection interviews were significantly more likely than others to develop psychological symptoms overseas. We need, therefore, to remember to ask candidates not only what work they do, but also how they are getting on, and how stressful they find it. These days nearly everyone seems to have stress at work, but those who are obviously distressed by it should have extra care and counselling in stress management before final selection. As the previous paragraph shows us, learning how to handle occupational stress at home may well protect people from more serious psychological troubles overseas

Missionary finance

Before looking in more detail at overall working problems, mention should be made of the problems associated with missionary finance. In two questionnaires large numbers reported this as highly stressful, especially when they came home on leave. Missionaries have always expected to live at sacrificial levels as far as finance goes, but as the years have gone by personnel unease at the system appears to have increased. Methods of financing missions vary enormously. In the larger denominational churches missionaries are paid from central funds allocated to mission. In some of the interdenominational and 'faith missions', all monies received by the agency are pooled, so that personnel receive regular monthly allowances. In other groups missionaries receive only personalised donations, so income level may be very irregular. This pattern is obviously closely related to the individual's fund-raising skills and the attractiveness or otherwise of the project concerned.

Some people have told me they have no problem with the current personalised fund-raising pattern and have lived happily with it for many years. They see it as a way of building up a wonderful relationship with home supporters. However, many have said to me, 'I wish I could earn my bread honestly by getting a regular salary for what I do, and so feel I am caring personally for my family', and I know what they mean. The worst aspect for most is having to raise funds during home leave, which has been described as a 'boiling point issue'. In some home countries, giving a talk about your work is automatically equated by the audience with a need for personal donations, even though this may not be mentioned. This is becoming increasingly repugnant to many workers. They want to inform people of the need overseas, and what they are actually doing to meet it, without their talk being confused with personal fund-raising. Deputation-related stress on home leave emerged in my research as significantly related to the development of psychological symptoms, but whether or not this is related to fund-raising requires further clarification.

Another problem concerns the willingness of supporters in some countries to donate only to the religious aspect of the work, which they call 'ministry', and not to the other things missionaries may do to serve their people in the name and spirit of Jesus Christ. Hence medical care, creating a library, digging wells, and many aid projects would be classed as secular, not 'ministry'. I have never been able to agree with this outlook. As a missionary doctor this would imply that when I am handing out aspirins, or operating, or lecturing to staff I am doing secular work, but when I am taking a Bible study or preaching a sermon in church I am doing spiritual work. There is no way that I can accept this, for it implies that I can divide myself into two parts, one that works 'in the Spirit' and one that is secular. I am one person, totally committed to serving Jesus Christ through the power of his Spirit. I have given myself to him, and therefore believe that whatever I do, whether it be seeing patients, jogging, fishing, swimming, going to the cinema, taking a Bible study, giving a lecture, going to a prayer meeting, or sorting out my many mistakes, these are all part of my life as a committed Christian, despite my multiple weaknesses and failures. The secular versus spiritual view causes much hardship to some missionaries on home assignment as they try to explain to their supporters how they actually spend their time, and the importance of the holistic ministry they engage in.

As I discovered on my recent travels, some of the new-sending countries have an even more serious problem. Missionaries and their families are sent out to nearby countries, or interstate in their own country, and are supported by their churches for one year. In that time they are expected to acquire a working knowledge of language and culture and to find ways of supporting themselves. At the end of the year they are cut off from their allowances, and many have a very difficult time indeed, especially if they work in a hostile atmosphere. In an excellent paper on mission problems in one of the new-sending Asian countries, the speaker quoted results of interviewing their missionaries about financial problems:

> Several missionaries who were interviewed agreed that missionaries and Christian workers were the ones who did not have much savings, or any health insurance, or retirement benefits, or death relief schemes. The consensus was that this state of affairs resulted from a false theology called 'faith', until some disaster struck them such as a heart attack... Many missionaries did not speak about funds for fear of being branded as unspiritual, but quietly suffered the insecurities. They endured much in the name of spirituality and faith... these situations lead to problems when the missionary faces a crisis, or when he retires and has no place to go, or when he dies and his family are left stranded in the streets with no sustenance. (Rajendran, 1999)

Missionaries are not lacking in financial faith, as exemplified by a household I stayed in where the children knew that periodically money did not arrive, and were quite used to asking their parents if they could have second helpings of food at the meal that day. There was no tension, it was just a fact of life, and they were not harmed by it.

All my friends know I am hopeless about finance, and I was always thankful I worked for missions which did not demand personal fund-raising. However, I have had opportunity to observe many different financial support systems. One of the best I have known is the unit support method. The cost of absolutely everything required by a single missionary or missionaries with families is worked out and divided up into units. At the candidate stage, efforts are made by management and candidate in a very unpressurised way to raise the number of units that will be required, the unit amount being kept small enough not to put people off! The local sending church has become increasingly involved in raising the money their missionary member will need, and often accepts responsibility for raising most of the units required, the shortfall sometimes being made up from agency general funds. Should the missionary's circumstances change, such as getting married or having children, then prayer supporters and home churches are informed, and further units allocated. From that time on missionaries are not expected to fund-raise every time they come home on leave, which frees them to talk about the work they are doing without it being inevitably equated with raising money. There have often been problems with this method, much faith is required to raise the units, but it seems to work better than most current systems in the interdenominational group.

No one doubts that God looks after his servants, but if we are to fulfil the God-given task of spreading the gospel, then something must be done to reduce the unease that personnel are expressing over the current financial system. I have heard that in some countries an association of Christian businessmen has been created to act as a think tank and to give advice to agencies on handling missionary finance in the new millennium, and this would be a most welcome development.

The components of other forms of occupational stress

Many people say things like 'I feel stressed out by the work', but analysis of exactly what they are reacting to has thrown up some interesting points. The components of occupational stress will be discussed in three sections: the work itself, the working environment and working relationships. Material for this has been obtained from 397 missionaries who consulted me for depression, and from questionnaire responses submitted by 150 currently serving partners.

The work itself
Overload is right at the top of the list, way ahead of anything else. After this comes national working conditions, followed by

job mismatch and instability. Next came communication problems, not only on the job but also in poor pre-service job descriptions.

Clearly, overload needs further investigation. In secular aid projects many personnel said they worked in excess of 70 hours a week and admitted that more breaks and less work would have been more efficient as they were all burnt out (Macnair, 1995). For mission partners the problem seems to be predominantly related to having too wide a role, one person having far too many different things to do. There is the visa-related job which is usually much broader than in the home country, plus church, plus home and family, plus friends, plus all the other things expatriates get asked to do. Difficulty in balancing all this is much the same as in the home country, but is complicated by adverse climate, strange diseases, poor communications and the problems of working in a foreign language. In addition, the nature of the work may be such that it cannot be reduced. For example, there may be an epidemic in the area and the hospital is swamped. Nothing can be done to control this, unlike the more chronic overload conditions which with a little juggling can be spread out more evenly during the week. I saw another example recently, where missionaries involved in building a hydro-electric dam had to cope when their senior technical officer went off sick. The project was time-related and had to continue without him, which was very stressful. I add hastily that all went well in the end.

The second highest complaint concerns **technical problems**. Job mismatch was a cause of stress, as were false expectations from the nationals as to what the expatriate was actually going to do, but the major ones were inadequate training for the job and inadequate equipment on arrival. This type of stress can be reduced by good job description and clear explanation of technical problems before the job is taken up. However, doing the work with the equipment provided overseas may prove very difficult. The missionary may be over-trained for the equipment available and find it hard to adapt. The opposite may be true, national equipment being far advanced and with cultural additions, which the cross-cultural workers do not understand and so feel disadvantaged. This creates added conflict between older workers and generation X personnel who usually know a great deal about certain kinds of advanced technology. As the idiom says, 'they drank it in with their mother's milk'. If they decide to enter the ordinary work scene they may become more important resource people than the older generation, and to accept this demands a good deal of grace!

The final factor that requires comment is **professional isolation**. A recent survey reveals that although most partners are satisfied with their professional development, certain inherent stressors emerged (Foyle, 1999). The major one is difficulty in maintaining and developing professional skills in long-term overseas service, usually for financial reasons. Little has ever been written about this, but many long-termers remember the time when they could never afford to go to a national or international professional conference, or to buy new textbooks, or to do reputable courses during home assignment. These days most agencies have changed their financial policies to enable serving personnel to keep up to date, and of course the Internet has been hugely beneficial. One agency sets an example by sending all its professional workers a textbook every year. It is essential that those with professional training be enabled to attend national conferences, where they not only learn something new, but also contribute and make many lasting friendships. Recently someone asked me why I went to professional non-mission conferences, and my reply was 'to mingle'. To attend as an ordinary human being doing admittedly a rather odd job, to learn what is new in the profession, and incidentally to befriend lonely foreign nationals striving to cope without their families and with no apparent support systems, is a real ministry which every professionally trained partner should consider.

Two other aspects of professional isolation are the lack of professional support and of audit. Personnel are used to both of these, and would value their inclusion in personnel care policies. Visiting support is better than none at all, and audit serves as a learning process and an encouragement to continue. One agency has allocated an experienced person to visit on a regular basis every isolated mission member of his profession, and this has been most successful.

So far we have thought of the problems of those accustomed to a regular work pattern, but in generation X, work-related occupational stress may take a different form. Their generational custom is to change jobs, to move on and to be much more flexible about where they work and how they do it. One very reputable group currently has 200 vacancies for established posts, probably because generation X does not feel called to serve God in that way, or to get involved in projects that are either not primarily evangelistic or not fully church-related. They want to be free to serve for a time in one area and then move on, to concentrate on relationships and simply change jobs when they feel it is right to do so. In addition, they are not always used to authority, and since national working conditions tend to be based on an authoritarian structure they find it almost impossible to fit in. Their occupational stress has yet to be studied, but so far it appears to be predominantly related to the conflict between established old-style work and the totally different pattern on which they wish to work. Agencies are increasingly having to come to terms with the fact that some of their long-established work which for various reasons has not been adequately nationalised may have to be closed, for we cannot rely on generation X to slot into the gaps left when long-termers retire. This has been well-outlined by Dr Harold Adolph (2000) who relates these difficulties to the need to pay off educational debts after graduation, and the changing attitudes of different generations. Interestingly, forty years ago one very well-known agency foresaw this dilemma and closed down all its old hospitals, thus releasing staff for a new-style medical missionary enterprise in other countries, and opening new doors for short-term generation X-style ministry.

An even more difficult problem is related to the entrepreneurial gifts of many in the modern generations. Almost as soon as they arrive in their location they may see better ways of doing things. But being able to say so is not always part of the accustomed pattern, for in many parts of the world new people are still expected to accept things as they are for some time before they begin to express their opinion. In some groups personnel are not allowed to take part in planning and other meetings until they have been working on probation for three to five years, while those in the new generations have worked through three different jobs by that time!

Basically, attitude is all-important. As Gish wrote (1983), those who saw working problems as a challenge, rather than something negative or threatening seemed to be more success- ful in keeping stress at bay. Missionary training therefore should incorporate an attitude of accepting work difficulties as a challenge rather than a problem. This encourages creative enterprise rather than a defeatist problem-based attitude. God did promise us that we would be able to do all things through Christ who strengthens us, and accepting challenges may help us to prove this, although of course the verse does not mean we should take everything on without first asking if God wants us to do it.

The working environment

Certain other stressors have emerged in connection with the environment in which missionaries work, such as the overall arrangements for workers, general frustration, inadequate finance and cultural adaptation.

While not everyone will agree with me, in the current work- ing environment overseas I do not feel it is wise to locate mis- sionaries to certain kinds of jobs. For example, sometimes an expatriate missionary with office and financial experience may be asked to manage national church and diocesan funds. In countries where there has been a strong colonial past and the church is settling into its new pattern without the old-style missionaries, such an appointment is potentially very stressful, for the working environment remains loaded with old cultural misunderstandings. I believe such an appointment should only be permitted for a short time to help out in emergency, not as a longer-term appointment.

The local culture is a vital part of the working environment, and as an example I will use food. Every nationality has its own food patterns, which differ from country to country and are usually rigidly adhered to. For example, in some parts of Asia workers eat a large meal before going to work, have a snack lunch and then another large meal in the evening. Consequently official meal breaks at work are very limited, and the Westerner used to a reasonable lunch break has to change his eating habits. This is not an easy task, and is by no means confined to expatriates. Mumbai (Bombay) seems to have worked out how to manage a mixed society with a plethora of local food rules. Workers buy 'tiffin-carriers', little round boxes of food in a stand, and after they have gone to work their wives cook lunch and fill the tiffin carrier. People are paid to collect these from homes all over the city, and they all meet at a large railway station in the city, sort out which box goes where, and then deliver them to the workplace This gives the recipient an opportunity to eat a home-cooked lunch during the very brief lunch break, as well as reducing the amount of snack food he eats. This very successful culturally appropriate take-away system is repeated every working day.

Visas in most countries remain difficult. It is right that national rules are strict, but sometimes the bureaucracy can be deadly. Hours of time are spent in offices waiting for the right official to put the right signature on a document, and often a multiplicity of documents must be signed before the final visa is given, all demanding visits to different places. This is an area where national friendships help, for friendly local people may know the best path through the maze, and how to avoid the problem of bribery, this being an honourable social pattern in some countries which many Christians do not feel free to utilise.

Working relationships

Relationships with leadership

Relationships with national and expatriate leadership appear to be more difficult for missionaries than those between colleagues, and both are significantly related to the development of psychological symptoms overseas. The major problem with **national** leadership is the under-use of positive feedback. In some countries it is considered dangerous to praise anyone. I learned quickly in India that it is not good to praise a baby because the people believed such praise was an open invitation to hostile gods to bring evil on the child. The other cultural belief in some countries is that by working well you are building up heavenly merit, and if it is praised the benefit will be negated, so they do you a kindness by not praising. In one country I worked in the locals believed that I was the first wife of the senior doctor who had thrown me out because I had no children. By working so hard I was trying to appease the gods for my bad luck. Hence if they had praised my work at all, or said thank you, it would have destroyed the merit I was seeking to build up!

Even among the Christian community little praise is given until after you have gone. Disgruntled people will say, 'Things were all right when Y was here [your predecessor],' and this gets under your skin after a time. We need therefore to remember that the day will come when you will be Y, and the new person is having to cope with how marvellous you were. Meanwhile it is better to smile sweetly and say, 'Oh well, I am so glad you enjoyed working with Y, I will just try to do my best.' In my time I have taken over from a famous doctor after whom the locals named the hospital, a doctor who spoke the language like a national due to being born in the country, and a famous doctor who was one of the very first missionary psychiatrists in the world. I became immune to 'the marvellous Y', and just tried to do what I could, this being the best way to handle the problem without being permanently discouraged.

The problems with **expatriate leadership** are different. As has been said, there is a significant relationship between being dissatisfied with the expatriate leader and the development of psychological symptoms overseas. In addition, those who were conditionally selected due to personal problems found at selection were also significantly more likely than others to have a poor relationship with the expatriate leader, but not with the national. Relationships with the **home office** were satisfactory on the whole (Foyle, 1999).

The problems missionaries experience with their expatriate leadership have been outlined as poor communications, domination, policy disagreements, uninformed criticism of the work the missionary is doing, and incompetence (Foyle, 1999). The problem is exacerbated by different expectations of management from different nationalities (Neale et al, 1992). I have always had great sympathy with missionary complaints, but in this case my loyalties are divided, for I also have a lot of sympathy for the poor expatriate leaders. Usually they do not want the job, and it is tacked on as an extra to an already heavy work-load. Most of them have had no special training in leadership. In addition, expatriate leaders have to cope with financial stringency, inadequate office staff and equipment, and too broad-based a role. In some cases unsuitable leadership has simply been imposed on the group by the home office, personnel not being allowed any part in the selection process. I have known some absolute disasters from this policy, for often the person seen by the home office as suitable is not so in the eyes of the personnel concerned. In one group, the appointment was so unsuitable that the overseas missionary group collapsed entirely through mass resignation. Dodds (1995) has put the matter succinctly, 'Mission leaders are seldom actually hired for competency or job experience. They are usually promoted through the ranks and may lack training and experience as managers and people nurturers, even though proficient in other areas of work.' We should remember that this problem is by no means confined to missions; business and secular overseas aid groups publish papers describing exactly the same problems (Foyle, 1999).

The only thing to do at present is to await the results of an investigation of this problem that I have heard is under way. Current expatriate leaders themselves need to enter this field much more strongly, seeking to find through study and discussion possible solutions to a new style of leadership in the millennium. Generation X is not going to listen to old-style leadership anyway, and maybe the millennium generation will be even less interested. Meanwhile can personnel and expatriate leadership be patient with each other? Can we do anything to help our administrators? Can we pray for them especially, and ask them to send us prayer requests so that we can support them? I know that sometimes their inadequacies impact on us and our families, and that research has shown that anything impacting on the family arouses excessive anxiety, yet both sides are trying to get on with God's work, and a little compassion and patience would go a long way. We also need to balance what has been written by remembering the superb expatriate leadership many of us have had. I for one owe my 51 years in missionary service to two wonderful leaders who nurtured me through difficult times and taught me so much.

Relationships with colleagues

Differences in **type and use of equipment** already commented on may provoke poor interpersonal relationships, and a meeting point has to be found. The major problems are being personally over- or under- equipped for the job in hand, or else the equipment may be unfamiliar. When we do not know how the local equipment works it is much better to say so, with a laugh at being just an ignorant foreigner, rather than to become all superior and say, 'Of course we understand our work, it's just the equipment which is peculiar.' It may have taken years of struggle to produce that piece of equipment within the country, and to undervalue it is distinctly harmful to national-expatriate relationships. Conversely, where local technology has outclassed our own home technology, we need to explain that we do not know how to use it, and ask to be taught.

What I have written seems almost patronising, but in reality there are still a few who go overseas feeling they are God's gift to the country and have little to learn. A humble respectful attitude is the key to good working relationships. It is interesting that just as expatriate personnel have courses to explain working practices in other countries, some host national leaders are also being given courses to help them to understand the expatriate background. I have twice been asked to give a short lecture-course to national teachers in an overseas language school to help them understand why expatriates behave the way they do. In the secular world, one UK group organises a periodic joint conference of national and expatriate leadership to increase understanding of each other as they work together overseas and to build those friendships which so greatly enhance working harmony overseas.

Problems also arise between **older expatriate partners and the newly arrived**. As has been mentioned earlier, many generation X people have entrepreneurial gifts and have little patience with what they see as old-fashioned stuffy ways of working. What they do not realise is that the older people are reacting in a way that helps them cope with fatigue. Many have been grossly over-stretched, and have learnt to cope with it by setting up routines that can more or less run themselves. Unfortunately routines can get out of date, and the new people spot that very quickly. They then rush in with suggestions which the older person sees as criticism, and reacts by becoming even more rigid. This is specially true if there has been, in psychological terms, an over-investment in the work, i.e. the older person's ego strength is bound up in what has been accomplished. Thus a suggestion becomes a threat to the person, rather than a professional matter. A vicious cycle then develops, with increasing rigidity on one side and an attempt at suppression of new people as 'too young to know what they are talking about', and anyway what they suggest is 'not in accordance with the local culture'. As a result there is increasing anger and frustration on the other side. The truth is that quite often local methods are old-fashioned, but this has often been unavoidable, due to financial constraints and the problems of keeping up to date while working so hard. This sort of relationship may take time to sort out, and demands good will and humility on both sides, but real harmony and mutual respect can be achieved with a little love, respect and give-and-take on both sides. The young should never wipe out the old, and the old should listen carefully to the young — they may be right!

Handling occupational stress

Occupational stress is usually the chronic kind, not the emergency alarm type, and therefore demands a great deal of personal commitment to God and dedication to the job in hand as the basis of all coping strategies. As explained in Chapter 2, the first thing is to decide whether it is right to stay on and cope or if you should take steps to leave the situation in a controlled way. As was mentioned before, never rush away when emotionally upset, do it 'decently and in order'.

If you decide to stay on there are many things that can be done to help cope-ability:

Set up a personal support structure. Get in touch with your home church and prayer partners and tell them the situation. Ask for regular prayer as you continue to deal with it. It helps if someone promises to pray for you at a certain time on the same day of the week, which gives a wonderful sense of continuity of support. Make certain your leader knows about the situation and is in agreement with how you plan to cope. Ask for someone to visit you on a regular basis to provide professional support.

Support other staff members. If you are responsible for them, encourage new expatriates to write down all the changes they would like to make, discuss them and see what can be implemented. Look after the needs of national staff by regular meetings, knowing their families, and integrating as fully as possible with local cultural life. Delegate as much responsibility as possible.

Safeguard your personal spiritual life. This may mean changing long-established devotional habits. One thing is to establish a prayer pattern that suits the job. For example, when I was overloaded at the hospital I developed the habit of praying silently as I walked from one department to the other. I also kept in my pocket a small devotional book called *Daily Strength* printed by Scripture Gift Mission, and during the day meditated on the printed verse for that day. We can spend more time in prayer and Bible study when we have a little more free time, meanwhile the emergency rations keep us going. My mobile praying bore dividends. I told the gardener I prayed for the dahlias he so lovingly grew, and when we put them into the annual flower show at Government House and they yet again won first prize, I heard him tell the Governor's gardener that of course we won because his Doctor Miss-Sahib prayed for them every day!

If married, **be sure you and your spouse are in agreement** about staying on in the same job. The last thing to add onto occupational stress is marital disagreement, and if one partner feels strongly that you should leave, and continues to feel like that after a period of time, then it is better to leave and get help than to stay and argue about it.

Eat as well as you can and get all the **sleep** you can. If any **physical illness** occurs get it treated quickly, for stress is a potent cause of repeated physical illness.

Look at your overall stress load. In India we used to say, 'It's all on my head' if we had an awful lot of stress to carry. We need to look at the total load and reduce where we can. Nepali porters do this when assessing a load they are about to carry. If it is too much they simply remove part of it, for they know their own carrying capacity. Reducing the load may involve pulling out of other things for a time. For example, a mother who has two children and then produces twins is going to have to reduce her outside occupational load. This may mean she has to give up her Sunday-school class for a time, and cut down on the pastoral visiting she did for the church. You never know what help is going to turn up, so instead of saying to the pastor, 'Sorry, I must pull out,' it is better to pull out 'for the time being' thus keeping options open, and making the problem of finding a permanent replacement less urgent. If you finally have to pull out altogether it is then less of a shock to everyone.

When looking at the overall load it is helpful to see if the overload is recurrent or present all the time. If recurrent, then special plans can be made for the heavy time ahead. A good example is the annual board meeting before which budgets have to be prepared and future planning documented. This is a temporary overload, and support can be found to cover for the necessary period if you usually control your routine work load wisely. Too often, alas, no advance planning is done and the situation becomes more and more stressful as you try to shed something at the last moment.

In addition, the whole of life needs to be scrutinised to see which other stress areas can be reduced. You need to find yourself a little more space to allow for the heaviness of the occupational load. If there are interpersonal tensions with anyone try to resolve them. Brief quarrels can be resolved simply by saying sorry, more severe areas need working on. In long-standing disputes, a frank approach can often be made to the other person. An explanation that both of you have too much to do at present, and a request that the hatchet should be buried for the time being till both have leisure to discuss the matter will usually be very acceptable to the other party.

Where your own **past problems** are revived during this period of overload, as is very common, try to shelve them temporarily. I find this can be done by handing them over to God, asking him to look after them for a while, and then taking them out to deal with later on when things have quietened down, taking proper advice if necessary.

If your job is permanently heavy, do **short terms** overseas with shorter home leave until the load is easier. Jesus and the disciples seemed to follow this pattern, travelling for certain periods and then having a rest time. As indicated earlier, management should consider not locating personnel to places where they will be permanently overloaded and there is a history of a high rate of psychological malaise or breakdown.

Be extra careful about time off. If you have to carry a heavy load for a long time, agree to it on the condition you can have extra leave, and take it no matter what happens. One mission hospital I worked in had to close for six weeks every summer, making other arrangements for their patients over the interval. This way all the staff got a holiday and were ready for the extra load on return. Local leave is mandatory when the work is too heavy. It is more difficult if you are self-employed overseas and have few colleagues, but it is better to do less and allow for a rest period than to go on too long and begin to suffer stress symptoms. Use the system of short end-points as described in the 'fish and chips' section of Chapter 3 (p. 61). To think three years is an eternity, but to think a week makes it bearable.

Avoid the guilt of the undone. Some things will have to be either inadequately done or not done at all. It just cannot be helped. The personality structure must be controlled here. Those with obsessional or type A traits find it very difficult to settle for second best, but if you recognise it as a life-saving manoeuvre then usually the personality can cope with it.

Use good ways of handling tension. This will be further discussed in other chapters, but here it should be emphasised that some form of regular relaxation is essential. There are no rules, it is a matter of personal choice, but some time should be set aside for it every week. One man I knew used to ride a bicycle over newspaper covered with different coloured paint, and create lovely patterns, which he found very restful. Another used to skip on the roof. If there is a young family a communal project is very relaxing, such as building a shed in the garden or painting fences in bright colours. In my last hospital during the hot weather when everyone got fractious we did a marvellous project. Once a week in the hot evenings all the staff did Batik work, and found that tensions disappeared like magic as we fought to scrape wax off the huge picture we were creating.

Use a quick relaxation technique. This one takes about five minutes.

1. Select a comfortable sitting or lying position.
2. Close your eyes and think about a place you have been to before where you felt relaxed.
3. Imagine you are there, imagine the sight, the smell, the colours, the atmosphere.
4. Feel the peace and calm, or the sheer happiness of the place, and imagine yourself being totally refreshed by it.
5 After five minutes open your eyes, stretch, and go back to the rat race!
6. Remember, you can go back to 'your place' at any time. You can even withdraw mentally from a difficult committee meeting for a few minutes refreshment!

My own place is a lovely lake in Scotland, with rhododendrons blooming, birds flying round, and a nice trout rise developing. The sun is too hot to fish so I am lying on the bank doing nothing but listening, smelling the scent, and resting. But now I must open my eyes, get up, and return to my current rat race, the computer. Perhaps next time I'll catch a fish.

6

Interpersonal Relationships

Wherever I go people ask me to talk to them about interpersonal relationships, hereafter called IPRs. They complain that the energy expended in trying to get along together depletes the energy available for the job they came to do.

In reality they are being more successful than they thought. With the exception of relationships of personnel with leaders, interpersonal relationships between nationals and expatriates and expatriates and expatriates did not prove significantly stressful in my recent research (Foyle, 1999). In other words, despite their complaints of IPRs being difficult, the personnel I studied had obviously been well trained, took great care to try to get on, and probably prayed a great deal about relationships. Most complaints were related to the presence of one person with whom they had difficulty rather than with a large group, and this may be the reason they managed to cope — ultimately the person moved on, or went home, and things improved.

Most Christians naively expect to live together in constant harmony. We forget that even in the presence of the Lord the disciples quarrelled about who got what in the coming kingdom. If I had been there I would have been furious with James and John for asking Jesus for the best positions (Mark 10:35). It appears that they also asked their mother to use her influence on their behalf (Matthew 20:20). They were entirely ignoring the fact that all the others had made similar sacrifices and equally deserved special privileges and were therefore belittling the achievements of their colleagues, a sure way of producing interpersonal anger! The way Jesus dealt with it teaches us something. First of all he did not chop them off and just say 'certainly not'. Nor did he scold them for asking. He explained the implications of their demand, and its constitutional impossibility. 'It is not for me to grant this' put the request into its correct administrative background. He then called the whole group together and explained the vital new principle that in the coming kingdom the greatest people would be those who were servants of all (Mark 10:35-45). Presumably James and John, and possibly their mother, made humble apologies to the whole group, for nothing good can be achieved by role-grabbing, self-seeking, and minimising others. As we look to him to teach us what we need to know, we often find we learn something new about IPRs. This helps us to resolve the problem rather than it remaining as a constant irritant.

One of the basic causes of problems in interpersonal relationships is that we are all **different**, and it is worthwhile examining these differences in some detail. Differences cause friction between us for two reasons. One is that due to our early life training, in the depths of our hearts we think our ways are both right and better than others, and this is usually picked up by our colleagues who find it very irritating. The other reason is that differences upset our framework. The mind likes to organise things, to make them into wholes. When someone comes along with a new idea we feel threatened because it means we have to adjust our framework. The threat is worse if we are already feeling stressed, for then we may only be able to manage life by keeping everything controlled and organised in our own minds, and fear anything that could upset the equilibrium we have created. So we may hang onto our own rigidity and react to new ideas with severe criticism, which in turn often leads to eruptions of anger, jealousy and frustration.

This was one of the problems missions had to face after the watershed of the Second World War. Before that missions had gone on within quite a secure framework with a fixed working hierarchy. After the war, when new personnel began to come out as missionaries they proved to be an entirely different breed of people. Some had seen war, bombing, hunger and atrocity. Others had been bereaved and had to mature very early. If they had served in the armed forces or the civil defence they had had enough of rigidity, and certainly did not expect to find it in mission. So an immediate generational division sprang up between the old and new workers which demanded much love and charity on both sides, together with a degree of administrative modification. One mission I knew took the unprecedented step of allowing new missionaries to meet together during the annual conference, and to present their own agenda and solutions to the problems facing them. Some of the old guard were not pleased! This is understandable since they had survived equal difficulties, and kept everything together without collapsing under the strain, As a result they were very tired, which in turn reduced their ability to change their framework. The same sort of upset is now occurring due to generation X, one of whom has written, 'Our motivation for mission will be different, as will our understanding of what mission actually is. We will be able to accept different visions, goals, styles and so on from different people, and aim to combine the strengths of each into a wider whole' (Tiplady, 2000). He then goes on to say that gen X is now out of date anyway, and the millennium generation is arriving, so many further changes will be required of us, as discussed in Chapter 1.

The message of all this is that missions can never stand still, they need constantly to rethink how their task is to be done, and to pray for adaptability. This does not mean abandonment of the past, for good principles and practices are a permanent requirement, but they 'wear different pyjamas', i.e. are expressed in a modern comprehensible way.

Behind the need for change which each generation brings lies a helpful fact. God has created all of us for an individual and corporate purpose, and the task of mission is not only to fulfil God's purpose for the lost world but to enable personnel to achieve their fullest potential. It is interesting that very little has been written about personal development in God's service, as if sacrifice was the only possible end result. For this reason I asked a group of 150 missionaries to tell me to what degree they were professionally, emotionally, spiritually and overall satisfied with personal development during missionary service. The results showed they expected to develop, and were much more satisfied with this in the professional and spiritual areas than with emotional and overall development, stress in these last two areas being significantly related to the development of psychological symptoms during service (Foyle, 1999). We must therefore be prepared for things to be different as new generations come along, and should seek not only to do the work but also to enable all personnel to be more satisfied with their in-service development. However, while the new methods and patterns younger missionaries wish to institute may be the way God has chosen for them to fulfil their greatest potential for him, they must remember that for some the older pattern of mission is the right way to achieve the same thing. So instead of generational differences creating IPR problems, a mutuality of understanding should be achieved, each side giving a bit and taking a bit, so that all are fulfilled and God's work is done.

Differences between us have practical implications, and these will be discussed under three headings: physical, cultural and personality differences.

Physical differences

Dr C.B. Dobson has written an interesting book called *Stress, the Hidden Adversary* (1983). One section deals with research into stress in the working environment. He explains that some people function best in the mornings and others in the evenings. In addition, some are at their best at the start of the week and others towards the end. These differences are related to our hormonal patterns, which are in turn related to our genes. Anyone who lives with a companion will know what he is talking about. Imagine a husband and wife with different genetic hormone patterns. He is a slouch in the mornings, staggering down to breakfast unshaven and not really wide awake. Conversely, she is bright and breezy in the morning and wiped out in the evening. So she comes down to breakfast like the traditional 'Kellogg's Golden Cornflakes Girl', irritatingly clean and tidy with even a bit of make-up on. Unless they love each other a lot, and respect each other's genes, they could well quarrel every morning and evening! Similarly, there are people who insist on holding planning committee meetings on a Monday afternoon. This means half their members are not really with it, they only begin to come to life about Wednesday noon by which time the other half are starting to go down. So a wise leader plans committee meetings on a Wednesday afternoon when there is a hope of getting something out of all of them. We should never, of course, use our physical structure as an excuse for behaving badly, we should try to do our work at all times, but it does help to have a bit of understanding and to plan sensibly.

As a spin-off from this, there is interesting research on absenteeism from work the day after the weekly holiday. Some people who are stressed or nervous cannot cope with only the national statutory weekly time off, and tend to report sick the first working day more often than those with different personality structures. So if you are responsible for others it is worth keeping an eye on Monday absenteeism (Sundays in Nepal, Saturdays in Muslim countries). It gives you a shrewd idea who is over-stressed by the work and needs to have an eye kept on them.

Finally, mention must be made of those whose physique is weaker than others. They simply cannot cope with a driving untiring boss, and should not be located with one unless agreement is reached beforehand about how much the weaker person will be expected to do. Probably they can do a full working week quite easily, but cannot work the same 7 days a week and 365 days a year schedule as the boss, which will, of course, ultimately have a detrimental effect on his own health and family relationships. The best remedy is to be honest, never to use physical patterns as an excuse for laziness at work, but arrange the work load to suit your own pattern as far as you can. I hated finance, so I used to do it on a Tuesday afternoon when I was reasonably productive. Try to maintain a sense of humour in your attitude to physical differences, rather than constantly feeling ill at ease with your colleague who has a different pattern. It's not always deadly serious, make a joke of it together.

Cultural differences

Many of these problems are caused by what was mentioned earlier, the secret thought based on our childhood training that our way is not only the best but also right for everyone. People are not always aware of this, but in reality it impacts hugely on working cross-culturally. Thankfully the days are gone when new missionaries sometimes thought of themselves and the way they did things as God's answer to local needs, and now understand that initially they really contribute very little. The best thing I was ever told was on our first day at language school. The principal got up and said, 'Thank you for coming, but I hope you realise that by coming here you are merely adding to India's illiterates.' And so we were, we could neither read, write nor speak the local language. Mercifully nationals read our hearts and could tell that we wanted to love people even if we could not communicate, so we did not feel as demoralised as we might have done.

There are three problem areas in considering cultural differences, problems between nationals and expatriates, and problems between expatriates and expatriates. The third is problems of expatriates with national and expatriate leadership, which has been discussed in Chapter 5.

National/expatriate relationships

The modern generation has less difficulty with this for they are often brought up in multicultural societies and are travel-wise from an early age. For many expatriates, however, the difficulty is that our kind national friends are very hesitant to tell us when we do something that offends their culture. That is why in Nepal the current system of sending expatriates to live for a time in a Nepali home during orientation courses is so beneficial. They can actually see how the set-up works, learn what is acceptable and so feel more confident. The great mistake is to try to make ourselves exactly like the nationals. We can never do that, but we can make ourselves acceptable as friends from another culture coming to live with a different people group. Sometimes we get disheartened, but as indicated in Chapter 5, in some cultures we never really know how we are doing because of culture patterns which rarely include praise and encouragement. Usually it is some time after we have left a location that we hear the encouraging things. I shall never forget going back to Nepal several years after I had moved back to India. I was not marvellous at the local language although I could get by, and always wished I could have done better. When I went back I heard that people from the villages had often come to the hospital and said, 'Where's that doctor who speaks like a baby, she understands us.' I felt as if I had been given a bouquet of flowers.

There are certain things we can learn and practise which keep us from being offensive. One concerns national social customs. We never get these just right, but efforts to do so are respected and enjoyed by our kind national friends. Incidentally we never stop making mistakes! I made the worse social mistake of a thirty-year career the day I retired from India. I was at home relaxing with my feet on a table before going to the airport, and an old friend came to say goodbye. I sat him down with some tea, and then unthinkingly put my feet back on the table. In many parts of Asia it is a real insult to show the soles of your feet to someone else, and I immediately realised what I had done and apologised profusely. He said to me, 'Well, I minded, but then I remembered you are only a poor foreigner after all,' at which we both laughed and proceeded with our final chat and goodbyes. So you never do it perfectly, but at least you can show willing and try. Nationals have said to me that what matters to them is knowing that expatriates love and respect them, and this is far more important than behaving correctly. So whether or not you wear national dress, speak the language fluently, and always eat national food, these are no more than polite externals.

It is the degree of heart-integration with the nationals that really matters. This requires a qualifying word. There are things in our own countries we do not like, yet we still remain integrated. Similarly, to be integrated with a different culture does not mean we will like all of it, there are things which never cease to shock us, but this makes no difference to our hearts being oriented towards the people God has called us to work among.

National family pressures are not always understood by expatriates. There are communities where everything has to be done by the man of the house, and things like dental emergencies in a female member of the household or problems at the children's school will therefore impact on his ability to turn up to work that day. It is not until expatriates themselves begin to experience the conflicting demands of family/church/job overseas that a meeting place of understanding is found. Linked with all this is social shame, which is well understood by African and Asian nationals but not so well by Westerners from a more fluid society. If nationals are seen not to be as careful of family and social customs as the community thinks they should be they feel ashamed before their group, yet to observe the custom may conflict with the demands of the working situation, or in the case of converts with the demands of their new faith. They may therefore have to struggle with both social shame and individual guilt for hurting their families by not conforming, and both are highly stressful. Expatriates need to be very understanding and sympathetic with the nationals' social and religious dilemmas, and to provide a security of love and care while the individual works out what to do.

Expatriate/expatriate relationships

It is interesting that missionaries seem to prefer working in a multicultural team rather than a monocultural one (Roembke, 1998). However, language may be just as much a problem between expatriates as between nationals and expatriates. I once worked in a location where people came from nine different countries. Initially English was our *lingua franca* until we had learnt enough of the local language to communicate together. When English is incorrectly understood or utilised people easily get offended. A nurse working with us said a ward into which we had put a lot of work was 'revolting', at which we all bristled. We had learned enough to ask what she meant, which was only that it needed a new coat of whitewash, so that reminded us of the first cardinal rule in expatriate relationships: when you don't understand, ask for clarification.

The social situation can be affected by language because the same word in English means different things to different people. Tea to Australians is a large cooked meal, to southern UK folk it means a cup of tea and a biscuit, and to Americans it is sometimes a new thing anyway to take a tea break! So if you turn up at an Australian house for tea do not eat before you go, for you won't have room to cope with the large amount of food you will be offered. I have long ago learned to clarify what I am being invited to, and to explain what I mean when I am giving the invitation.

Working patterns are affected by nationality, and problems are usually based on different training methods. I belong to the era when temperatures were taken in Fahrenheit, whereas most Scandinavians and continentals were trained in centigrade (as we are now in the UK). But until I discovered a chart which had both centigrade *and* Fahrenheit on it I was in deep trouble with my mainly Scandinavian colleagues when I unwisely tried to persuade them to change rather than changing myself! Compromise is the usual answer, finding a mutually acceptable way round the problem. In this context it is also important to understand qualifications from different countries, otherwise staff can feel minimised. This all sounds very petty, but not understanding differing educational patterns can influence behaviour. When I was head of an Indian hospital, two expatriates refused to keep their appointment with me because I was an MB.BS doctor (the medical graduating degree in the UK), and they wanted 'a proper MD doctor' which was the US degree! I was personally secure enough to feel nothing but amusement, and after explanation of the system they were happy to continue with the consultation. But this re-emphasises the original rule quoted: when you don't understand, ask for clarification.

Social and national customs

We should never make stereotypes, expecting people to be what we think they should be. We had a disastrous experience when we heard a Welshman was coming to join us. I got all excited and explained to my multinational colleagues that all Welshmen were good singers, so we organised a choir and waited for him to arrive. When he came he was tone-deaf and could not sing a note! This is an example of a stereotype, and we should therefore never expect anyone to be anything but themselves, uncoloured by an often erroneous national characteristic. Certainly few Scots are as tight with money as the old stereotype says, and not all Texans are boastful!

Financial disparity

This can cause disharmony. Some mission partners have bigger allowances than others, and some have no fixed allowance at all, living on what comes in every month. This usually leads to different life-styles on location, and differing holiday patterns. The fact that in the eyes of the people all foreigners are equally rich makes things all the more difficult for those on lower incomes. My only advice is to live in the way you feel right, and if you are on a low income try to handle the shame you feel when the richer missionaries give generously to things at church and you have to contribute something smaller. Probably no one will ever understand, so just accept it as a *fait accompli*.

Missionary subcultures

This is a rarely mentioned danger. The term 'subculture' indicates a type of group thinking and behaviour that can develop when missionaries live in a small group separated from the larger outside group, from which they remain detached. It is made worse when partnership with the local church is not yet well developed.

Subcultures may provide support for their members, but have inherent dangers. For various reasons it may become increasingly inward looking, interest in the outside world becoming progressively decreased. As an example, in one place I visited the country was having the first ever national election, but the missionaries in the group did not even know about it. Some of them had good language, but due to inward preoccupation with subcultural concerns they neither took a local newspaper nor listened to news on the radio. (There was no TV at that time.) Such inward-looking thought patterns can lead to over-concentration on interpersonal relationship problems or the community spiritual life to the exclusion of other topics. Within the subculture accepted norms frequently develop, such as how you pray, dress or behave, and the content of your faith. I remember once being asked unexpectedly to give my testimony to a mildly sub-cultural group, presumably to discern whether or not I was an OK Christian!

The greater danger is that the norms of the subculture may be imposed on new members joining the group. Those who accept them are considered spiritual and therefore in the group, the others being unacceptable. Under these conditions unhealthy emotions such as depression and anxiety readily arise, together with a growing sense of inferiority, and these may be infectious to the rest.

Two things help to avoid an unhealthy subculture when living in an isolated situation. First of all, a balance should be maintained between the outer world and the missionary community. Mixing with all sorts of people is a very healthy thing to do, and joining a suitable local community activity is a wonderful way of integrating with outside people. In one isolated area the missionaries were asked to host the first ever music group to which caste nationals invited outcaste musicians, and it was a very good experience. Going shopping in the local market is also a great way of making friends. I was walking down our shopping street in India the day after the traders' new year festival. I did not realise how many people I knew until they all began popping out of their shops to ask me to buy something and bring them good luck for the year ahead. Mercifully they were satisfied with a very small purchase!

The second thing is to maintain the integrity of your own person. To avoid the worst of the sub-cultural mentality we need to care for the whole person, body, mind and spirit. The mind is often the neglected area, usually due to sheer overwork. We have doctors to help us look after the body, and God himself, the church and our friends help to keep us alive spiritually, but we often forget that expatriate service should also be mind-enhancing. In culturally suitable places where the locals will not find our possessions offensive, TV, video, radio and computers are God-given, for by selective choice we can remain in touch with the world. Not only do they keep our minds fresh but we are also less boring when we go home on leave. I have never forgotten turning to my brother at the opera when I had just got home, and saying to him, 'Isn't that Alexander Gibson conducting?' 'How would you know that?' he asked. 'BBC world service' I said, 'they had a talk about this opera and how good Alexander was.' I felt positively brilliant! I also believe that we should use our opportunities overseas to enhance academic development. We may stay long enough to do a simple research programme, or study briefly something unusual that will look very nice on our c.v. Due to our heavy work-load this will probably have to be somewhat low key, nevertheless it keeps our minds alive.

I have been travelling world wide to care for missionaries for the last twenty years, and have been amazed at what they do in their spare time. I have met artists painting Russian Orthodox Church icons or local views, excellent carpenters and embroiderers, people studying local history and music. All these were done in a low-key way as time allowed, but were all of amazingly high standard. In some areas cultural interchange is often difficult due to inherent spiritual problems, but the situation is easier these days due to the global village atmosphere of so many countries, and the increasing feeling that we as mission partners are world citizens who are privileged to have a unique knowledge of the area where we live.

Personality differences

As we work together personality differences can cause great problems. Basically, we think it would be easier if we were all just the same (usually just like us!) but in reality that would be dead boring. God gives infinite personality variation, and this can be an exciting experience. It may also cause much stress, and this section will attempt to look at why personalities are different, why some are very difficult to handle, and how we can strengthen and protect them.

Personality structure

Personality is made up of the genes our parents gave us and the environment in which the genes develop. People often wonder why siblings are so different and there are two reasons behind this. The first is that not all parental genes are used in the production of each baby, there being a sort of gene bank from which the 'genes of the day' are selected. How this happens I do not know, but my scientific friends tell me it is so. Secondly, no child's experience of its environment is ever exactly the same. We need therefore to learn to respect the individuality of other people's personalities, and particularly their efforts to improve them. When we become Christians the Holy Spirit moves into our lives, and slowly begins to work on all areas including personality. He will take infinite pains to help us rectify the difficult areas, and to develop and strengthen the whole, but it takes time and we need to be patient with each other.

People with difficult genetic and environmental backgrounds have real struggles in this area. Their personalities may be damaged and they often do not understand what God has in mind for them. Psalm 139 gives us the first clue. 'You have laid your hand upon me' (v. 5) is the basic wonderful fact of coming to know the Lord and the power of his Spirit. Furthermore, 'you [Lord] created my inmost being; you knit me together in my mother's womb. I praise you because I am fearfully and wonderfully made; your works are wonderful, I know that full well. My frame was not hidden from you when I was made in the secret place. When I was woven together in the depths of the earth, your eyes saw my unformed body' (vv. 13–16). This relates to our genetic structure being created during conception, and to the nine months of human pregnancy. None of that was without God's knowledge and care. The Psalm then goes on to speak of the environmental effect as part of God's plan. 'All the days ordained for me were written in your book before one of them came to be' (v. 16). So from conception to death, God is involved.

Problems arise when things go wrong. The baby may be born 'differently-abled' as the modern term has it, or the personality may be deeply damaged by very adverse early environmental factors. I believe there is a partial answer, and interestingly enough had my opinion strengthened by hearing much the same testimony from two different men living on different continents who had never met each other. I quote one of them with permission, having made a few changes to prevent identification, but the facts of the story are true. There was once a man who was the product of rape. An invading army had come into his country and one of the soldiers got hold of his mother. He was the result, and because of his parentage the villagers did not like him, and because of the rape his mother found it very difficult to love him. So he grew up damaged in personality and so lacking in social skills that he felt acceptable neither to his community nor to himself. One day things changed. He met someone who told him about Jesus and his love, he asked Jesus into his life, and slowly began to live in a totally new way. He joined a church where he was loved and respected as a fellow believer, was able to begin to grieve for his lost years and to rebuild his life. During this period he struggled with why it had all happened to him. Was God so unfair as to give one person a square deal and refuse it to another?

The answer both men found to this problem was contained in Psalm 139, and was much the same as I had worked out. I will try to make it clear by using an example drawn from what we call in the West DIY — (Do It Yourself). Many people world-wide like to keep some tools and repair and decorate their own homes. For example, in Nepal the villagers often wash the outside walls of their homes with a mixture of manure and water, which strangely enough keeps flies away, and they add on pretty yellow patterns. In Hong Kong, where the people may live in one square room, there are all sorts of individualised efforts at improving electrical systems and curtain arrangements. For Western people DIY may either be a family joke or else save them a lot of money, depending if it works or not.

A very common DIY feature is a big board in the garage with cut-out features into which each tool is slotted. If one tool is missing the board does not look right because of the gap. To turn this picture into helping us understand what God has allowed to come into our lives, we need to realise that everyone of God's servants has their own spot on the DIY board. However, people with tragic backgrounds and damaged person-alities often feel that God has been unfair to them in allowing so much suffering in their lives, which may well have had an adverse effect on their personality structure. They feel they can never be useful to God, cannot understand why he seems to have been so unfair, and feel bitter and resentful because of it. So they never feel they really slot into the big board.

The men in the example I gave found an answer that really helped them. They felt bitter and angry against God until they really understood that God had something personal for them to do, and that it was because of the suffering that they could slot into his big board so wonderfully. With the deepest reverence I say that while God does not want people to suffer, suffering is still in this world and cannot always be avoided. But when people have suffered, that is not the end. As they come to God for his love to enter them, they slowly realise that they can be uniquely useful in his ministry on earth just because their past lives have not been easy, and they have needed such a lot of help to restore aspects of their damaged personalities. It is a wonderful day when they realise that without them, despite all the pain and damage they have endured, the board would have remained incomplete, but by trusting the God of love with their whole story, and turning to him for forgiveness and empowerment, they pop right into their empty slot on the DIY board and he clips them in! That's what I call security.

Practical advice on interpersonal problems due to different personality types

- Respect everyone else's personality type. Remember they may have past and present problems you know nothing about, and are probably all too aware of their own deficiencies and are working on them.
- If in charge of teams, try to make suitable personality matches. Two people with obsessional traits in one office are a disaster, whereas mixing an obsessional person with a mildly hysterical personality type can be great! Similarly one mildly manic type works best with a mildly depressive person. Have only one hyper-driving Type A in any location, and help them try to learn not to impose their patterns on others.

- Look frankly at your own personality type, learn its strengths and weaknesses, and never stop working with God on it. More will be written about this topic later.

Personality maturity.

There are many different views on the development and maturation of personality, and usually people pick out the bits that fit their own ideas. I have selected Eric Erikson's description, mainly because it is simple, clear, and continues personality development right up to old age. Most of the others seem to stop at adolescence, which is very disheartening as you get older. With Erikson I have a clear picture of myself sinking into my grave at a ripe old age waving the last diploma — 'Final stage of personality maturation accomplished'!

In Erikson's pattern, personality development is accomplished in eight stages, and at each one a particular task has to be learned, certain persons being important to us at that time. He called the stages 'The Crises of Life', the word crisis indicating normal events in our development such as first going to school or entering adolescence. The following table outlines the stages, which are not clear cut, and there is a lot of overlap. In addition, there are generational changes to be made. Adolescence now starts earlier, and important persons in childhood backgrounds have changed. In some communities Fathers, and tribal aunties, have become just as important in stage 1 as mother, supplying security but not, of course, breast milk and that special maternal smell that makes babies feel secure.

The Crises of Life

Stage	Age	Task to be learned	Result of inadequate learning: a tendency to:	Important persons
1	Birth-2 years	Basic trust	Mistrust	Mother
2	2-4 years	Autonomy	Shame and doubt	Both parents
3	4-6 years	Taking the initiative	Guilt	Parent of opposite sex
4	6-12 years	Industry	Inferiority	Peers, teachers, parents
5	13-19 years	Personal identity	Identity diffusion	Everybody
6	20-30 years	Social intimacy	Isolation	Husband, wife, partners, friends
7	30-65 years	Social responsibility	Self-absorption	Family and society
8	65-death	Integrity	Despair	Family and society

Taking stage 1 as an example, basic trust is developed through immediate bonding with mother, and to a lesser extent father. I am in entire agreement with the current pattern of fathers being present at the birth, and experiencing those moments of bonding when the baby is put into their arms, even before the placenta is delivered. The child's experiences over the next two years will create a capacity for basic trust in the personality, which develops steadily throughout life. Substitutes for own parents can also achieve this developmental stage, but where the society is too fluid for substitutes to be available then later trouble with trust may result. One wonders what the final impact of the Rwanda massacres will be on the children, many of whom were not only orphaned but had witnessed terrible crimes against their parents. Due to the strength of tribal and community links, situations like this may sometimes be easier for Africans and Asians than for Western children, but grave developmental problems can arise when all family members are wiped out. We can only go on praying and trying to find adequate parental substitutes for a wounded generation.

This book is not the place to examine all the stages in turn, but further information can be found in *Childhood and Society* (Erikson, 1950; Hayes and Orrell, 1987). The important point about personality development is that failure to learn enough of the task may occur, leading to immaturity at that particular stage. None of us completes each task perfectly, but we manage enough to be reasonably normal. Some people, however, have such poor experiences in their lives that large areas of the task for that period are inadequately developed, resulting in areas of immaturity in the personality that are too large for them to cope with. Common indications of immaturity are persistent difficulty in trusting anyone, boastfulness, over-dogmatism, over-dramatisation of events, persistent exaggeration and over-dependence on friends, colleagues or family. The major thing is over-reaction.

There is another spin-off from developmental immaturity, in that it is usually accompanied by an overload of persistent negative emotions such as bitterness, resentment, irritability or jealousy, and it is these things that impact on interpersonal relationships more than the failure of the developmental stage itself. We can usually cope, for example, with people who have persistent inferiority, since it is obvious and we can understand and sympathise. But in a small community we have real problems in coping with constant eruptions of bitterness, resentment, jealousy, hatred or anger. They may be present to excess in those with damaged personalities, being long standing reactions to difficult past events which are transferred onto present situations.

Just what does the Scripture say about negative emotions? In a long list of acts of the sinful nature, Paul also includes negative emotions as something we need to deal with, hatred, jealousy and fits of rage being specially mentioned in Galatians 5:20. In Ephesians 4:31 he tells us to 'get rid of all bitterness, rage and anger', and in Colossians 3:8 we are told to put off anger and rage. Hebrews deals specifically with bitterness: 'See to it that no-one misses the grace of God and that no bitter root grows up to cause trouble and defile many' (12:15). To these I would add resentment, a word not used in the Scripture but which indicates constant anger and bitterness related to a particular thing (*Collins Concise English Dictionary*, 1992).

This is not the way God wants us to live. He tells us in the Greek tense used in Romans 12:2 to 'go on being transformed by the renewing of our minds', and in Ephesians 4:22–24 to 'put off your old self... to be made new in the attitude of your minds; and to put on the new self created to be like God in true righteousness and holiness'. It is so easy to despair of ever changing, but I have learned that after we have become his children there are ways of working with him as he moves into our lives, and seeks to free us from our emotional weaknesses and to lead us on to maturity.

Basically, as one of the pathways towards achieving greater maturity we need to work with God to rid ourselves of overloads of negative emotions, which have been called 'the poisons of the soul'. They often stem from past experiences, and although we cannot remove the experiences, we can, with God's help, change our reaction to them and hence stop negative emotions from further damaging our personalities and creating difficulties in our daily living. Herewith some practical suggestions:

- **Acknowledge before God** that you have persistent negative emotions within you that you want to be rid of. Offer yourself to him for the change to begin.

- **Learn to understand your own over-reactions.** Sometimes things happen that could be handled by a sensible discussion, or a gesture of impatience, but because of our negative overloading due to something in our past we set off an atomic explosion. I once saw this happening. Two staff members, both of whom struggled with inferiority and were also somewhat stressed-out, wanted to have the same day off from work. Instead of talking it through and compromising, they ended up shouting at each other and having childish temper tantrums. I knew their backgrounds and realised that in two stressed-out people difficulty in getting their own way over off-duty time had reactivated old buried feelings of inferiority and resentment, hence the atomic explosion! Happily it led to a profitable discussion, compromise, and a little increased learning of how to cope better.

- **Determine to work with God** to reduce your own past negative emotional overloads using the following method:

  - *Spend a little time daily* asking God to show you which events in your life have caused you negative emotional problems, e.g. what made you furious, or jealous, or resentful. Sometimes this starts with recent things, which opens the door to remembering past events. I underline that we should not try to poke around our whole memory bank. Never brood about it and become over-introspective. If you ask God he will show you what is important, so relax, chill out, and let God do his gentle work within you as you try to sort it all out. If you find it easier, find a counsellor or trusted friend to discuss it with you.

  - *Write down in detail* all you can remember of the incident. This may take you some weeks to accomplish, for it is amazing what you remember once you start. Never mind if it seems petty, write it down. Note especially people involved in the event.

  - When you feel you have written down all the major things, look over it and see *who was involved* in the event. Begin to ask yourself why you think they behaved that way. Remember, children can never understand adults, and automatically think that if things go wrong they are to blame. In reality, the adult who hurt you may have had problems, and now that you are also an adult you can sometimes think your way into these. Did the teacher who treated you with constant sarcasm have personal problems? Often one can only guess at this, but sometimes on mature consideration it becomes obvious. A very good teacher unfortunately known to terrorise children by getting angry caused real upset to a child from a broken home. In later years, as the person began trying to cope with her long-standing bitterness against the teacher, she realised for the first time the extent of the teacher's own problems: she was separated from her husband, which was a source of playground gossip among kids in those days, and was trying to educate her own children while working all hours to earn enough money, plus being of menopausal age. Realising this added the oil of compassion to the person's thinking about the teacher, which is the first stage to healing old negative emotions.

- Accept that *you yourself have to be forgiven* for your own emotions. Because children cannot understand the wider facts they simply react with personal pain, or hatred or bitterness or jealousy. Adults, however, are more responsible for their reactions, and I feel therefore that wounded people need to accept responsibility for what the child within them felt and still feels. This sounds a bit peculiar, but it is true. These old childhood reactions often persist into adult life and may have an adverse effect on our adult mental health. As Christian adults we need to do something about them, and the following section explains a method that may help us in this task.

- Set about putting things right with God and with our memories, using what I call *The Forgiveness Technique*:

  1. *Write a list* of the people who have hurt you in the past, with brief mention of special events you remember. Add on reasons for their behaviour that you may have understood when you thought about it as an adult.

2. *Understand what forgiveness means.* It does not mean you forget, the memories remain, but the pain of the accompanying negative emotion tends to wither away. In addition you need to understand what you are going to forgive. When we forgive people, we forgive the debt they owed us. The Scottish version of the Lord's prayer makes this clear by using the words, 'Forgive us our debts as we forgive our debtors.' Usually what has hurt us is situations where people owed us better treatment and did not give it. For example, it is not right for children or adults to be minimised, terrified or abused. They deserve better. What needs to be forgiven, therefore, is people's debts to us, what they owed us as parents, teachers or fellow human beings and did not give us. This makes forgiveness much more concrete and therefore more comprehensible.

3. *Seek an occasion to make an act of forgiveness.* Some people use the communion service to do this, taking their list of events with them. First ask God to forgive you, as an adult, for continuing to react with negative emotions towards the people who hurt you. However justified they were the emotions are still wrong. Then read over the list, and say to God, 'I forgive that person for hurting me in this way' and if you like, ask God to bless those people if they are still alive. Then having completed your act of forgiveness take communion or do whatever you feel will act as a symbol that you have made a full act of repentance and forgiveness.

This method has proved helpful to many people since it is a definite act at a definite time in their lives, and forgiving old negative emotions and attached memories is decidedly stress-relieving. As I wrote earlier, we still remember the events and it takes some time for the pain to wither away. But because we have wiped the slate clean, we shall gradually be freed from the negative emotions, and thus advance more rapidly to greater personality maturity.

Protecting our personalities

God has built into our minds methods of protecting them from overload which switch on automatically. They are called the ego-defence mechanisms. There are many of them and the ones we habitually use are related to our genetic patterns. They are just like the fuse box we have in our house. If anything goes wrong such as overload, the fuse switch goes down, or the old-fashioned ones break, and the implement they protect is saved from damage.

To explain how this works we need to remember that there are two major compartments in the mind. The smaller one, the **conscious** mind, deals with what is going on now, and its memory is usually about ten days. It resembles the day-to-day work we did on our computers if we had forgotten to save it for the last ten days. The **subconscious mind** is the recipient of important things which we need to retain, these being transferred there by the conscious mind. It resembles the hard disc on our computers. Traumatic and pleasant events that are important to us are all kept there in store, and may be recalled when a memory link triggers them off. For example, many missionary language students find themselves remembering French they learnt years ago at school and had not used since. They have opened the relevant section in the subconscious mind, just like opening an old computer file that we made years ago. So computers and the Internet are really utilising in modern form principles that have operated in our minds since creation!

The subconscious mind automatically switches on mental mechanisms when there is a danger of overload. However, as I have thought about them I have come to believe that just as they come on when emergencies occur, so we might learn to use them voluntarily as a way of protecting our minds. It is with a description of these healthy personal uses that this chapter closes. I shall describe only three of them, all capable of unhealthy and healthy use.

Repression. This means pushing various things out of the conscious mind into the subconscious, and keeping them there. Two kinds of things are deposited. One is things we need to remember, just like saving important material on hard discs. The other is painful material that we have not really processed, so it is pushed away into the subconscious where we hope we can forget about it for the time being.

Repression is usually presented as the villain of the piece in terms of mental health, but that is true only of unhealthy repression that never deals with past trauma. Good forms of repression are used all the time. As an example, in our offices most of us have an in-tray containing what we are going to deal with very soon, and a pending-tray which is the ever-hopeful repository of things we hope to get round to doing some time but very rarely do. The in-tray represents healthy repression, temporary storage which is rapidly processed. Prayer lists are a form of healthy repression. We pray for someone when the name comes up on the monthly list, then forget about them until they come up again next month, thus reducing the load on our memories. Similarly, in times of severe trauma where we have to remain functional, we repress the emotional aspect of what is actually happening and just carry on with our work. In the UK this was experienced in World War 2 when people were bombed every night, but there was work to do so they automatically repressed the actual experience and got on with the job. It was only after the War that they began to take it all out, and then talked and talked endlessly about where they were when the big bomb went off, describing in great detail what they did. Healthy repression is a comforting concept for modern mission partners. We never know when we will be caught up in wars, or revolutions, or natural disasters, and sometimes fear we shall not be able to cope. Healthy repression will help us to do so, being given by God to help the mind cope with severe unavoidable stress. After the event is over we need to talk over what we have experienced with a trained person to help us ease the mental load and avoid unhealthy permanent repression.

The pending-tray represents permanent repression. It contains unfinished business which because it was unpleasant we have just pushed down into our minds in the hope it will go away. Unfortunately it never does, and periodically comes up in an unpleasant form when we are under other forms of stress. Clearing out the pending tray is accomplished by following the advice given in the earlier section on negative emotions, and we again need to remember that it may be wiser to talk with someone reliable if there is a lot to clear out.

Regression means behaving as if we were much younger than our actual age. This can of course be unhealthy, resulting in the kind of temper tantrums I described earlier, and in some cases of mental illness it can be a prominent feature. There are, however, excellent uses of good regression which should be regularly practised. Do not always relax with sensible adult things. Have a few 'adult toys' and use them regularly. One of my friends was described as a marvellous dad because he regularly took his young son to the swings. What people didn't know was that he went with his son not only to give him pleasure but also because he needed to become a child for a time and to use the swing himself! I have recently acquired the art of snorkelling, and the other day in Greece while floating gently about looking at the underwater scene, I felt as if I was a little girl again just gliding over water and playing hide and seek with a fish, not an elderly adult! In our busy lives we need some form of voluntary regression to use at least once a week. Try walking through the park eating a childish form of ice-cream. If you meet a respectable church member they may be a bit startled, but never mind, it is good for you.

Displacement. This means transferring painful emotion from its place of origin onto a person or an object. By this I mean that when you feel stressed you can either yell at someone nearby or else use a displacement object to get rid of the tension until you have time to think about it more calmly. There was a well-known saying among expatriates: 'Beat the cake not the cook' i.e. take out your stress on an inanimate object, which then becomes the 'displacement object', rather than on your nearest and dearest. An old-fashioned typewriter was marvellous for displacing tension. I did all my notes on one, and when I had finished with a really difficult patient used to make myself feel a lot better by banging the keys as hard as possible while I wrote up the records. One of the best ways of dealing with anger and tension is baking bread, the kneading dispersing excessive tension so that we calm down enough to think rationally — and no one has got hurt in the process.

Having read this last section, maybe you would like to sit down and think of a good displacement object, and a regular form of healthy regression. Promise God to use them, rather than taking out the tensions of an ordinary working day on others.

CHAPTER
7

Parental and Home-country Stress

Parental stress

To the best of my knowledge, nothing much has been written about helping missionaries to cope with stress relating to their own parents. This was one of the unexpected findings of my research, and emerged in several places.

A group of missionaries were contacted for whom I had provided mental health screening during the candidates selection process and who had later gone overseas. They kindly filled in a questionnaire which I analysed. One of the questions was about their own parent-related stress. The results showed that both those who were experiencing problems with their parents *at the time of selection*, and those with *current* parent-related stress during missionary service were significantly more likely than others to develop psychological symptoms overseas (Foyle, 1999). Lest serving personnel get anxious about this, it is important to remember that while both these groups were more at risk than others of developing psychological symptoms overseas, it was not inevitable. Fifty per cent of those with severe parent-related stress in both groups coped very well.

The major difficulty in the selection group was a poor relationship between the parents which created a home background of quarrelling, violence, infidelity, separation or divorce. We know how traumatic these things are for families, and it is not surprising that if people are still wounded by the effects of this major stress, adding on expatriate stress may prove too much for them. So the candidate period remains important, this being the time when people can be encouraged to examine the stress and find a better way of coping. It is likely that this will prove to be one of the major problems for generation X, with all mental health workers currently reporting a marked increase in dysfunctional family backgrounds. This, together with the research findings, would appear to emphasise the importance of continuing the current screening policy of making enquiries about family backgrounds and personal and social histories.

In the serving group the major parent-related problems were bereavement, parental illness, continued parental opposition to what their children were doing overseas, and continuing poor relationships between parents themselves.

The effects of parental stress

Some people handle life-long parental problems with little adverse effect on themselves. These people have an in-built resilience and just accept it as a fact of life, finding their emotional support elsewhere. Others, however, are deeply wounded. As children the domestic strife made them feel inadequate, frightened and helpless because they had no control over what was going on. They felt somehow as if they were to blame, which made them overdo efforts to be good so that the problem would go away. Worse than that, they felt responsible for protecting one partner against the other. One person told me that when she was ten she told her grandmother that she did not want to follow the family pattern and go away to boarding school because she feared her father would try to kill her mother if she was not there, which later proved to be true.

The outcome of such a childhood varies, some people being badly traumatised and others becoming cautious about making personal relationships. Finding security, peace and support through knowing the Lord is a great panacea, and in addition a lot of human talk may be needed. This is one of the major reasons why a history of parental conflict should be disclosed during selection. It enables the candidate to look at the situation with a trained person, and to assess what can be done about the remaining damage. In addition, the candidate may be strengthened by discussing new tactics for helping parents resolve or improve their problems. This will be further discussed in Chapter 13.

Parent-related stress arising during overseas service does not influence the personality structure, but it certainly creates much anxiety. One of the hardest things is **bereavement**, which may be expected or totally unexpected. If the bereavement is expected, then advance planning is necessary to decide whether you will go home early to see your dying parent, or go home for the funeral, or not go home at all. Similarly, in unexpected deaths urgent decisions have to be made, and it is the greatest possible help to be able to communicate rapidly through e-mail or telephone. Most mission agencies have contingency plans to enable bereaved missionaries to do what they feel is right. I am aware that generation X does not usually like books of rules, principles and practises, but they certainly defuse a lot of the anxiety aroused when you are uncertain how to set about things like emergency leave. Incidentally, one sending agency rule book went a little over the top in providing information for all eventualities, and I had the feeling that if you looked up 'socks' in the index the book would have told you how to buy, mend or wash them!

One helpful strategy is dealing with the possibility of bereavement at the time of selection. Sometimes candidates' parents have an incurable illness, but they agree it would be right for their children to go overseas for the time being. In these circumstances I have advised what I call a gentlemen's agreement (not sexist, but 'gentleladies' is a clumsy word). Candidate, agency and parents agree that should the worst happen the missionary can come home immediately, returning to the overseas appointment when circumstances allow. This contingency planning has proved to be a very good way of reducing avoidable stress.

When missionaries decide not to go home following parental death, special plans are needed. The stages of grief described in Chapter 3 should be respected, and the tendency to rush back into a pattern of overwork as a way of handling grief be avoided. Take a little time to cry, to look at photos, to talk about the dead person. Explain things to the bereaved grandchildren even if they did not know their grandparents well. Use the valuable resource of the national community. Due to shorter life expectancy in many Afro-Asian countries, nationals are wonderful at helping people handle bereavement. In India it was the custom to sit beside the dead person and pray, and then show your sympathy with the crying relatives in another room. Crying, grieving and talking about the circumstances of the death, combined with a real joy because the dead person had gone to God, was the normal pattern for both men and women, accompanied by a lot of demonstrative affection. When expatriates lose a parent, then national sympathy and affection wells up. My mother died when I was in India with very poor telephone communications, but my family managed to get a message to me. I sat in my office stunned, looking at my work, till a colleague came in and said, 'Marjory stop work, we will take you to your house and look after you,' which they did. Many church members and local friends came to see me, and I felt surrounded with loving care.

Once the grief has begun to settle down, it is good to have some sort of ritual. It is recognised that rituals are the culturally compatible way of getting through bereavement, hence the funeral service and other burial rites. When we do not go to our parent's funeral we are denied this, and it should be replaced by any sort of ritual with which we are comfortable. Some people give a memorial gift to their local church in memory of the dead person. Others have held a memorial and thanksgiving service with their colleagues, and this all helps the grief process to proceed normally.

Another potent stress factor during service is **continued parental opposition** to what you are doing. Jesus did warn us that being his follower could lead to trouble between parents and children (Matthew 10:21) and implied that we would have to be prepared to leave them (Matthew 19:29). It is hard enough to leave our parents, and even worse if they do not agree with our course of action, but if we really feel the Lord has called us to a cross-cultural work we may have to do exactly that.

I have long felt that such leaving must be honourable, for Jesus never said we should leave parents unsupported and in need. This raises the problem of which comes first, obedience to parents or to God. In the old sending countries parents often have financial and personal needs that in our fractured society demand extra care from their children. The situation may be even worse for some of those from the new sending countries where the children may have become better educated than their parents, who in turn expect them to go on with education, get good jobs and look after their future needs. So when their child says he or she feels called by God to be a missionary this dashes all parental hopes, and the candidate has to find a way of resolving the fierce family disappointment that results.

Years ago mission agencies did not see it as part of their role to support parents, and where links with the local church were not strong parents were often left out of the equation. Today, the local church staff consider parent care to be as important as member care, unless of course the parents refuse to have anything to do with them. In Hong Kong, a special parental allowance is paid to parents of cross-cultural workers, thus fulfilling the cultural obligations for children to support their parents. Not to do this would involve missionaries in a total denial of their cultural obligations, which is in itself a potent stressor. In this generation sending agencies often encourage opposing parents to take a short trip overseas to see their children in action, and help them with their travel arrangements. This often results in a total change of attitude, and I have heard of long-standing poor relationships between parents and missionaries being resolved by a visit of this kind, the parents turning into whole-hearted supporters of their children's work

In the Scriptures this is all rather confusing and takes some sorting out. We are told in Luke 18:29 that it is right to leave parents for the sake of the kingdom of God, yet we are also told in the Epistles that we should honour them and not be disobedient. 2 Timothy 3:2 gives a clear indication that what matters is our motivation for leaving our parents. The verses indicate that the motivation described was greed and self-betterment, illustrating people who walk out on parents without caring for their welfare, and go off to better themselves in their own way. Missionary motivation is not usually like that. We certainly are not bettering our incomes and our material and professional provision for our futures, but we are putting first what we feel God wants us to do. If God is to bless our work, however, all of us need to check that our motivation is honourable. We must be sure that we are not just trying to walk out of an unresolved problem or difficult situation, but are genuinely seeking to follow God's will as far as we understand it.

The answer lies in compromise between honouring God's call to work overseas, but at the same time ensuring that we are honouring our parents by making some provision for their needs. One of my friends decided she would not go overseas until she was able to give a small monthly allowance to her widowed father. She prayed about it privately, and one of her friends spontaneously decided to give her some extra money every month, which enabled her to contribute to her father's support. Thus 'honour' and 'call' were satisfied. This was a precursor of what I now call the 'Hong Kong system' whereby agencies incorporate care for the parents as part of their obligations in accordance with the cultural needs of the community. In meeting parent's needs, however, it must be remembered that these vary a great deal. Some need money, others need personal support for living without their loved child, or not being present when a grandchild is born, or being deprived of watching them grow up. Nothing can replace this, but if parents of missionaries are willing, incorporating them into the agency and church families is a vital part of meeting their needs. Where parents are non-Christian and their only response to agency and church is anger, then approaches can still be sensitively made, and evidence given that both will stand by to help should need arise.

Home-country stress

This term means stress experienced by missionaries serving cross-culturally who also have problems in their home countries for which they feel some responsibility. In a study of missionaries with a depressive illness, there was a significant relationship between the adjustment type of disorder and stress related to the home-country (see Chapter 2). In another group of serving missionaries who were not clinically depressed, home-country stress was significantly related to the development of mixed psychological symptoms. It is therefore important to consider what it is that is causing the stress reactions and to see if anything can be done to relieve them.

Part of the problem is related to modern technology. Before aeroplanes and good communication systems, when missionaries went overseas they were often away for many years. New missionaries and their relatives therefore had to accept that should trouble arise at home the person overseas would not be available to help. Postal services were poor, air mail was only just developing, and it might take six to eight weeks before news of illness or death at home reached them. As they waited to board their ship at the docks people used to feel that they really were burning their boats, there was no turning back, and very upsetting it was too. Now things have changed, communications are easy, air travel has shortened journeys, but the flip-side is that when missionaries board an aeroplane they tend to take all their home problems with them. News comes to them instantly by e-mail that someone is sick, they can use the telephone, and so end up carrying not only the home load, which makes them feel helpless because they are not right there, but also the load associated with their work overseas. Consequently if there is trouble either at home or overseas, or both, they can get really overloaded.

The major components causing missionaries severe home-country stress were family social problems, sickness and bereavement, and problems with their home church Some of these overlap with parental stress, and require no further discussion. Social problems of the family at home are a growing cause of home-country related stress, although I have found no literature about it. These include family members in prison or with a prison record, young relatives on drugs or in trouble with the law, unemployment, the legal hassles connected with divorce and severe financial problems. The overseas cross-cultural worker may have been the major support to other family members as they coped with their troubles, hence even though they are overseas they are contacted constantly for further support and guidance.

Problems with the home church provoke much stress. The missionary concerned may have taken a lot of time to build strong relationships with the sending church, and is usually officially commissioned by them for cross-cultural service. This provides a strong undergirding for them when things are tough overseas. Sometimes changes occur in the home church, such as a split in the congregation or the loss of the known pastor who is replaced by a new one not so interested in cross-cultural mission. Hence personal prayer and financial support may be reduced or lost, leaving the person concerned feeling really bereft.

Under such circumstances it is vital that the sending agency covers financially until the missionary goes home on leave and can sort out their church membership. Personal prayer support can, of course, be continued by retaining the old church members' names on the list for receiving the regular prayer letter.

As I write this I am aware that much more research needs to be done into this interesting topic. The influence of parents on their children is incalculable, and where the background is so fractured that this has been almost non-existent, or where the relationship between parent and child remains problematic into adulthood, the expatriate experience may well provoke the development of psychological malaise. It would not be surprising if such parent-child problems proved to be one of the major causes of missionary attrition in the future.

CHAPTER
8

Stress and Singleness

The meaning of the term 'single' has undergone a remarkable change over the last 60 years. It used to mean an unmarried person, and usually implied virginity. This definition still holds good in most of the new sending countries. In traditional India, for example, virginity is still highly prized, and major steps are taken to preserve it until legal marriage has occurred. In many of the old sending countries, however, the word 'single' now has many meanings. It may still be used in the traditional way, although as a rule it no longer implies virginity but a break-up with the current partner with whom there has usually been a sexual relationship. So the ex-partners describe themselves as 'being single now', or 'being on my own', which usually implies they may be looking for a new relationship. The word 'single' is also applied to divorcees, widows and widowers, anyone in fact without a permanent partner. It has the same meaning in both the heterosexual and homosexual communities.

In this chapter 'single' is used for those who have never married. They may have lost their virginity at some time in their lives, but because they now believe that God's pattern is celibacy unless married they commit themselves to observe this. These days this is usually dismissed as a very old-fashioned view, nevertheless I believe it to be what God planned when he ordained marriage as the basic permanent relationship between man and woman as they commit themselves to each other and create a home and family unit.

The New Testament has something to say about singleness in the passage on eunuchs in Matthew 19:11–12. To us, the word 'eunuch' indicates those who are unable to have sex relations due to being castrated. Jesus, however, used the term in a much wider sense, aiming it at those who for various reasons live celibate lives. 'Some are eunuchs because they were born that way' indicates those men and women who usually for some physical or mental reason are unable to have sex relations and therefore have no choice but to remain celibate. 'Others were made by men' indicates boys who were castrated to preserve their singing voices, or older men castrated so that they would be safe to care for the king's harem, as portrayed in the movie *The Last Emperor*. In modern times the words include those for whom sexual relations have become impossible due, for example, to accidents, injuries such as the atrocities perpetrated during the last war where the genital organs were damaged or removed, or to the need to take certain medicines that interfere with sexual functioning. Also included here are the psychological casualties such as those who have been physically abused, resulting in such serious psychological problems that sex relations are difficult or impossible.

The third category in Jesus' teaching is relevant to the majority of longer-term single women missionaries, and the occasional man. 'Others have renounced marriage ('made themselves eunuchs' is the footnote version) because of the kingdom of heaven. The one who can accept this should accept it.' This applies to those who voluntarily take a vow of celibacy, such as members of the religious orders, and also to missionaries whose response to the call of God may include involuntary celibacy. No vow is taken, they are quite prepared to marry, but in reality they accept that under the usual conditions of longer-term missionary service marriage becomes less likely.

Orientation courses in the home country usually include teaching on sexuality which would include discussion of the meaning of singleness, and how to cope with it. But it is not until after arrival in the host country that singleness becomes a practical reality and an issue that has to be dealt with. This involves more than just accepting that celibacy must be the order of the day. It may also include loss of male company even on friendship terms, for in the average village 'goldfish bowl', and even in big cities, cultural customs have to be observed especially if you are working for the church. Having been to a female medical college, trained in a female Bible college, and joined a women's mission where we treated only female patients, I sometimes used to go into the garden to talk to the gardener just for the pleasure of hearing a male voice!

Our attitude to singleness may be the biggest issue we face and it is here that singles sometimes make their biggest mistake. There are few Protestant missionaries who take a vow of celibacy. Usually they just drift along waiting for the right person to cross their path. But faced with the involuntary celibacy of their overseas lives, they may rush into making vows to God that they will never marry, hoping this will make them feel a bit better. In reality it may not be very wise. Two of my friends made such vows quite early in their missionary careers, and told some of their friends what they had done. Both married when they were over 60, and said they felt decidedly foolish going down the aisle when all their friends knew of their earlier vows to singleness! It is much better to commit yourself to being single for the period of time you feel you can manage. This may be a day, a week, six months, a year, but it works much better to chop it up into small chunks of time and renew it if God has not provided a marital partner when you come to the end of it.

The menopause may be a difficult time for single women. They have reached the age beyond which it will not be possible to have children, unless they marry late and their conscience allows them to use the modern techniques which may soon enable even geriatric women to have babies. But for most singles the menopause is a watershed, and many have told me they had a little weep on their 45th birthdays as they saw their hopes of motherhood vanishing. It is at such times that a new act of commitment to God is so useful, based on faith in words used in another context but which illustrate a principle of how God acts towards his children. 'I know the plans I have for you... plans to prosper you and not to harm you, plans to give you hope and a future' (Jeremiah 29:11). In the end a place of maturity is reached where singles truly understand that God has no favourites, and that being single is his best plan for some but not for others. As they mature they also discover that marriage is not an automatic bed of roses, and that everyone engaged in God's service, married and single, may have to face severe problems demanding an equal need for coping strategies. So the end result for long-term singles is usually real confidence that God has planned wisely, and a sense of peace about the whole issue that is not just loss of hormones!

Special problems of single missionaries

This section applies more to longer-term missionaries than to those going for a few weeks. However, something of each section may be relevant for both groups, or else will help the short short-termers understand the rest.

Social peculiarity

Many cross-cultural missionaries live in societies with different customs from their own, and suitable behaviour has to be learned. Of course we can never be considered as totally one with the other society, our skins may be the wrong colour for one thing, but we can be recognised as politely trying to behave acceptably, and can be loved even when we make mistakes. The trouble is that single people, especially older women, are not always understood in a host society which is predominantly couple-oriented. Many of these communities practise arranged marriages. If you are still single the people automatically think your parents have either failed in their duty to arrange a marriage for you, or else for some unknown reason you have been weighed in the marriage scales and found wanting. Perhaps, they think, your dowry was not enough!

Much has changed in the past 60 years. For example, at one time young Indian Christian women had to choose between marriage and the mission. If they wanted to serve God on the staff of mission hospitals treating only women there was no work for men and therefore no married quarters. This meant they had to choose between leaving to get married, or staying single and remaining in the hospital. To make things even more difficult, in a few places there were some who thought that leaving to get married meant you were abandoning God's call. That era passed many years ago, and it is now common to find married women working in Christian programmes of all kinds, often with housing available to the whole family.

It is still difficult for the older professional woman in some societies. In India when I was middle aged I used to be invited to doctors' dinners. We all got together and spent about two hours talking before the meal was served. All the male doctors gathered at one side of the room and their wives at the other. Since I was the only woman doctor, where was I to go? If I joined the men that was seen as forward, but if I joined the women they imagined I could only speak in English, and if I spoke in the vernacular they felt branded as uneducated. Finally we would reach talking stale-mate. I felt like a real party-pooper until I decided to resolve the problem by taking a female national staff member with me who broke the ice in the women's group. The situation is much the same today unless several women doctors are present or the conference is international.

A major change has resulted from the influence of television, which can be good and bad. The good side is that previously isolated communities may learn a lot about other countries which is helpful to them when they welcome a single foreigner for a short-term work project. They have a vague idea of their background. The bad side of course is that many TV programmes lead them to expect the foreigner will be promiscuous, so the elders take precautions against them getting off with their children. Of course despite the parents' best efforts, if the stranger is a man the girls develop feminine wiles, and if a woman the men dress themselves up a bit and look hopeful. Generally speaking, however, the foreigner is welcomed very warmly, nationals going out of their way to provide friendship and companionship as they work together.

Accommodation

Accommodation on return home will be discussed in Chapter 12, but accommodation overseas may be even more stressful, and has a great impact on personal relationships. Thankfully it is not as great a problem as it used to be. Communal bungalows where missionary women all lived together are nearly dead, and single people usually have a choice. In countries where it is safe to do so single women can live alone, but usually they live with another single person which may turn out to be fine or full of trauma. Despite believing that God is basically in charge of their lives and circumstances, singles sometimes feel that who they share with is more a matter of pot luck than anything else. The other person may prove to be a wonderful friend or there may be total incompatibility. To make things worse, living companions change frequently as people come and go on leave. This means that if one person remains stable in the home, she is always having either to welcome newcomers and help them adjust, or else to adjust to another experienced person who is set in her ways. One woman I met said, 'I have had so many living companions in the past 18 years that I can't remember their names let alone their backgrounds.'

The one situation that should normally only be allowed for a very few days is a single person living with a married couple. It is all right if they have a separate apartment and privacy is respected, but to live there as a permanent paying guest is good for nobody. Married people cannot maintain and develop their relationship if a third party is always present, and single people cannot develop to maximum potential if they have no freedom and privacy to do their own thing. Sometimes a sexual attraction develops between the single man and the wife, or the single woman and the husband. Missionary marriages have to cope with enough stress as it is, and it seems to me pointless to add on third-party stress for more than the initial few days after arrival. It seems to work better for a single man than a single woman, but even so can be hazardous to the marriage. The only exception is in countries where it is too dangerous for anyone to live alone, and if going to this situation all parties must be willing to take it on, and to exercise discretion and restraint so that each has some sort of privacy.

Part of the problem of two singles living together is that both are reasonably mature. They have their own customs and habits imported from home, and these may unconsciously irritate their companions. Take, for example, eggs. There are so many different ways of eating them. Punjabis eat them hard boiled, Chinese eat them raw dropped into soup, the British eat them soft boiled for exactly three and a half minutes and take the top off either with a little knife or a spoon. Americans never use egg-cups and find them ludicrous, but the British would find it difficult to eat a boiled egg without one. Older people even make little woolly caps to put over the egg to keep it hot! This all sounds very funny, and it is. It is material for a hundred jokes, but in the pressurised situation of sharing an apartment with a total stranger it can escalate into a blood-feud!

Various things can help. Someone living with an uncongenial companion should not feel compelled to prolong the situation for too long. Initially real efforts should be made to overcome the problem. A pair of women I knew had problems getting on, and they decided to meet every day except Sunday to talk for half an hour. They did this, and discussed their mutual problems, and learnt about each other's backgrounds and needs. The end result was the forging of a firm friendship based on real understanding. However, if it is not working out there is no sin in asking for a change of housing. If you have tried to share a house together, and prayed and tried again without much success, speak to your leadership about it and make a change.

The danger of living alone is that if you are overtired you tend to become reclusive. You just cannot be bothered to entertain. This is understandable, but if it becomes a permanent state then something should be done about it. Get a take-away if they exist and ask someone in to eat it with you. In this context a word should be said to those who live alone for quite a long time, usually single women. We need to avoid becoming more peculiar than our job makes us anyway! We are oddities in the host community, but that does not mean we should be oddities elsewhere, other than in the basic oddness connected in some circles with being a Christian. We should really work at this so no one is ashamed of our appearance or behaviour when we rejoin the wider world. I have never forgotten a missionary who came to speak to us at Bible college. She had obviously done a marvellous job somewhere in the heart of Africa, and we who heard her speak were not worthy to lick her boots, as the saying goes. But her hat, which she had to wear to meetings in those days, was at least 30 years out of date, as were her clothes, and we were so entranced looking at what she wore that what she said made little impression on any of us. I do not recount this with pride, I am ashamed of my reactions, but it did speak to me about the importance of trying to remain basically compatible with the society in which I was living. Mercifully these days most missionaries look very presentable thanks to easier fashions, charity shops, and regular sales, but we do need to keep an eye on it and have an adviser if possible. My sister-in-law who had the reputation of being able to 'wear a dishcloth and look marvellous' used to give me great advice every time I came home.

Personal relationships

In addition to personal relationships with living companions, problems arise in other areas.

With married people

Proverbially there has often been tension between married and single women missionaries, although this is by no means the norm, and Korean leaders have commented that there is less tension between singles and wives than there used to be. It has always been held that single women have a more difficult time than married ones, but my own research has shown that married people have many more problems than singles (Foyle, 1999). However, in some of the new sending countries there is only a small difference between attrition rates of married couples and single women. For Brazil the figures for those returning home early are 47% married couples, 39% single women and 14% single men (Limpic, 1997). In Korea those who returned home early were 54% married couples and 36% single females, but they comment that the early return of singles was often related to parental pressure to marry (Moon, 1997).

The basic difficulty is one of role. In earlier years married women were expected to look after the home and to add on extras as time allowed. So the burden of work and many extras fell on single women who were supposed to be free of the burdens imposed by domesticity and the needs of the children. The latter is certainly true, but not the former. Any single woman will tell you how much time it takes to cope domestically in some overseas situations. To quote two single ladies living in a very isolated situation, 'We find it takes us most of our time just to live.' Be that as it may, the expectation was that singles would fill in gaps whereas the married women would be too committed to the home needs even to be asked. For example, someone in hospital service told me she had been approached by the senior doctor who said, 'I have put you on duty every day of the Christmas festival because you are not married and so Christmas is not so important to you.' She went home simply livid, but finally decided to be charitable and to do what he had arranged.

This is not the modern situation where there is greater insight, singles understanding the obligations that home, family, and possibly a part-time job put on the married women, and they in turn understanding that singles also have private lives. The end result is a sharing out of all the extras that have to be done, with no one feeling put-upon.

One further problem may arise when a single woman works

with the husband of the married couple, or vice versa, and because they work together they quite rightly become good friends as well as colleagues. This is great, but care needs to be taken that because the single and the married person talk the same professional language, the other marital partner does not feel excluded and hence undervalued. This problem usually occurs when the working area is isolated and there are few people to relate to apart from the job.

Another situation that arises is what I call the 'let's be kind to the singles syndrome'. Married couples understand that singles can be lonely, and may invite them round for that reason alone. This is most kind but it is not enough. Singles need to be asked because their married friends like to have them as people in their own right, not just as needy singles, although of course really difficult singles do have to be asked from time to time! Singles have a return obligation. They too must invite married people into their homes, and periodically offer to baby-sit, which should not, however, be regarded as automatic since singles also have private engagements. The basic principle, therefore, is dealing with the situation on the basis of social equality.

With friends

Singles can make friends overseas in the place where they work, in the church, and in culturally compatible areas through social occasions in the wider community. It was great to see a senior member of my mission playing the lead role in *The Pirates of Penzance* put on by local expatriates, and similarly friends can be made by sharing in suitable events in the national community. This may sometimes be hazardous, as a friend and I found in one country where we worked. It was a small town, and an important festival was on. We wandered out to have a walk and greet our village friends, and seeing an open door onto a grassy space went in to take a short cut over to another house. As we arrived we found the local governor and his friends all waiting on some steps, and they called us over to stand with them. Then the outer gate opened, in came a procession of idols and a goat which was sacrificed before our eyes. Now in accordance with the Scriptures we would never attend idol worship or share in sacrifice of this kind, so we hurriedly said goodbye and left, and asked a male member of our staff to try to explain why we did this next time he met the governor. Despite the odd hazard, however, in village settings culturally suitable social contacts outside the home may be very rewarding. One person I know got one of the women to teach her weaving, and she taught the woman to read so they became firm friends. The keynote is to respect such aspects of the local culture. Then you are welcome, and not regarded with suspicion by anyone.

Being friends with a member of the opposite sex, especially if you are getting interested in each other, is more difficult. For expatriates, dating patterns of the home country are usually inappropriate unless it is in a big city setting. People just have to work this out the best way they can. In one isolated area where male-female conventions were very strict, a married couple invited a couple in this situation to their home in the evenings and then tactfully busied themselves with something in the next room so that the couple could at least talk together. This may all seem incomprehensible to younger people today, but as I learned overseas, no matter how old you are, breaking the cultural custom invites unpleasant misinterpretation. I was once standing near my own home talking about business matters to a national man I had known for many years. It was dark, and despite being well over 50 years old, the darkness still made it culturally inappropriate for me as a single woman to be talking alone with a man. The business was finished and as I said goodnight and began to go home he said in a suggestive voice, 'Can I come up to your flat?' I realised my mistake, which actually was very amusing at my age, and said in the politest possible way, 'When your wife comes back from her mother's home I will be very happy to have both of you round for tea,' and that was that.

In connection with relationships with the opposite sex, special problems arise for single missionary members in some of the new sending countries (personal communications). Where arranged marriages are the norm there is often much confusion over who will make arrangements for the single missionary. The parents may be from a village background and so only have access to eligible village brides, yet the young man continuing in mission service needs a more educated wife. Some missions in India have appointed a person specially to care for singles, but the marriage problem remains very complex.

Friendship problems can also arise in normal daily life. Every expatriate longs to make national friends, and to learn from them about their lives and culture. As a rule this is one of the best things about living closely with nationals of another country, and is a real privilege. But there are a few things to remember that may keep friendship in the right perspective. One is the danger of singling out one national or expatriate as a special friend to the exclusion of others. It is the exclusion that matters, so you need to share out your time between your friend and other people. The other is the danger of being 'taken over' which is an offshoot of the first problem. It becomes very difficult to extract yourself if you have allowed the friendship to become possessive. So spread yourself out and make friends widely.

The final comment concerns the behaviour of singles in a strange country. The first thing is the danger of predators. In many countries of the world there are people who make friends with a foreigner of the opposite sex in the hope of contracting a marriage and so getting a visa to their country. Do not let this put you off making national friends, but handle the opposite sex in a way suitable to his or her cultural background. Ask a trusted senior person for advice if you find you are falling in love and there is a possibility of a cross-cultural marriage. In most cases this is truly of God, but you need to look into it carefully, meet the family, and make sure you understand what you are taking on by joining another community. This sounds harsh but it is wise. In addition, it is good to have advice from senior people about how singles should behave in general. You probably can do most of the things you would do in your own country, but not all. For example, one young girl came for a short-term appointment and behaved with a national young man as she would in her own country. To him this came over as a sexual invitation, and he finally asked her out in a boat and tried to rape her, thinking this was what she had indicated, although this did not excuse his behaviour. So a general understanding of how things tick in the area you work in frees you to enjoy national company without fear of danger. You will still do the wrong thing but this enables your new national friends to teach you a bit and you all have a good laugh together.

Loneliness

Although a decision to live alone may be the right one, it does open the door to loneliness. Single missionaries have to learn to cope with a variety of practical and emotional problems. They cannot, and should not, always be asking for help. Skills suitable for the location have to be acquired such as what to do when the fuse goes, minor carpentry, filling the oil lamps and trimming candle wicks. Skills such as managing e-mail and laptop computers demand the ability to find out from books what to do if it goes wrong, which of course is more difficult for older long-term missionaries. I do not know if managing a computer is taught during orientation, but it would certainly be good if it was.

One aspect of singleness which is usually related to long-term service is loneliness due to the lack of a permanent confidante. Singles have to learn how to be a unit of one and not a family, and it is not easy. My family saved me from danger by coming to visit me every Christmas or Easter for my last ten overworked years. By that time I was the only expatriate single woman left in the district, the only other one leaving seven years before I did. I am eternally grateful to them for coming to the rescue, for at festivals, although one longs for a family atmosphere, one does not like to intrude on national families at a time when they have their own visitors, despite the loving invitations they give you.

In isolated locations loneliness can lead to another problem. Due to lack of a permanent confidante, a lonely single can have an almost compulsive desire to share everything should someone move into the apartment. This usually gets sorted out between them as they settle down, but trouble can arise if the older person not only continues to over-share but also expects the newcomer to do the same when it may not be her nature to do so. She could be a rather private person who keeps her thoughts to herself, and handles her own problems within her own coping strategies, but in this situation if she behaves in accordance with her personality structure she is made to feel guilty. I once discussed exactly this situation with a young single missionary whose obviously over-stressed senior companion expected her to share everything the whole time. If she did not, there were tears and accusations of not being a good prayer partner, and she felt she could no longer cope with going against her own nature just to keep the peace. 'If only she'd leave me alone to get on with my life. She's always at me to tell her what I am thinking or why I react the way I do. I never have any peace or private life' is a telling quote from someone who could not take it any more.

This situation of course is an unhealthy one, for everybody has a core of privacy that must be respected. As Anthony Storr wrote (1963), 'To know that another person accepts one just as one is, unconditionally, is to be able to accept oneself and therefore be able to *be* oneself, to realise one's own personality.' It is therefore important that any attempt at this kind of over-dominance should be dealt with firmly. The problem will not just go away, for the location is still isolated and personalities do not change all that much. The matter should be discussed with the field leader sooner rather than later. The dominated person should not hesitate to do this because of feelings of loyalty, but if uncertain should remember that a useful guide as to whether sharing is healthy or not is the degree of anxiety or other strong emotion aroused by it. I have written about this at some length because I once witnessed the results of not handling such a situation soon enough, although I was not involved. Both the people concerned were of the same sex, one older than the other, their location was isolated and rarely visited by anyone from management. The problems of the older one progressed into a frank mental illness, and finally the younger one developed a stress-related depression. At this point, following a suicidal letter from the younger person, their leadership was informed and they were removed from the location for adequate care. I do not think this would happen in modern times for overseas member-care is generally so much improved, but it is quoted as an example of when not to be unwisely loyal to a colleague, and the importance of widening one's interests when living in an isolated situation. Birdwatching is highly recommended, providing an endless relaxing occupation, and keeping down interpersonal tensions by giving a respectable reason for disappearing into the local fields for a time!

It is important for missionaries to understand the difference between loneliness and solitude. The *Collins Concise English Dictionary* (1992) defines loneliness in a negative sense, but indicates that solitude can be used in a positive sense. I am using loneliness to mean unhappy at being alone with yourself, and solitude to indicate being alone with God, which can be a very positive experience. Stephenson agreed with this when she wrote (1981): 'Loneliness can become enjoyable solitude.' Single people often find the pains of unavoidable loneliness are met by remembering that God is with them in the house. I do not think the pangs always go away, but they are certainly relieved. In addition, two practical things are helpful. The first is keep clear of self-pity. God is not being unfair to you, your present isolation and loneliness will be revealed later to be a part of his loving and creative plan for you. The second is do something creative and active that is people-oriented. I realise in some very difficult or dangerous locations this is not always possible, but a little inventiveness may work. There may be culturally suitable local interests to share, or others in need of a bit of friendship, and it is sometimes possible to get round the local culture. I never forget a wonderful party a few of us had in an isolated area when we managed to have an evening of Scottish dancing without upsetting anyone.

Handling sexuality

Single people sometimes think that if they answer God's call to service, and this proves to involve singleness, then sexual feelings will either automatically go away or at least decrease enough to cause little trouble. This of course does not happen, for people with no sexual feelings are either very sick, extremely old, or very dead! If God took away our sexuality we would not be fully human, and he of course plans for us to be whole people in every sense. Single people can be helped to handle their sexuality by remembering it consists of two parts, which I have termed biological and creative sexuality. These are not very good terms for biological sexuality is also creative, but they are the best I can do.

Biological sexuality

This is the instinct to mate and reproduce the species, and in God's goodness is often accompanied by love and tenderness. If we neither mate nor reproduce due to our views on being single, then we are of course seriously frustrated in this area of our lives. It is good to remember this, for many people try to be brave and say that despite being single they are totally fulfilled. Personally I doubt this, for their biological sexuality has never been utilised. If God in his wisdom and love has decided that people should remain single, that does not mean there is no pain or frustration involved, and certainly many singles do find it painful to live without sex and without the opportunity to have children and grandchildren. The important thing is to accept it from God himself. It is so easy to think you must be totally unattractive and this is why you have never married, but in reality behind your looks, or personality, or any handicap you may have there is the loving, discerning hand of God. He has planned our lives, and if that includes biological frustration, then that is his first-best loving will for us. If singles can accept this, then frustrated biological sexuality can become a pathway for personal growth and development. Because it is in God's loving plan for us, although it is very hard to believe, we shall do better without marriage than with it!

Creative sexuality

By our definition this excludes creating children, but includes every other aspect of our working lives. Relationships, work, hobbies and personal development are all a part of our creative sexual activity, and in this area single people can be totally fulfilled. Of course abstinence from biological sexuality remains painful and difficult at times, and we never lose our sex desire despite all that is written about sublimation, but as we move through the difficulties and go on with our personal development under the guidance of the Holy Spirit, we shall come to know more and more what creative fulfilment means.

The trouble is that some single people hinder their creative development by remaining bitter over singleness, and never really coming to terms with it as God's best plan for them. Dedication to it for as long as it lasts remains the best thing to do. 1 Peter 4:1 is very helpful, for it explains that since Christ suffered in his body, we should 'arm ourselves' with the same attitude, or mind. To arm yourself means to pick the weapon up, something we actually do, and for singles this may include the act of making a voluntary commitment to God to be single for as long as he wishes. As we do this we must never forget that we are doing it for a God who loves us, who has called us into his service, and who can be trusted to fulfil his first-best plan for our lives.

I think this is illustrated by Jesus' own life on earth. When he was offered a human body by God the Father, he accepted it with the words 'a body you prepared for me... Here I am... I have come to do your will O God' (Hebrews 10:5,7). I am sure that he would understand part of that will as remaining celibate during his time on earth, despite having all the normal feelings and desires of a human being. There is an interesting reason behind the celibacy which Dr Paul Blackham enlarged on recently when we were discussing Jesus' singleness (personal communication). He said, 'When Jesus came to earth he knew he would remain single because he was already engaged to be married! The church was to be his bride', the church being those people who would accept Jesus as their Lord and Saviour, and be born again by the Holy Spirit. Therefore, because Jesus lived a sinless life on earth, and was an engaged man living in a strict sexual culture, he would obviously not engage in human sexual activity until the time of his own marriage, which will come when the church is complete.

I write with the deepest reverence on this difficult topic, but I remain sure that Jesus' original act of commitment to God the Father to accept a human body in which he knew he would remain celibate was the greatest help to him. He lived surrounded by women helpers, one of whom, Mary Magdalene, was clearly crazy about him. Yet his dedication to God for the ultimate task of going to the cross for our salvation, even though this involved celibacy among many other things, was what must have helped him to cope with his normal human sexuality. I am sure that this concept can help those of us who in our own small way are involved in a work for God that has included singleness as part of the package. God knows better than anyone else how hard it is, yet he did it for us and by his strength we can do it for him.

One big problem is that in the modern generation many people have sexual experience, often from quite an early age, and accept it as the normal thing to do. When they become Christians they usually decide to give this up, and to accept the traditional position of no marriage, no sex. This may involve breaking up quite a long-standing relationship, the break being followed by a real bereavement reaction. In addition, it is harder to be celibate when you have had previous sexual experience than it is for virgins, this being confirmed by the experience of the staff in modern missionary training colleges where many fairly recently converted young people are attempting to live celibate lives. A lot of care and help is needed as they prepare to work cross-culturally. Others with a firmly Christian childhood have usually received sexual guidance from their parents, but then decide for themselves what they will do when they come under pressure to have pre-marital sex. They have experience of how difficult this is at school where they may be the only one who refuses to engage in sexual activity. Christian fellowship groups for young people are the greatest help in this situation, the mutual support enabling them to hold firm to their convictions about correct sexual behaviour.

Masturbation

This may be a problem for some Christians, their background teaching being that it is not honouring to God. It creates anxiety not only because of the act itself which causes guilt, but also because it may be accompanied by fantasies. Various Christian writers have held widely differing views on it. I tend to adopt a middle position, in that I think what lies behind it is more important than the act itself. Usually it occurs as the release of a pressure cooker, and indicates too much stress in other areas which gets added on to normal sexual pressures. It is often a sign of an imbalance, and if the problem is getting worse you should talk with a wise person and look round your life to see what steps you can take to reduce other tension areas as well as urgent sexual pressure. The old Victorian idea of a cold bath is not much good, but a run or a swim may get you over the immediate struggle. If masturbation becomes out of control then help must be obtained, for many other things can lie behind it if it reaches this severity.

Homosexuality

For the last few decades, changes in sexual mores have resulted in much discussion in Christian and secular groups on hetero-sexual and homosexual orientation and practice. This book is not the place to discuss these at length, but John Stott in his book *New Issues Facing Christians Today* (Stott, 1999) has an excellent chapter on same-sex relationships where the biblical aspects are clearly expounded. These changes have impacted in missions, and I therefore feel it right to include in my discussion of singleness and marriage some comments on the problems experienced by homosexually-oriented Christians.

Initially I must make it clear that I believe what the Bible teaches us, that homosexual practice is not God's pattern of human sexual relationships, and therefore not an acceptable option for evangelical believers who take the Bible as their authority. It is therefore taken for granted in this book that missionaries who have a homosexual orientation or tendency which may prevent them from marriage have decided to live celibate lives.

Some people through no fault of their own have never known heterosexual impulses, and appear to have been pre-dominantly homosexually oriented throughout their lives. Many have a deep Christian commitment and have tried various physical, psychological and spiritual methods of increasing their heterosexual orientation. Some do experience a degree of change, and may even be able to marry, but others remain almost totally homosexually-oriented and therefore celibacy becomes their only option. Missionary sending agencies differ on their policies about sending such homosexually-oriented celibate candidates to work cross-culturally, their decision depending on their own views and those of the host country. In general, while both agencies and the church overseas are not willing to accept homosexual couples, they may accept a single homosexually-oriented person who has made a commitment to the Lord to live as a celibate, and whose sexual orientation therefore remains a private personal matter.

Many such people make a fine contribution to the Lord's work overseas, but problems may arise when they come under very heavy pressure, usually from a combination of the stress of cross-cultural living combined with loneliness. This may lead to severe temptation to find a local same-sex partner. This in turn increases their stress, for they know that to yield to the temptation would be entirely unacceptable to themselves, to their sending agency and to the local community they serve. The same also applies to the celibate heterosexual, and should members of either group experience prolonged temptation to break their commitment to celibacy, and they feel it is becoming stronger than they can control, I believe they should exit immediately from their location and go to the nearest qualified person for help and support. (The same of course applies to married couples where one partner experiences strong temptation to an act of infidelity.) Incidentally, some preventive help can be given during the selection process, in the form of advice not to locate a celibate person who has other areas of potential vulnerability to an isolated place with only a few colleagues. A wider social circle often helps them cope better when outside stress impinges on their commitment.

It is interesting that this problem has also been noted in training colleges in the home countries, where, when life gets tough, both heterosexually and homosexually-oriented persons who have decided to remain celibate because of their faith may experience severe temptation to break their commitment. Thankfully there are usually staff available to whom they can turn for support. In fact it would be wise for all singles overseas to have a lifeline of support for times when the going is particularly difficult.

Several other situations can cause problems overseas. Single heterosexuals of both sexes can be attracted to a person of the opposite sex, not knowing that he or she is a homosexually-oriented celibate. They may easily misinterpret friendliness as a romantic interest and begin to hear wedding bells, and when nothing happens can get very upset. It is interesting that the principal of a well-known missionary training college told me she has had to cope with distressed students experiencing just the same problem during candidates' orientation.

Another possible difficult situation involves what is called 'opportunistic homosexuality'. This happens in prisons when opposite-sex partners are not available, and can happen in single-sex boarding schools when hormones are rampant. Opportunist homosexuality may also occur among missionaries, although it is not very common. The usual scenario is that severely stressful situations arise in their location, such as prolonged interpersonal relationship problems or long continued work overload. Nothing they try seems to reduce the load they are carrying, and everyone begins to feel very stressed out. As their coping mechanisms begin to break down two people of the same sex may develop an intense emotional attachment. If one person has had previous homosexual experience and the other is exceptionally vulnerable, the attachment may become physical. The partners know that their relationship is not in God's will and usually feel very guilty indeed, but because they are so pressurised by the current stressful situation they find themselves unable to break it off. The result is massive guilt, and often the development of a depressive illness, usually in the more vulnerable partner.

This is a very serious situation and needs urgent care and attention. Some training colleges discuss such a possibility with missionary candidates, dealing with both how to prevent its development and how to deal with it should it arise. I believe that when such a situation occurs during overseas service the couple should seek help immediately rather than trying to handle it on their own. They must speak to someone locally whom they can trust, or else send an urgent message to their field leader for help. An even more difficult situation occurs if the couple are unwilling to seek help, and others in the location know about the relationship. (The same difficulty arises of course when a heterosexual single develops a sexual relationship with an opposite sex person in their location.) I have reached the conclusion that management should be informed, even though it is always very difficult to break our loyalty to our colleagues. Nevertheless, such severe mental health tragedies can result, together with an adverse effect on the spiritual health of the whole community, that steps must be taken to deal with it. The usual pattern is that the persons involved are withdrawn from their location to receive proper help and care, those left behind are counselled and supported, and steps are taken to reduce any problems that have acted as immediate precipitants. It is good that the organisation Membercare (Memca) is now setting up accessible care centres for missionaries in an increasing number of countries.

Practical suggestions for dealing with singleness

- Single men and women should discuss their sexuality and proposed coping strategies with the selectors during the candidates' period. In my own practice I used to ask about sexuality as a routine question, and found that candidates were really relieved to be able to talk about their sexual orientation and other fears and problems. In addition it gave them someone safe to contact should problems develop overseas.
- Single people should understand the possible difficulties that could arise during cross-cultural service, and work out some plan for finding a confidante to give help and support overseas. Should their coping strategies for living a celibate life begin to break down, they should seek help as early as possible.
- It is very important that people make up their minds what they believe about sexuality before they enter missionary service. Whether they are going short-term or long-term, they should discuss it with the tutors and decide how they would manage potential heterosexual or homosexual advances.
- Most agencies foster a climate of trust between themselves and their personnel and it is very important to maintain

this. For example, where a homosexual situation has developed it is easier for the persons involved to consult their leadership if they have already learned to trust them. It is important also that leadership has access to suitable counselling help for distressed celibates, such as the centres for missionary care that have been established in many parts of the world.

Conclusion

Sometimes people wonder whether any good can come out of singleness, and I want to assure them that it can! So far we have discussed problems and some of the creative possibilities. Stephenson wrote (1981): 'Hundreds of men and women past and present have done a work in the world and for their fellow men in every sphere of life which has only been possible because they stayed single.' On a personal level, however, I have come to see that being single enables people to explore other channels of love even though the channel of sexual love is denied to them. Our Lord was the best example. He loved people, his disciples, parties, flowers, birds, fishing, the sea and his surrogate family in Bethany. Although his life was tough as he went towards the cross, he never seemed to lose his love and zest for human life, going from hours of prayer with God back to meet the people who needed his help. We can share some of this, so that our lives of personal sexual denial as single workers in his kingdom can be as full of dedication, love, fun and fulfilment as his was. We may also have many children, people we have helped know a little more about God. There is a lovely sentence to illustrate this in *Goodbye Mr Chips*, the novel about a boys' boarding-school master who married late in life, which was made into a famous movie in 1939. When he said to his wife how sorry he was they had no children she said to him, 'What do you mean? We have had hundreds of children, all boys' (Hilton 1987). The Scriptures give us a lot of help at this point. In Hebrews 2:13, a passage from Isaiah 8:18 is used to refer to Jesus which speaks of 'I and the children God has given me'. He was not referring to ordinary human children but the many he had 'brought to glory', as verse 10 says. In our own humble way, we whom God has chosen to remain celibate will also find some of our children, those we may have helped along their spiritual pathway, present with God when we all meet in heaven.

CHAPTER 9

Missionary Marriages

Missionary marriages are usually very impressive. The partners have their troubles like everyone else, and there are some marriages that do not work out, but by and large there is a quality of dedication to each other, to the children and to God's calling that is special. The first word of this chapter, therefore, should be one of encouragement. Sometimes couples feel their marriage is in a mess and so they are not providing a good witness, but this may not be the whole picture. It is the way they overcome their troubles and cope with the stress inherent in missionary marriages that makes many of them so remarkable.

Research has shown that the major problem of married missionaries is their relationship with each other, this probably being made worse by seeing too much or too little of each other, and by role problems. The number surveyed was small, only 98 married individuals, but 27% of these complained of severe marital stress which was significantly related to the development of psychological symptoms overseas (Foyle, 1999), the other 73% complaining of no more than the usual moderate stress levels. Some of their problems will be commented on, but it should be remembered these are by no means unique to missionaries.

The impact of modern social problems

Current social backgrounds have a huge impact on the marital relationship, and since candidates have lived in this background, it's impact needs to be carefully explored during selection. To outline some of the problems:

Many young people live together without marriage

This is now almost the norm in many Western societies, although does not occur to the same extent in the new sending countries. It is an indication of how society has changed that the British government, in setting the syllabus for teaching sexuality in schools, has had to discuss whether or not they should 'promote heterosexual marriage' as the desirable norm, and whether they should accept the validity of homosexual marriage. As a result of this social situation candidates may have a history of having lived with several partners, breaking the relationship after some time and then forging a new one. Others have had multiple sexual partners and never really formed a stable relationship. When they come to Christ many rethink their position, and look to traditional marriage as the only possible future relationship, which involves acceptance of the idea that vows are taken before God and that Christian marriage is for life. For those converted out of the modern generation this demands real courage and dedication.

Additional problems are created by the fractured nature of their own childhood home backgrounds. If a relationship did not work the parents simply split up, and new males or females came onto the family scene as substitute parents. The results of this have recently been painfully portrayed on TV in a drama by Joanna Trollope, which showed how parental split-up affected children as they tried to adjust to the male or female who had replaced their biological parent.

Because of this background it is even more essential when selecting and training candidates to discuss sexual and other relationships with them, and their views on marriage. Few mission agencies will accept candidates living together without marriage although it occasionally happens in some of the old sending countries. To date I know of no examples from the new sending countries, but the literature on sexual and marital problems of missionaries from these regions is sparse. If candidates are already married, the strength of their bond and the problems they experience need careful discussion. Without a firm personal view of marriage and its importance in God's economy, surviving marital pressures overseas may be very difficult indeed. In this connection, marital seminars to strengthen the bond can be very helpful both during the candidate period and overseas. One of the best I know was led very successfully by a Roman Catholic Father in New Delhi, India! Another essential is the possibility of marital counselling somewhere near the working location overseas, so that serious trouble may be dealt with early.

Roles are no longer stereotyped

In some home countries the husband goes out to work and the wife is the housewife with possibly a part-time job. Conversely, the husband may now be the house husband with the wife going out to work, or both may work full time and use nannies or nursery schools to care for the children. When an expatriate appointment is considered in the business world, it is sometimes the wife who has the working visa, and her husband goes along as her spouse, and at other times the reverse. The non-visa partner is then rather unpleasantly called 'the trailing spouse'. Another common term used is 'dual career partners', indicating that one partner will have to give up the career if the appointment is accepted. In the business world the success or otherwise of an expatriate appointment is said to depend mainly on how they work out dual career problems: 'The dual career family is becoming a primary issue in relocation (overseas). Effective spouse assistance should not be considered a perk but an essential part to make the move work' (anonymous, 1996). 'A recent survey of 200 companies by Price Waterhouse's expatriate consultancy reveals that the prospect of loss of spouse earnings and loss of career progression is one of the main reasons why employees turn down assignments abroad' (Simpson, 1993).

In the missionary world the situation is the same but is approached differently. In most selection procedures husband and wife are usually considered to be two candidates, each requiring an independent call, being equally suitable, and with a realistic approach to their future working roles. They therefore fill in separate papers and have separate interviews, plus a joint one to assess their relationship and to give opportunity for three-way discussion. The situation varies so much that no more than a few scenarios can be mentioned. Sometimes it is discovered that the wife wants to go and is pressurising her husband to fit in, or the reverse. This underlines the importance of hearing both sides independently. Before I learned this I interviewed a couple together who seemed very suitable. On the spur of the moment I decided to see them alone for a time and then the truth came out. The husband had no clear leading to go overseas but his wife was the dominant partner and was adamant that they were called, and he had not really liked to say anything about his personal reservations. After that I always saw people alone as well as together.

Whatever the scenario, it is important that the 'trailing spouse' and dual career problems are carefully considered during selection. Plans must be made for the 'trailer' (horrible word) to find personal satisfaction overseas. I have known both trailing husbands and wives work things out very well overseas, thanks to long and careful prior discussion. So far I have found no mission literature on trailing husbands, but the business world has made the interesting comment that it is harder for them than for trailing wives since they do not usually have the social networks that are already in place for female expatriate spouses, and find it very difficult to set up their own support networks (Fletcher, 1993; Foyle, 1999). My gut feeling is that the average missionary trailing husband usually finds more to do than he could ever have imagined. I once worked with a couple in this situation and we could never have managed the work without the different things he did to help us.

In Muslim countries women are usually the trailers, and it is essential that they know what they are taking on. A preliminary look-see visit may help them to understand the reality. Such forethought enables them to make an informed decision about whether they feel they can, or cannot, cope with it. If they feel they can cope and make a definite commitment to God for their future role, even though their own career will have to be put on hold, they often feel abundantly satisfied with the overseas experience. Such commitment reduces the resentment the woman in this situation may feel, and increases a trusting relationship with God. One concept I have found useful is God's deepfreeze. In it he has many compartments, each of them bearing the name of one of his servants. If a role is taken on for God that necessitates putting personal talents and training on hold, then they will not be wasted. God will put them in his deepfreeze, and when the right time comes he will take them out better than new! This happened to a friend of mine who gave up considerable academic opportunity to go to a difficult part of the world with her husband where she could not really use her gifts at all. They did that for many years, but after returning home permanently she had opportunity to return to academia, and her gifts came out of the freezer fresh and ready for use. She made rapid progress, obtained new degrees, and ended up as a professor in a well-known university despite her age! If we honour God by our obedience he will honour our commitment. 'Those who honour me I will honour' (1 Samuel 2:30) is a key verse for a trailing spouse, combined with David's wonderful words in another context: 'I will not offer to the Lord my God burnt-offerings that cost me nothing' (2 Samuel 24:24, RSV).

People have different ways of resolving the trailing spouse dilemma. Some decide to have their children during this period. Others take up correspondence courses related to their location, and others get very involved in the local life and 'the ministry of the tea and coffee pot'. Whatever decision they take, research has shown that there is general satisfaction with the professional aspects of missionary life, and this included those who entered their profession as homemaker (Foyle, 1999). This may be evidence that the situation for wives has improved, for these results contrast with those from Bowers' questionnaire study of 98 missionary wives in the World Mission department of the American Lutheran Church (1984). She found that an overwhelming majority had problems or concerns relating to their roles, especially the lack of definition or recognition of their roles. The importance of development of wives' roles was emphasised by Harrison (1997) who felt that for the family in cross-cultural service one essential was for the spouse, most often the wife, to take courses with a view to upgrading ministry skills.

That wives' roles are vitally important is underlined by Maines (1983) when he wrote: 'What will happen if mission agencies maintain the same status quo, neglecting professional development of missionary wives and allowing a major percentage of them to remain uninvolved?' Part of the problem is that people still expect married women to behave in a particular way, and because the generational patterns have changed this stereotyped attitude may cause difficulties for married women considering their proposed roles in cross-cultural service. Donovan and Myors (1997) explained this clearly when writing about attrition. 'Booster women,' born 1927–1945, 'tended to be comfortable supporting their husbands and fitting into whatever role was available where they were posted. In many missions they were not eligible for council membership, and certainly not for leadership over male missionaries.' 'Boomer women' on the other hand, born 1946–1964, 'have very often had professional training and many expect to have a recognised role commensurate with their training.' They then comment on the current difficulties married women may experience in finding an appropriate ministry and conclude: 'Thus some cases of attrition occur because of wives' dissatisfaction with their ministries.' New sending countries describe similar problems. Belinda Ng (1997) writes from Singapore that 'the role of missionary wives is very unclear', and says this has an effect on whether the church supports her to the same extent as her husband.

Much of the remaining literature from other parts of the

world does not specify singles or wives but the quotes indicate some of the women's problems in cross-cultural team-based ministries. From the Korean perspective Sung-Sam Kang writes (1997) that 'women's abilities as leaders can be utilised in gatherings for fellowship and caring', and Cho and Greenlee (1995) comment that 'female leaders may be accepted by Americans and perhaps Brazilians. Korean men, however, would find it hard to submit to a woman unless she has significant experience to set her above men.' Rajendran (1998) quotes an Indian woman leader as saying that 'most women in mission in India are prepared to be assistants and wives' and another who says, 'The paucity of work among women stems from confusion on the role of women. With so much argument on the place of women in the church many are afraid to encourage women to upset the status quo.'

I suspect all this may be incomprehensible to new generations. They are brought up on 'political correctness' with regard to women, and in their churches are often accustomed to generational equality in church programmes. In some missions, however, women are still not allowed any input into administrative decisions, being permitted to sit in council meetings and speak if the issue concerns women, but not to vote. It is noteworthy that most of these women are single, married women having even less input. I am aware that this issue is fraught with denominational and scriptural difficulties and I am no theologian, but I have long thought that people need to remember that missions are not the same as the church, and using a missionary woman with good administrative ability does not indicate in the church sense that she is 'usurping authority over a man'.

One other group of married women requires comment. Some feel that after God their primary commitment is to their spouse. Consequently they are well satisfied to operate on the Ruth-Naomi principle, that where the spouse goes they will go (Ruth 1:16). They may not like it very much but that was what they committed themselves to when they married or when the role balance changed in their family. This type of commitment is not, of course, confined to missions. Many clergy wives operate in the same way, and it is a pattern that demands a lot of integrity, love and common sense if it is to work successfully.

In mission the Ruth-Naomi principle does not mean that spouses with this commitment are not treated as ordinary candidates. They must be selected in the usual way to make sure they are not just being dominated by their spouse, but feel a genuine commitment to the course of action proposed. Neither does it mean that the husband or wife can come home one day and say, 'The Lord has told me we are to go to Africa and we are leaving in a month.' That is domination not partnership, and I have seen dire consequences of such behaviour. But when the basis of commitment is mutual love, honour and respect for each other then a type of Christian marriage emerges that has a great impact on other people.

The importance of personal development in marriage

This generation expects that personal development will result from missionary service, and certain things can hinder or enhance such development.

Expectations

Some people expect more from a marriage than they should, thinking it will solve all their personal problems and so give lasting happiness. It comes as quite a shock to find that marriages have to be worked at like anything else, and nothing happens just automatically.

Equality

This is the normal expectation of modern marriage although Christians have to balance what the Scriptures say about it and this may cause difficulty. Basically the consensus of opinion is that both partners are equal, but should there be a long-standing difference of opinion between the two partners and a final decision must be made, then the wife should be prepared for her husband to decide. Those who suffer from inferiority as a marked personality trait may have problems here, for if they are not treated as equals they resent it, whereas the reality may be that they have real difficulties in decision-making.

Immaturity

This is a dangerous word to use for it means different things to different people. I am using it to indicate those who cannot cope with what the average person of their age can deal with without undue stress, and the problem can affect both sexes. For such people there are several pitfalls in marriage. One is over-dependency. The immature can rarely decide things alone and depend on spouse, friends and relatives for advice on even the most trivial things. Because self-esteem is so poor they demand constant reassurance through affection and approval. This puts a great strain on the spouse who may be the only person available to give such advice and reassurance, and it can become very wearing. The basic problem, therefore, is that the immature partner expects the spouse to supply everything they need psychologically, most of which they should have been able to provide for themselves if they had mastered earlier stages of personality development. As a practical example, in a good marriage the partners are free to say to each other that they do not like something. Their basic link is secure, loving and mature, and such criticisms are part of daily living. But where one partner is profoundly immature nothing can be said that could be interpreted as even the smallest criticism, for there would be anger, floods of tears, or both. As one man said to me, 'I have to pussyfoot around her all the time in case I hurt her feelings. It's very wearing.'

Few human beings could avoid becoming over-stressed if they attempted for a prolonged period to meet the excessive demands of a severely immature spouse, plus meeting their own needs, those of the children, and the demands of working in a cross-cultural situation. These days, due to better selection, gross immaturity of this kind would be picked up and prolonged help given before any final decision was made about cross-cultural service. However, if it has not been picked up and the couple are overseas, suitable help should be provided before the difficulties escalate beyond the moderate stress level. The first step, of course, is insight into the need to mature, and this may well demand quite prolonged help before it is achieved.

In-service problems

The double load

This is one of the basic problems missionary couples experience, and can be very stressful. The couple realise they have to fulfil a dual function and this creates the double load. They feel they should demonstrate two things through their marriage, the first being what Christian marriage really is. The second is that since the concept of marriage is used so frequently to illustrate scriptural truths, their own marriage should illustrate these vital truths to the people around. For example, the church (those who believe in Jesus) is described as the bride of Christ, and the parable of the wise virgins indicates the need for his future bride to be ready to meet him, the implications being the need for spiritual growth and personal holiness.

Using the concept of Christian marriage to explain such huge truths may create problems for a conscientious couple. There are few marriages that do not have periods of trouble, or at least occasional quarrels, and somehow that does not seem to fit what the Bible has been teaching. It may sound rather odd but there are some couples who feel positively guilty about needing a little personal space, a little time spent apart, for it does not seem to match up to the constancy of togetherness of Christ and his church which they are supposed to be illustrating! Couples need to understand that it is not physical presence that they are illustrating, that being impossible anyway in the normal working week. What God means was clearly demonstrated by Jonathan Edwards, a fine Christian athlete who has often spoken in public about his love for his wife. Her mother died in the UK just before the Olympic Games began, so Jonathan had to go alone to Australia. After winning the gold medal in the triple jump he was interviewed by the BBC, and almost the first thing he did was to look directly at the camera and speak to his wife . 'I love you and the boys very much,' he said, 'and this medal is for you as well as for all my other supporters.' Physically they were on opposite sides of the world but that made no difference to their inner union, and this is the kind of love we are supposed to demonstrate through Christian marriage. Of course there will be quarrels and disagreements, that's life, but they make no difference to the basic trust and love that cements the marriage. So next time you want a break from your nearest and dearest do not feel guilty about it, it does not indicate a poor relationship but just the need for a little space and peace to recharge the batteries. I specialise in taking wives on 'girls' days out'!

The other stress related to this dual responsibility is dealing with any marital problems that may arise, for missionaries fear these will destroy their witness. Privacy is required to sort some of them out and this is at a premium for many missionaries, especially those living in a small town or village goldfish bowl. They have to get used to being the source of the local daily news flash. So if husband and wife have a minor quarrel which is no more than the usual daily give and take of two people sharing a house, the word goes round the village via someone like the man who brings the firewood that there is a major problem. In the village this would usually result in the man beating his wife, so they wait for the next thrilling instalment. When they find that he did not beat his wife but that they sat down and talked it over, this becomes a testimony to a different way of living, with forgiveness and mutual understanding working much better than a beating.

The expatriate family's need for privacy is not usually understood in a village setting yet it is an important part of the way we strengthen the marital and family bond. Hence we need to make some arrangement for privacy that will not upset the locals. The best solution I ever saw was a typical village house like all the others that had two storeys, ground and basement. The locals knew they were welcome at any time on the ground floor, but that downstairs was kept for language study, children's education and sleeping. They were not at all upset by this and did not feel excluded, they just recognised it as something other people did.

Incidentally, we need to remember that a Christian witness is often given by the way we try to sort things out both in our marriage and in our individual lives. I remember a bad day in my hospital in India. I spoke sharply to the senior ward sister in public, which of course is a thing one should never do anywhere. I left the ward and then had to go back for something, and I stood quietly in a corner watching the result of my ill temper. The sister spoke sharply to the nurses who then scolded the servants. They took it out on the sweeper who had no one beneath him to take it out on so he kicked the cat. At this point I went and apologised to the sister, calmed the nurses down, spoke kindly to the servants and sweeper and stroked the cat. So I was forgiven and relationships were restored, all of us having learnt something (except the poor cat). When interpersonal relationship problems occur between married couples, and indeed between any colleagues and friends, the participants have a choice. Either they can stay angry and bitter or they can try a bit of humility, apologise and smooth things down and try to sort it out. If of course the problem is a constant one and is becoming seriously disruptive, then help should be sought. It does not always work, marriages cannot always be saved nor rifts in relationships healed, but it is the effort we make to put things right and the sincerity of our purpose that speaks to others.

Comment should be made here on a good way to deal with the anger and frustration that is a part of our daily lives. Married people, like singles, can so easily use others as a punchbag if they are not careful, taking out on each other things that are not relevant to the other person but reflect the difficulties and frustrations of the day. Suppose the wife is the working partner and her husband looks after the home and children. She has had a ghastly day, he is fed up with not hearing a sensible adult voice since she left the house, so both are ripe for an explosion. Prevention is much better than cure. If the wife stops off at a tea or coffee shop, orders a drink, adds sugar if she is not on a diet, stirs it vigorously and sits there for a bit with her Walkman playing soothing music and reading the paper, she will calm down, and on arrival home can say to her husband, 'What has your day been like,' and let him sound off a little. Then they will talk more quietly about her day, so peace is preserved and all is well. In addition, everyone working cross-culturally, whether married or not, should have an enjoyable hobby to keep stress levels down, preferably something to hit or throw so that tension is harmlessly displaced onto an object and not on a vulnerable human being. This has been further discussed in Chapter 6.

Coping with separation

During the working years of missionary service, or when working for a home-based agency, much separation may be involved, and for those overseas this can extend to one or two months. For convenience I shall use the wife as the stay-at-home partner and the husband as the one who is away, but this of course may be reversed.

A common scenario which still exists in several missionary locations is the one where the children are away at a boarding school, usually in a place with a good climate. The common pattern is that the husband stays on in his location, and the wife spends a few months in the school area so that the children can come and live with her for the rest of the school session. The husband comes when he can, and one man I knew spent most of each weekend on trains so that he could see more of the children. As a rule the husband comes to the holiday house for his mandatory annual holiday. In his absence the mother has had to do everything. She has been mother, father, homemaker, electrician, plumber, administrator of the household, disciplinarian and nurse. A house routine has developed and when the father arrives he has to slot in. He has an awful lot of trivia to learn about the house routines, and although they are delighted to be together they all have to make little adjustments to the new situation. As one wife said to me, 'It's marvellous to have him home but we tend to quarrel about where to put the toothpaste!' Sometimes the husband is so tired he does not want any role at all while the wife is longing to hand over half of hers, or the worst possible scenario develops as he sits down with his laptop and prepares to spend most of the time catching up on a work backlog, so the children see hardly anything of him. Compromise, therefore, is the essential ingredient of vacation or post-separation time. Difficulties in readjustment are resolved by patience, humour and mutual understanding. It is in such times that the quality of previous communication is revealed. After about the first chaotic day, old communication patterns are re-established and everything settles down into the old routines.

As a single woman I would not dream of giving advice to married couples on such domestic issues, but I have shared so many problems with wives having to cope with their newly arrived husbands that I will presume to make a few comments. Like most women I believe men love a bit of babying, and after arrival is the time to do it. A bath, clean clothes, a nice meal and a doting family hanging over him make him feel like a mixture of a baby and a Raja. Wise women never pounce on him immediately with problems like the plumbing or the cook, although they may be near desperation, they put it off till the next day after the Raja has had a good sleep. One thing that is valuable in the readjustment period is to avoid booking routine things the day after he arrives. I have known husbands be really disappointed because the wife and children were out for most of his first day for non-urgent dental appointments.

Both partners may have a degree of sexual urgency after a

long separation, but the opposite may also be true. They may both be so tired that immediate sex is the last thing they want. This is a time when previously learned sexual cues are invaluable, that instinctive understanding of the right time for both partners that comes with a good marriage. In this connection, one of the most difficult scenarios can occur when separation is prolonged. For those who believe in celibacy when the marital partner is absent, as most Christians do, prolonged separation can be fiercely difficult, and I have known cases where both partners have succumbed to the pressure of sexual temptation and been unfaithful to their absent partner. The grave danger is that either this is concealed, or if confessed is followed by such implacable anger and bitterness that discussion and the possibility of restoration become increasingly remote. In these circumstances I have known marriages break up and remain broken, although this may sometimes be the only solution to a very difficult situation. I have also known marriages restored after acts of infidelity, with forgiveness and willingness to try again being the keynotes. It is in these situations that the availability of proper marital counselling is so important to personnel, for an outside 'safe ear' is invaluable as they sort the problems out.

Sexual problems
Problems after periods of separation are not the only situations in which missionaries may experience sexual stress. Marital partners do not realise that sexual patterns may change during the early adjustment period to the new country. When they board the plane they are usually tired out, and the flight may be equally exhausting. (Oh for the wonderful days of sea travel, twelve days doing nothing but looking at the Mediterranean and Indian Ocean, swimming, eating and sleeping.) However, in modern times the couple often arrive exhausted, and have to cope immediately with many strange things and a hectic period of settling in at language school or on their location. The end result is often an anxious husband and an exhausted

wife. He turns to sex as a way of coping with the insecurity he feels, whereas all she wants is a hug, a 'Darling I love you' and a good long sleep. This may lead to a quarrel, with him saying, 'You don't love me,' and her saying, 'All you ever think about is sex,' both totally untrue.

It is important to recognise the different meanings of sex relations to a man and a woman. Although based on a mixture of love and hormones, there is a much deeper function within Christian marriage which is the reinforcement of the bond and commitment to each other made when the couple took their vows before God. The sexual relationship therefore includes several things: the satisfaction of a biological need, the fulfilment they have in each other, the pleasure God has provided through sexuality, and the partnership they have created under God's direction. As their sexual relationship matures both partners find increasing sexual fulfilment, but there are additional joys which are immensely valuable. Men often find in sex a loving restoration of their selfhood and identity, especially in the early days after arrival when they may be feeling a bit battered by life in a new country. The additional bonus for women is often the knowledge of being loved, and being important to someone. The cardinal thing couples need to remember is that variations in response should not be automatically interpreted as lack of love or commitment. As indicated above, one partner may be dead tired, or the wife pre-menstrual when sexual response is lower, or one or other may be feeling depressed which reduces sexual desire. It is good that as a marriage develops the partners become very much aware of these variations in response, and handle them with increasing understanding.

Certain things block progress in the development of a fulfilling sexual relationship. One is poor interpersonal relationships before going to bed. It is of course possible to have sex in this situation, but no one gets much joy out of it. The man does not get rid of his anger just by having sex, and the woman often feels assaulted. The lesson is that it is better not to have sex while the original quarrel is unresolved, but to first try and find as much of a meeting place between you as possible. The injunction 'Do not let the sun go down while you are still angry' (Ephesians 4:26) is as much applicable to marital partners as it is to general relationships.

A second block to sexual development is disagreement about having children, whether to use contraception and if so which method to employ. It is obviously essential to the growth of the marriage that agreement be reached. A third hindrance is ignorance, and it is here that cross-cultural marriages may have special problems. Each country, and often each segment of a country, has its own sexual norms and conventions that govern individual behaviour, and these affect not only cross-national marriages but also people coming from different areas of their own countries. It is therefore essential that the couple discuss their marital expectations and culturally induced beliefs, rather than letting them grow to a point of serious conflict and disappointment in each other.

Anxieties about child-related matters

These will be discussed in Chapter 10.

Despite the problems we have discussed and the fact that we do not know all the problems marital couples face overseas, the overall impression is that missionary marriages are indeed magnificent. Things are often tough due to the combination of the usual marital problems that would be experienced in the home countries plus those related to living in the expatriate context. It is a tribute to the selection and care process, to the personal determination and dedication of the couples themselves, and to their prayer partners, that most missionary marriages do so well. Their homes often become places where the family can develop, and outside friends find companionship and restoration. I personally remain deeply thankful for my married friends and their loving help to me. A piece of pecan pie and a cup of coffee round the table with the family does a lot for an exhausted single!

10

Stress and Missionary Children

Terminology

In this chapter, children of missionaries will be called missionary kids (MKs), or the later term Third Culture kids (TCKs), in accordance with the current fashion. TCKs have been defined as follows by Pollock (1999), based on previous work by Useem (1950):

> A Third Culture Kid is a person who has spent a significant part of his or her developmental years outside the parents' culture. The TCK builds relationships to all of the cultures while not having ownership in any. Although elements from each culture are assimilated into the TCK's life experience, the sense of belonging is in relationship to others of similar background.

The important point in defining who is a TCK is that expatriate residence must occur during the developmental years, from birth to age eighteen. These years are the important ones for gaining a sense of identity, learning relationship skills, and developing a personal view of the world. Hence to be resident in a cross-cultural situation, which may periodically be changed due to the mobility of expatriate life, means that the child is exposed to a constant variety of cultures, and yet does not fully participate in any of them. Hence they relate most easily to others of their kind and so the TCK culture becomes the one they adopt.

The biggest factor in the development of the TCK group is that TCKs have an overdose of mobility and therefore of transition experiences. TCKs are constantly mobile as missionary families commute between parents' home and host countries, and periodically move for the benefit of children's education. Each move involves repetition of the transition stages, which as Pollock (1999) explains include five different things: involvement in the place in which they currently live, leaving that place, transition to the new, entering it which includes much new adjustment, and finally getting reinvolved with the new one. It is no wonder that TCKs often remain somewhat reserved, fearing to make close new friends because either they or their friends will move on and they have to start from the beginning again.

With this as the background it is obvious that TCKs need understanding and care. As Pollock reminds us, the problems have always been there, but it is only comparatively recently that words have been put onto the experiences, and so they can now be verbalised and discussed.

The development of MK care

For many years missionaries' children were rarely professionally studied. As Bowers wrote (1998): 'Although the needs of missionary children were a primary concern of their families, especially their mothers, there was little attention given to them on a broad scale.' In 1984 interest in their welfare resulted in the first ever international conference on MKs, held in Manila. This was a watershed, for the organisers and delegates were astounded not only at the numbers of people who came but also at the content of the papers. People had begun to realise that MKs had problems, and to take a properly informed interest in their needs that went far beyond a merely local care and concern for them. The initial conference was succeeded by two more, one in Ecuador and the other in Kenya, following which care for MKs, called TCKs by that time, became the responsibility of each country. This was helped and boosted by the emergence of literature, travelling personnel such as Dave Pollock, and the formation of national or continental groups to look after missionary children's welfare. Perhaps the most significant development was the fact that the child's voice was heard, and people realised that they had shrewd observations to make, and had their own agenda for what they needed.

Related to concern for the children came concern for the parents' struggles to do the best they could for them. They realised that despite their good intentions mistakes had been made, the children's views had not always been heard, and that what they had considered secure programmes for them were in some cases stress-provoking. The development of the TCK concept began to address this in a most helpful way. Counsellors and parents understood and began to verbalise the fact that sometimes their children lived in a culture-related vacuum, and hence often needed to find their identity through linking with others like themselves. An additional development has been better support for parents who try so hard to care well for their children, often under very difficult circumstances, and experience much distress when their children are having problems.

Because of the plethora of published literature, I intend in this chapter to outline certain principles and special areas, and for wider treatment of the subject to quote useful references.

Children's reactions to stress

Missionary parents often feel isolated which makes their anxiety to be good parents all the more intense, and they often ask me how they can tell if their child is stressed. The symptoms vary in accordance with age, but there are certain common ones such as unexplained changes in behaviour, loss of appetite, change of sleep patterns, nightmares, unusual fatigue or weepiness, and unexplained abdominal pain or headaches. It is usually wise to have the child seen by the doctor to establish there is no physical cause for the symptoms if they are prolonged.

One of the most important signs of stressed children is loss of previously learned skills. Children learn something new at each stage of physical and psychological development. For example, bladder and bowel controls are learned physical skills, and in the psychological realm so is trustfulness as described in Chapter 6. When children are moved out of a familiar environment into a strange one they sometimes regress, lose a learned skill, and for example, start bedwetting again even though they have been dry for some time. Or they begin to suck their thumbs again or demand extra love and cuddling. This is nothing to get alarmed about, it usually settles down, but it is helpful to try to establish a secure routine as fast as possible.

When the family moves overseas, therefore, children may show any of these symptoms for brief periods, but once their environment becomes more stable they usually get over it quickly. Part of the problem is that they have to cope with national customs, and if the usual way nationals express affection is by patting and stroking children, and pulling their cheeks in a rather painful way, the children can react adversely. I know of one child who got so fed up with having his cheeks pulled that he bit the hand of the person doing it, and the parents had to make profuse apologies. In these circumstances it is better to keep them at home for a few days. Let them play in the garden if you have one, or in a safe nearby park where they will not be too disturbed by the locals. Look at home videos, give plenty of love and time to them, and if you can obtain it prepare some special food treat they used to enjoy at home. This usually settles the problem down in a reasonably short time, and they can gradually be reintroduced to the new world. However, if they are not improving, or getting worse, medical advice should be obtained using a local doctor and the Internet, and a wise local teacher or experienced expatriate mother.

In the next parts of this chapter we shall look at some of the common problems of missionary parents and their children, and try to outline a few practical ways to help.

The decision to move to cross-cultural service

Children's involvement in this depends on their age. Up to about two or three they need be told very little, for they are content to be where the parents are. Due to TV, video and earlier nursery school attendance than in older generations, children aged around three can understand aeroplanes, and different countries, and so need only a little explanation that they are going to go to places like the ones they saw on a video. This can be made more meaningful to them if a child at their nursery school comes from the place they are going to.

After the age of about five, children should not be involved in making the final decision but it should be discussed with them. In families who pray together regularly, a simple explanation of motivation can be discussed and made into a prayer item. Books, TV and video can be enlisted to help, as can fellow pupils at school. For children aged about five to seven, the teacher can help by telling the other children how brave, or lucky, Johnny is, because they are all going off to another country where their parents are going to work for a bit. This is usually well understood by children due to the large increase in occupational mobility. The major anxiety for children of this age is whether or not they will find a McDonalds, or whether their favourite TV programme will be there too, and will they go to school and be able to make new friends. One important thing is to help them understand the move is not just for a holiday, but that they will be staying for some time.

From about age twelve onwards, depending on the child and remembering that children mature earlier these days, children should have a share in decision making, and this becomes hyper-important for those already starting puberty. As a rule I am not in favour of a major move during puberty unless the children themselves are in agreement, for an unwilling teenager may have a very difficult time settling in. However, if they have a clear picture of what they are going to, their educational possibilities are discussed, and their likelihood of having a reasonable social life is explained, they will usually accept it. If they have a personal faith this is made easier, for the reason behind the move helps them to cope with it, but Christian pressure should *never* be applied. I have known this to be done in the most painful way for the child concerned, which left him with guilt if they did not go and personal unhappiness if they did. Sometimes it is possible for the whole family to go and see the place they will be working in, and such a look-see visit is as helpful to children as it is to adults (see Chapter 3).

The importance of including children in the selection process

In 1993 I carried out a survey of the problems of children reported to me by parents during the selection process (Foyle, 1994). Twenty-six per cent of 153 parents had problems with their children, and were concerned about them, but they did not always understand the impact such problems could have on expatriate life. Ninety-eight children's problems were extracted from the records with the following results:

Ten were apprehensive about the move combined with much distress, and nine of these were already drop-outs. Nine had personality difficulties; eight had conduct disorders; eight had learning disabilities; seven had some form of depression; seven had social problems; six had speech disorders; three had very high IQs and required special education; three had ano-rexia nervosa; two were schizophrenic; two had stress-related disorders. The remainder were a mixture of general medical problems of which asthma was the most common. It would be worth repeating and expanding this survey, but what is apparent is that questions must be asked about the children during selection, doctors and teachers reports obtained which comment on their fitness or otherwise for overseas service, and the selector's own knowledge and experience taken into account. In some cases the current care-givers were definite that the child should not be moved. In others a general decision was taken depending on where the parents planned to go. For example, asthmatic children should rarely be sent to live in the heart of Kathmandu where pollution is currently high.

The situation for those with unusually high IQs depends on

what both child and parents want. These children are academically older than their actual age, hence may have problems relating to children within their own age group. Without special care some can develop social problems as a result. Others do not like being educated above their age level and prefer to go along with the rest of their group, content to be top of the class all the time but not to move ahead. Therefore both children and parents should be asked what they feel, and if the child wishes to continue in the advanced stream of education then probably the family will be unable to go overseas unless suitable facilities are available. If, however, the child is content to be educated on a level with his peers then the problem is solved (Dr E.V. Fraser, personal communication).

Coping with disruption of family life

The selection and orientation processes may involve disruption of the established pattern of family life. The old house may be sold and the family moves nearer the orientation centre, or one or both parents are away a lot fund-raising which either leaves one parent to cope at home alone, or else to go with her husband and employ baby-sitters. This problem is easier for those who go with denominational groups and do not have to raise funds, those sent out by a local church without going through an agency, and those who go as 'tent-makers'. Some try to go to supporters' meetings as a family, but as will be mentioned in Chapter 12 this should not be overdone.

Children learn to cope with family disruption, which continues through the whole missionary career. For infants there is no problem other than a reaction to change of water and milk, for where the mother is there is security. But for all others during the transition period the question frequently arises, 'Where is home?' They move from the home country to language school housing, and then to where they will be located. Periodically they may have to migrate elsewhere if the older children are at school. Then they uproot and go home on leave, but what the parents call 'home' is the host country to them and the host country is home, so everything gets more and more confusing. I am endlessly amazed that they cope so well, and put this down to the careful preparation and devoted parenting they receive.

Certain things can be done to minimise disruption. In the suitcase you have on the aircraft put a few of the children's favourite possessions right on top. As soon as you reach your first stopping place, get them out, and at once the children feel at home. This is a also a good tip for mobile adults: take with you something that symbolises home. I used my old typewriter for this, putting it on the table as I moved into the umpteenth room, and it felt like home at once. Your toiletries bag may be just as symbolic.

Language school arrangements should be such that parents with children have privacy to bring up the family. This can usually be worked out in larger centres by having rooms for language school students where food is available, and those with children can eat lunch there, and have the evening meal in privacy. Arrangements for child-care are usually made in this sort of set-up. Where no provision is made, parents often take turns at going to the language teacher and looking after the children.

Mentoring comes in here also, and the person appointed as mentor to the new family should visit early and get to know the children. They will then be able to help with the children in an emergency.

Parental expectations

Sometimes parents expect too much of their children. They have read books about children of missionaries chatting to their friends about the Lord, and expect their own kids to do the same. But maybe they don't want to, and I have heard disgruntled TCKs say they never really saw why they were expected to do part of the parents' job for them. The secret is not to expect anything, but to wait and see what your child's gifts are, and do not pressurise them to do this or that for the Lord.

Children's education

In missionaries suffering from adjustment disorder depression (see Chapter 3), it emerged that one of the major causes of stress was children's problems, and in another study of missionaries using a questionnaire it was found that the major stress was children's education, this being significantly related to the development of psychological symptoms (Foyle, 1999). In a table listing all stressors in rank order, stress related to children's education came second, home schooling being the major difficulty. The numbers of those who commented were small, hence this requires replication but my impression is that the result would be validated.

Three major pathways of education are possible, home schooling, a local day school, and a mission boarding school which may be some distance away or even in another country.

Home schooling

This usually carried out by the mother or a group of parents, and the scenario varies. In some places there are few children being home-schooled, and they use their own national correspondence courses at home with their mother, which of course puts a big extra load on her. Where there are several families, a separate room is set aside for school work, and most parents are involved in oversight and teaching. The sheet anchor of this method is national correspondence courses, of which I have seen many. One of the best is the Australian course, based as it is on a national curriculum for children in the outback, with many methods of creating an artificial community. Computers are required, and periodically children are called into a central school for a short period of socialisation.

These views are supported by research done by Mutchler

(1997) on the key factors for success in home schooling among American missionaries. The following were found to be important: satisfactory curriculum and lesson planning, flexibility, home schooling as the mother's first ministry priority which she enjoyed and valued as her own role, specified study area properly furnished, good relationships between parents and children and husband and wife, understanding of the children's development and learning styles and regular class schedules.

Local schooling

There are several kinds. Some missionary children are taught as a group on location using a properly trained teacher who has offered to do the job as missionary service. This is an excellent system but the problem is that nowadays too few teachers are offering to do it, and there are many vacancies. Another form of education is using the local school where the language medium is national, but this only works for younger children. It is fraught with hazards in that the children become fluent at the national language but the horrified parents are informed by their national friends that the children have acquired a large vocabulary of swear words! The other problem is that one day they will have to go to school in their own language and with early schooling in a foreign language this may be very difficult. Other forms of local schooling are a local international school, and English medium national schools. The former is very expensive and only covers those who want to be educated in English, and the latter may not provide the necessary knowledge or qualifications for proceeding to higher education in the home country.

The problem of children's education is obviously compounded for those missionaries for whom English is only a second language, some of whom establish national schools, and this will be discussed later.

Boarding school

Many missionaries are very apprehensive about mission boarding schools, mainly because they involve separation from their children. For this reason many candidates have made clear that they will only offer for service until their oldest child is ready for secondary school, aged around twelve. I must admit that some missionaries have cultural misunderstandings about boarding schools. They still have the idea that it is 'OK for the British who send all their children to boarding school anyway'. This pattern died out long ago, and now it is only the very rich who send their children to the comparatively few boarding schools remaining, so the problem is just as acute for the British as for anyone else. Sharp (1990) has outlined research on the outcome of MKs sent to boarding schools, and concluded that the boarding school concept does not in itself produce detrimental effects but was related to the parental viewpoint. There were disadvantages such as delayed social maturation in some, but the overall result was that 98% of adults with MK boarding school experience said that if they could do it again they would choose to grow up as they did.

It is impossible to give firm advice, for the final pattern chosen depends on individual parents and children. I have long felt that the best thing to do is to go with the child to the nearest mission boarding school during term time. Let the child look at it, look at it yourself and ask a lot of questions. It is more than likely that your child would decide to go to the boarding school because of sports and other facilities, and this sways the balance in favour of the school versus the wrench of leaving home.

Non-English speaking missionaries have resolved the problem either by creating their own language medium schools in which boarding facilities are available, or making extensive use of correspondence courses. One of the most interesting schools is KISC in Kathmandu where children of all nationalities study in their own language using computers, and come together for tutorials and group activities. The results have been good, figures from the British students showing high levels of success in the official British school examinations, and others doing equally well (McIlhenny, 1998). Many MK schools have established courses in the mother tongue to enable Asian MKs, for example, to remain in contact with their own culture. There is real eagerness in the new sending country communities to solve the problems of MK education without their children having to sacrifice the national culture (Chan, 1998). The situation remains fluid and circumstance-bound, nevertheless there is real dialogue and a desire to make MKs education as worth while as possible.

I once asked two groups of people what they thought about the boarding school experience. One was a group of 'twice-born' — those who had been MKs and had returned to the same country as missionaries, and the other was the graduating class of a well-known mission boarding school. Both groups said it had been a good experience though they had reservations about the hostel system however good the dorm parents were. They felt their international education gave them a breadth of vision and understanding that non-expatriate children lacked. They were in total agreement that children should not be put in boarding until they were aged eleven. On the other hand a group of Western missionary doctors working in Africa said they did better if they went at six! One thing there was agreement on was the need to maintain standards, and that those whose education had not been good due to lack of equipment were more likely than others to resent the financial stringency that had spoiled their education.

School holidays

Children at boarding school tend to come home for a long period at Christmas, so that they can have quality family time together. This does not always work out. The parents may be so overworked that the children feel neglected and bored, or the parents take time off and the children get the impression that they are worried at what they are leaving undone. In addition, the kids may be genuinely bored because compared with school there is nothing for them to do. I think various age groups need different handling, but sometimes the kids can do a small job that pleases them and get a bit of pay for it. Best of all, the whole family may be able to take a part of their annual leave during the Christmas period and try to go to a nice place. I know the financial problems, nevertheless it is amazing how God can work this out. Another thing that works is if each parent takes each child out separately to some local place. They do what the child requests, within reason, and this often works out as a really special time for them.

Coping with parents' anxieties about children

Because missionary parents take their children overseas they may experience suffering that they would not have done had they remained in the home country. At a conference in Holland the following question was raised by a missionary parent: *'When does suffering become unethical for our children?'* I was asked to respond to this, and after considerable thought was able to work out the following principles (Foyle, 1992).

Obviously we cannot protect our children from suffering throughout their lives. It is known that children grow through problem-solving relevant to their age group, although this does not mean we create problems so that they will grow! What it does mean is that we seek to protect them and also to stand by when they face the inevitable problems of growing up.

Suffering becomes unethical if the underlying family platform is seriously inadequate so that the child not only faces the current problem but has to operate from a most inadequate support basis.

A healthy family platform is based on humble parents who recognise their own inadequacies yet rely on the grace of God to give them what they need to rear their children. It has several important components:

Caring

The basis of the home is love, natural and God-given, and this loving pattern of care is made up of different components:

- *Predictability.* This implies regularity but not rigidity. Children will always accuse parents of changing their minds, and indeed sometimes they may have to, but the basic platform of family life should be predictable in routines and patterns.

- *Discipline.* This must be comprehensible to the child within the age group. As the family get older it may be wise to work out a family charter by joint discussion, and this should be reviewed regularly with all the children participating.

- *Communication.* There must be enough trust to facilitate communication. As indicated in Chapter 6 this begins to develop early, but needs to be maintained through the turbulent years of adolescence. In this connection never get upset if your teenager says, 'I can't trust you, you never do the same thing twice.' This is usually a projection of their own turbulent feelings, rather than the truth about your management. However, review the family charter and check if you are keeping your side of the bargain. In addition, children need to understand some of their parents' problems, thus keeping open doors of communication between the family. However, they should never be the recipients of confidential communications from one parent against the other. This is an unacceptable load for any child to bear, and it is better to use an outside confidante if things are not going well between parents.

Sometimes children do not want to communicate with their parents, but the doors should be kept open, BE there, wait patiently, and maybe one day they will talk to you more freely. This is a very normal thing, and you should not feel hurt or jealous if you find your child tells their best friend or favourite teacher everything, it is just a part of normal development. You will gradually return to being the 'flavour of the month'.

- **Affirmation.** Nothing can replace this, the combined knowledge of being not only God's much-loved child but also the joy of the parents' hearts! This is highly supportive of the necessary development of self-esteem, as Wickstrom and Fleck (1988) found in their research on MKs. Their results showed that self-esteem was positively correlated with the perceived approval of others, parental acceptance, and identification with parents. Affirmation includes learning personal controls, understanding what is acceptable behaviour and what is not, but behind it all is the security of knowing you are loved, good or bad. Interestingly, affirmed children also give affirmation to their parents which is very comforting however it is worded. 'Your mum's not bad' is the highest accolade a child can give to a friend's parent, and sometimes children will give huge joy to their parents by a spontaneous hug, before dashing off to the next vital thing they have to do. Such family affirmation is often increased if parents and children are free to admit they have been wrong, which releases them all from that nagging feeling they may have made a mistake but don't know what it was!

- **A workable Christian foundation.** Truly a family that prays together stays together, but the prayer time has to be chosen carefully. In the current pattern of family life it is hard to find a time when everyone is together, but something could be worked out at least once a week. For younger children, bedtime is prayer and talking time, and many of them never forget how wonderful this was.

- **Good parental relationships.** This is a difficult area, and cannot be handled fully in this book. However, it is axiomatic that parents who love each other will convey security to the children. This needs to be qualified, for there are some parents who think if they express one angry word to each other the children will be harmed. That is not so, for children need to see how parents handle each others' bad moods as they grow in their own interpersonal relationship skills. But constant quarrelling may be devastating to a child's growth and mental health. Advice from trained marital counsellors should be sought early, before the persistent quarrelling has a chance to do real damage. In this context, however, parents who quarrel and then divorce or separate should not carry an overload of guilt. Despite the pain, a reasonably secure pattern can be developed after the separation, and God will often provide special coping abilities to the children. What is devastating is constant recriminations against the other parent following the separation, and this must be dealt with by seeking proper trained help and not by sounding off in the home.

Developing

A healthy family platform provides an environment for growth. It is in this context that rigidity is so disastrous. Children need an opportunity to experiment, to learn to accept family limits as well as making their own personal ones. Parents can be helped here by a working knowledge of scriptural family teaching, for this contains a balance between absolutes and 'sweet reasonableness' that needs to be explored and practised. To enable the children to develop, parents need to balance their working lives and extra curricular activities with the needs of the home so that they can spend quality time with the children.

Understanding

Parents may get very upset when teachers point out the child's weak points, but in reality to understand your child's strengths and weaknesses is very helpful. One of the main reasons why parents get upset about what they interpret as criticism of their children may be their own insecurity. In these circumstances, the success of their child becomes doubly important, not only because of what the child has achieved but also because their own battered ego is strengthened. This situation puts a great strain on children who need to be loved just as they are, success or failure, without having to contribute ego strength to an insecure parent by always doing well at school.

Another area is understanding those needs which children may not always be able to verbalise. Understanding their nature often provides the clue, and they can then be helped to deal with their weaker points. A timid child can become braver by being useful to mother at home, and being given responsibility for some small household task plus lots of encouragement. Special support needs to be given at crucial times such as first going to school, when the timid child may lie awake at night with stomach ache or some other sign of general panic. To link going to school with some special treat helps such children enormously. Confident children have a different problem. They may have been accustomed to ruling the roost at home, but when they go to school they have to cope with much bigger children and to come down to a subordinate level. Not easy!

Providing specific training

It is tragic in our modern era that children need to be taught to distrust approaches from strangers and to beware of walking alone in certain areas. The TV does help here, for they become used to hearing about things like sex attacks and child murders, and they may vaguely understand the word paedophile from quite an early age. It is wise if parents try to get over to their children, in easy, non-frightening language, the need for care, and this is often supported by special lessons given at school. As a rule, it may be wiser to give sex education at home before the children are exposed to secular teaching at school which may promote sexual activities of which the parents disapprove.

The major danger is keeping the Christian child in ignorance of these facts, for then they are merely confused and upset by their school lessons.

Results of being a TCK

On balance, TCKs describe their experience as positive and are proud of their parents. They feel their lives have been enhanced by living overseas, and that they are more mature in many areas of their lives than their peers at home. Wrobbel and Pluedemann (1990) have done extensive research on TCK outcome, with mainly positive results. Missionary parenting is usually excellent, they are knowledgeable about possible dangers for the children and take every possible step to prevent them impacting unfavourably on them. Similarly they are skilled in making the experience a positive one. Despite this, however, some things will be disliked by the children, just as much as parents dislike parts of their expatriate experience, but this is a normal part of life and development that everyone experiences at some time or other. At the Manila conference in 1984, Sharpe (1988), having reviewed recent literature stated that 'we have every reason to be confident that MKs benefit from life overseas'. We need to remember this whenever our parenting problems and the problems of the children themselves appear to overwhelm us. That is not usually the end result, for which we thank God.

CHAPTER
11

Special Forms of Stress —
Burnout and PTSD

This chapter aims at helping serving missionaries understand the principles behind what they are experiencing. The purpose is to assist them in finding out if they are in danger of developing one of these special forms of stress, what they can do to prevent or treat it on location, and how to know when they should go for professional help. Detailed technical descriptions of treating things such as PTSD and burnout are not explained here, but attention is paid to general advice on the type of help needed, and to various practical suggestions.

Burnout

One thing must be clarified at the outset of this chapter. Until fairly recently, young Christians in some countries got the idea that if they committed themselves to God for cross-cultural service they were really committing themselves to burnout. This of course is not so, there are thousands of missionaries who remain happy, fulfilled and successful. What we are all committing ourselves to is the calling of God to do a specific job for him, and this certainly does not automatically equate with burnout.

Burnout is defined in the dictionary as 'to cease functioning as a result of exhaustion of the fuel supply' (rocket technology), or 'to become, or cause to become, exhausted through over-work or dissipation' (*Collins Concise English Dictionary*, 1992). Incidentally, dissipation here does not mean 'unrestrained indulgence in physical pleasures' but 'scattering over a wide area' — an experience common to many missionaries, especially the longer term ones. Freudenberger, who originally coined the term burnout, defined it as 'to deplete oneself, to exhaust one's own physical and mental resources, to wear oneself out striving to reach some unrealistic expectation imposed by oneself or the values of society' (1974). I do not entirely agree with this: we are all trying to do what God has asked us to do, but certainly there are some of us who try too hard to keep up with the image of what we feel a missionary should be like.

The term burnout became popular when rockets were invented. The major rocket took off with smaller booster rockets attached for extra thrust, and as orbit was achieved these dropped off and as they were useless bits of rubbish they burned out in space. This is the reason I have never liked to apply the term to Christian believers. I do not believe that the Holy Spirit who guides and indwells all believers would allow any of us to become 'useless bits of rubbish', although sometimes we may feel like that. What happens to us is that our bodies and minds get exhausted and begin to operate on reduced power. My life in India taught me to call this 'brownout'. I would sometimes be sitting in my home with a reading light and fan working nicely and the refrigerator humming away comfortably in the background. Suddenly everything dimmed alarmingly, the refrigerator coughed wildly and the fans moved very slowly. Nothing had gone out, but everything had dimmed down due to poor power supply from the electricity company, usually related to overload. This is what happens to us. We may be living in overload put on us by others and have just gone on with it too long, or we may have voluntarily overloaded ourselves, sometimes as a way of overcoming personal problems. Occasionally we may be living in a situation which we know to be wrong, and yet choose to remain in it. In writing this I am choosing my words carefully, for the last impression I wish to give is that we are to blame. Usually we are not, we have just gone on trying to make the best of a difficult situation, but it has all got too much for us.

The result is we 'brownout', we cannot try any more. Many people have explained what happened to them by using terms such as 'I was too tired to stop', 'I was on a treadmill and couldn't get off', 'I was absolutely knackered the whole time until I just had to stop. I couldn't do any more'. These are clear indications of the need to pause, take stock and see how we can set things up better. In this sense, therefore, a 'brownout' which leads us to reconsider what we are doing can be a Godsend.

Despite my not believing in the meaning behind the word, I shall use the term 'burnout' because it is compatible with the rest of the world. Burnout itself is not an illness, and to date is not included in any world classification of diseases. It is what we call a 'syndrome', a collection of symptoms that often occur together. The causes of burnout are not really known. As Mayou wrote (1987), 'The most important factors are probably person-ality and the characteristics of the job such as responsibility, variety of tasks, hours involved, poor support and rewards from others,' this last indicating praise and affirmation from time to time, as well as better support and reasonable conditions. The theory is that there has been an excessive outpouring of adren-aline for too long, plus other hormonal changes in a prolonged high-tension situation. The symptoms are usually described as 'trying to work through a blanket of cotton-wool', 'feeling dead inside with no interest in things', 'work is an effort, and it is easier just to stay in bed'. The general impression is that the main spring has gone, there is no inner drive left. To use another metaphor, all the water has drained out of the tank and there is no more in the reservoir. This is not a depressive illness, although some of the symptoms are depressive, but they do not usually all add up to a depressive diagnosis as dis-cussed in Chapter 3.

A major thing to remember is that after recovery people may feel they are not the same as they were before they burnt out, and they worry about it. The reverse is usually true, that although they are operating on reduced voltage, they have learned such a lot through the experience that God can use them even more effectively. By this I am not implying that God causes burnout but he does seem to allow it, and then uses it to empower us in a new direction.

I never forget what Geoffrey Bull wrote in his book *When Iron Gates Yield* (1955). He was alone in a Chinese prison, battered by brainwashing and many other hardships. One day he felt he had reached the end of his endurance. His Bible had been taken away years ago, but as he was sitting on the floor feeling totally broken up God put into his mind a verse which was like a shaft of light to him. 'Jacob worshipped as he leaned on the top of his staff' (Hebrews 11:21). He realised that Jacob had to lean on a staff (a crutch in modern speech) because he had been wounded during a struggle with the angel of God, presumably over the way he had spent much of his past life. His thigh muscles were damaged and he would never be the same again, but after the struggle God gave him a new name, Israel, 'because you have struggled with both God and human beings and have overcome' (Genesis 32:22–28). Hebrews tells us (11:21) that despite his permanent weakness, which was a great handicap to a man living in the desert, Israel ended his life still worshipping God. As he thought about this Geoffrey said to himself, 'What does it matter if I am never the same again, provided my name is Israel?' To modernise his language, he committed himself again to God saying, 'All right, despite my wounds let me go on leaning on my staff and worshipping you until the end of all this comes to pass.' Then he remembered that as Jacob left the place where he had been wounded the sun rose on him. 'From that time on,' he wrote, 'I viewed everything as walking into the dawning.' He was going to need this confidence, for even more terrible experiences were to befall him before his final release. But in the last prison, one of the worst he experienced, he sat and examined his faith:

> All the waves and the billows of the past three years had gone over me. Satan had brought to bear every device upon me. My mind had been so battered and I was now so fatigued that I hardly knew how

to think. Yet as in that dark cell my vision cleared, I could not explain it nor did I need to do so, but I knew that I believed my Saviour risen from the dead. I knew he was the Son of God. I knew he had shed his blood for me. I had been shaken, torn and wounded but I was conscious still that round about me were his everlasting arms. I knew... that underneath my feet, impregnable, unshaken and strong as ever, was the rock of ages, Jesus Christ my Lord. And as I sat there, from the wellsprings of my soul surged up the words that God is pleased to honour above all human utterance, 'I believe.'

This took him through the closing stages of his imprisonment, and in later years his writings were to prove a help and strength to many who were undergoing very difficult times. We should take heart. While most of us never experience imprisonment of this kind, we do suffer as we try to serve God, and may have very difficult things to cope with. The same Holy Spirit who enlightened Geoffrey and strengthened him in such terrible circumstances will do the same for us, processing the love of God in our hearts and increasing our trust in him as we soldier on through the difficulties.

Some causes of burnout

Normal wear and tear
Elijah is the best example. He had not done anything wrong, he had done a terrific job and then suddenly ran out of energy. We shall look at Elijah again later in this book, for it is a wonderful story of burnout plus depression plus restoration with a purpose behind it all. Here it is enough to say that sometimes in situations of unavoidable acute or chronic overwork we are enabled by God to work far beyond our own human resources. The important thing to remember is that this is a potentially dangerous situation, and that we need to ask God to show us what steps to take to curtail it as soon as possible. This principle is very important in disaster areas. The team has to work full stretch for a long time to bring some order into the situation, to organise how the relief is distributed, and to cope with ever-

increasing numbers of needy people with limited resources. Workers in this situation have told me how guilty they felt when management sent them off duty to a reasonable bed and adequate food and water. Yet without this 'rest therapy' they would burn out prematurely. I believe firmly that we should take breaks from the situation, even if the cover we leave behind is not really numerically adequate. I noted this in the media transmissions from the Sydney Olympics. The BBC did magnificently, their team of presenters was not all that large but they were on air for hours. Towards the end I noted that for some of the less important programmes they used only one presenter not two, presumably to allow the others to have a break, and we can do the same without feeling ashamed of our need for rest periods when there is so much to do.

In considering burnout we need to be very careful of our theology. Years ago there was a popular saying that you committed yourself to 'burn out for God' as you took up the ministry he gave you. I do not think this is God's usual pattern. We need to do the work God has given us as conscientiously as possible, but to balance it most carefully. I have the impression that Jesus was very careful of his strength. I think he used the house in Bethany as a sort of bolt-hole where he could go and relax and recharge his batteries. Similarly, his common use of flowers, fish and birds as examples in his stories may well indicate that he used his times on the mountains not only for prayer but also to wander round looking at natural history. As a fisherwoman myself I have long believed that when he was travelling by boat he went fishing just for fun. We know he got tired just like we do. 'Jesus, tired as he was from the journey sat down at the well' (John 4:6). But possibly one of the reasons he never burned out was because he was very sensible, and sat down whenever he could. For example, the sermon on the mount was to be a very long one, so he made himself comfortable by sitting on a hillside before he began.

Moses is another example of a man who took on too much. The people had been complaining about lack of variety in their diet. They got manna but wanted fish, garlic, fruit and vegetables (Numbers 11:5). God supplied quails, but they still complained, and Moses began to find it all too much. He complained to God, 'What have I done to displease you that you put the burden of all these people on me?... I cannot carry all these people by myself; the burden is too heavy for me. If this is how you are going to treat me, put me to death right now' (Numbers 11:11,14–15). Just after all this Jethro his father-in-law arrived and saw how hard Moses was working (Exodus 18:13 onwards). Being a sensible man he said to him, 'What is this you are doing for the people? Why do you alone sit as judge while all these people stand round you from morning till evening.' Moses' reply indicates the trap we can all fall into. 'Because the people come to me to seek God's will. Whenever they have a dispute, it is brought to me, and I decide between the parties and inform them of God's decrees and laws.' Note that it was 'me-me-me'. Jethro hit the nail on the head when he said, 'What you are doing is not good. You and these people who come to you will only wear yourselves out. The work is too heavy for you, you cannot handle it alone. Listen now to me and I will give you some advice, and may God be with you.' The advice? Train and delegate. This advice remains good to the present day — one way to prevent avoidable burnout is to train and delegate. We found this a good policy when we set up a primitive hospital in a very isolated area. The doctor in charge selected local young men who were literate, trained them in a particular task in the hospital and let them get on with it under periodic supervision while he attended to the work no one else could do. It appears Moses learnt the lesson, for as far as we know he never came so near to burnout again.

Physical illness

Inadequate convalescence is just as potent a cause of burnout as it is of depression. Unless we have to deal with a really serious emergency that no one else can handle, we should take time to recover from illness of any kind, especially viral illnesses.

Overwork

This has been mentioned several times in this book, but a little more needs to be said. Some people overwork because they are highly conscientious and the more work is put on them the more they do, resulting in overload. Others are workaholics, finding psychological fulfilment and personal satisfaction mainly in the amount of work they can accomplish. Usually their self-confidence is bound up in success, leading to an over-investment of energy to try to prevent failure. It is because of the psychological need to succeed that they cannot accept advice to cut down the amount they do, and to look after other areas of their lives. This situation usually leads to many casualties. Colleagues are driven almost to death, and families suffer. I remember one young lady who worked with a workaholic man. She got up at 4 am every morning to scrub floors so that her workaholic boss could come in and start his daily routine without undue temper tantrums. After a series of young women had breakdowns within six months of arrival, management intervened and things changed.

Herewith a few little bits of advice, mostly from experience!

- If you are subordinate to a workaholic it is better to discuss it with your leader sooner than later. If you have no team leader, consider carefully how long you should stay. Design reasonable coping strategies and make it plain to your boss that you must take this amount of time off if he/she wants to keep you functional. Do not let the Protestant work ethic prevent you from doing this, for you have a responsibility to yourself as well as to the work.
- If you yourself are overworked, but not a workaholic, look at it carefully and see if you can train and delegate. This is hard to do when you are in charge of the work and yet feel personally very insecure, but must be done if you are to survive without burnout.
- If there is serious job frustration, do not moan about it all the time, and do not react with overwork as a way of coping.

Live sensibly, and get all you can out of the work by designing side programmes to make it more interesting. If you feel it is not for you, try not to walk out but to wait for a natural break such as a short leave at home, and make the change then, which avoids jeopardising the work.

- Take regular 'pyjama days'. By this I mean days with no programme. You and the family get up when you want to, dress when you want to or else lounge around in pyjamas. Stay at home or go for walks, do whatever will relax you, but with no fixed programme and no pressure. I gave a talk on this once and next day a very senior person rang me up and said, 'Marjory, I'm having a pyjama day,' and I said, 'So am I. What are you wearing?' 'The kids and I are all in pyjamas and my wife is in her dressing gown and we are doing nothing.' 'I'm in joggers and my oldest sweatshirt, have a good day,' I replied, and we laughed and put down the phone.

Psychological problems

Several kinds of psychological problems tend to make burnout more likely. These may be part of our excess emotional baggage, those extras we take with us on the plane which are packed in our minds and not in suitcases. Some of these have been discussed in Chapter 6 on interpersonal relationships, and only inferiority will be mentioned here. Some of the *causes* of inferiority include the following:

a) Childhood factors. Unresolved sibling rivalry is one. Jealousy complicates this, but there are children who are always made to feel inferior to another sibling, and this may handicap their on-going psychological development. The inferiority can be reinforced as they grow older. For example, teachers may say, 'What a pity you are not such a good athlete as your brother,' or, 'Why ever did you fail the exam, anyone could have answered that paper?' Sometimes if we feel nervous starting a new job and have teething problems, a fellow employee may say to us, 'The last person had no trouble with the filing system, what's wrong with you?' Most unkind of all, people we thought were friends can sometimes make critical remarks about us behind our backs. Because we felt so inferior during childhood, remarks like these make us feel even more inferior, whereas they would be taken in their stride by those with a secure background. There are also *adult causes* of inferiority, such as unemployment and failed marriages, poor housing and lack of what others have due to poverty. To be unable to afford many of the things others regard as normal, essential household possessions, may become a powerful drain on people's psychological health.

b) Personal handicaps. Physical or mental problems, and things like social status are all involved. They cut people off from a peer group, and at school may result in bullying which further reinforces inferiority.

c) Poor family relationships. Children from homes where parents quarrel constantly and where there is a lot of violence always feel to blame and hence feel inferior to others.

d) No religious faith. This may involve not believing anyone loves them.

The content of inferiority

There are two important things to note. One is that inferiority may be a *reality*, although it is very difficult indeed to admit this to ourselves. We are very rarely brave enough to look our inferiority straight in the face for we are afraid to disrupt the coping mechanisms such as denial that we commonly use. As a result we feel miserable about ourselves, and if we are justly criticised for anything, can often become defensive or angry in the effort to avoid an overload of inferiority which is beyond our coping strength. Alternatively we may overcompensate for our load of inferiority by becoming brash and over-confident.

In God's goodness, sometimes events compel us to acknowledge our feelings of inferiority and the limitations they put upon our development. This gives us courage to seek proper professional help, to work on it with God, and to emerge stronger people. We then find out how relaxing it is simply to accept that we are not as well qualified, or as beautiful, or have such pleasant personalities as others! Such a realistic approach makes life fun, and enables God to teach us how to value who we are and what gifts God has been pleased to give us.

Certain things help us to deal with our feelings of inferiority. One is to understand God's gifts. The Lord chooses which he will give us, and everyone has received something. When we are learning to handle our own inferiority we should remember the gift of the ability to help others (1 Corinthians 12:28). We may not be much good at preaching or teaching, but everyone can help even if it is only washing the dishes. The problem is that we usually despise such a gift and wish we were evangelists, or teachers, and so feel jealous of others who are good at these things. I was once travelling with someone gifted in evangelism, at which I am hopeless. I had been talking to God about this for years, because missionaries by tradition are supposed to be good at evangelism. Seeing my gifted friend in action caused me to start moaning to God about it again, and suddenly he put a new thought into my mind. If he had wanted me to be a good evangelist he would have given me the gift, but what he had given me was the gift of healing through my medical knowledge and my prayers. I should therefore concentrate on trying to be as good a doctor as I possibly could. From that time on I stopped worrying and got on with my God-given job to the best of my ability. As an added bonus, I have recently understood very clearly that if evangelism means presenting the claims of the whole gospel of Jesus Christ to individuals, then as a psychiatrist my work of supporting missionaries and helping them deal with some of their problems is really the second half of evangelism, for it opens the door to a fuller impact of the gospel in their lives. So my job is to add a few more bits of brick to the foundation others have laid, and with that I am more than satisfied.

Another thing that helps us as we try to deal with inferiority is to recognise that there are many things in our past lives which may have produced the problem. We then need to try to work out exactly what made us feel like this, and whether there are people to forgive, as described in Chapter 6. If we follow the technique of dealing with our negative emotions as described there we may experience much relief and gradually be able to recognise that we do have strong points and that we are highly valued by God. After all, he paid a great price for us.

Much of our inferiority is related to not loving ourselves. Jesus commanded us to love our neighbours as ourselves (Matthew 19:19), yet all of us have unloved compartments in our lives which contain things of which we are ashamed. We never seem to open these up so that the love of God can penetrate them, but just put a label on them called 'Before I was a Christian', or 'What I did before until God taught me something new'. Tragically we not only do not love these areas but we can be fiercely critical of them to the point of positive dislike, which is not what God intends. He loves the total us, not just certain areas, and before we can love our neighbours properly we shall need to learn to love ourselves as God does.

There may come a time in our lives, often a crisis experience, when we become aware of the need to open up these compartments, to understand and deal with their contents and thus let the grace, love and compassion of God into them. It is wise to seek help from a trained person at this point, for thinking of the content of the compartment may be painful and we need someone who will, to quote a fine psychotherapist, 'tolerate, contain and accept us' as we work out the realities of the situation. As was indicated in Chapter 6, often the first stage is to try to gain insight into the origins of our problems, to think of them in adult reality, and to start understanding the devastating effect they may have had on our emotional life. For example, a long-continued hatred of someone, or resentment for what they did to us, may seriously hinder our emotional and spiritual maturation, and the same applies to constantly feeling ashamed whenever we remember some of the things we ourselves have done.

With a growing understanding of the problems and their origins comes a new realisation that the compartments contain hurt areas, and therefore we need to feel just as much compassion for ourselves as we would feel for any of our friends in the same situation. Instead, we just regard our wounded parts as areas of failure, and, as has been said, often combine this with a severely self-critical attitude which in turn feeds our inferiority. We need to acknowledge that we have been wrong to be so critical of ourselves and thus to shut off an area of our lives from the inflow of God's compassion, and this is often the start of the healing process. Someone said to me recently that once he realised he had been so critical of the areas of which he felt ashamed, he felt he needed to beg his own pardon for being so unkind to himself! That was exactly what he did, and slowly he began to experience an amazing relief that he could start to love and respect himself for the heroic efforts he had made to cope with a very difficult time in his life, even though they had been a bit misguided in some ways. He said he felt as if a flood of loving and compassionate understanding came into his life, and for the first time he felt like a whole person.

This experience exemplifies an important truth. Jesus loves the total us, so much so that he died on the cross to deal with our sins and to restore us to fellowship with God. His intention was that those who accepted his forgiveness and asked him into their lives would be transformed into a new creation, as Paul underlined when he wrote: 'If anyone is in Christ, there is a new creation; the old has gone, the new has come' (2 Corinthians 5:17). There is no need to remain ashamed of our past, it has all gone, created anew and growing steadily under the Lord's careful and loving hand. There is no better medicine for inferiority than that!

The second big thing to note is that *inferiority is not the same as humility*. The former is destructive and the latter constructive. Some people hide inferiority behind a religious catchphrase. One young man did this by a 'worm complex'. He used to pray the same thing every day when he and his colleague met for prayer, using a very gloomy tone of voice, 'I thank you God that I am a worm and no man.' One day his colleague could stand it no more. He jumped up and said, 'I thank you God that I may be a worm but I am a resurrected worm, a new creation in Christ Jesus.' Then they had a bit of a talk together. The problem was that the first man's statement came over as what the Bible calls a 'voluntary humility' rather than an inner reality, and this gets very wearing. It is a sort of con job to help us handle inferiority in a 'religious' way.

The difference between inferiority and humility can best be explained using a small table:

Humility	Inferiority
A new creation within us.	A lifelong problem, often with old psychological causes.
Increases our understanding of grace.	Leads to voluntary humility, an effort to appear humble which blocks the operation of God's grace.
Reality based. Gifts are recognised and accepted from the Lord, their absence is also accepted. Increases understanding that we are all parts of the body of Christ.	Unrealistic. Often a total denial of anything good within us, or the opposite, a brash over-confidence. Little understanding that we have the gifts God wants to give us.
A constructive force.	A destructive force.

Some practical advice for handling inferiority

- *Never live in the if-only's.* If only I had been this that or the other. That implies God has favourites and the Scriptures assure us he does not. He knows us and he knows what he is doing in our lives.

- *Handle inferiority by the forgiveness technique* described in Chapter 6, and remember always that he loves the total us. Remember too that as God works with us, anything unpleasant we learn about ourselves is the door to a new creation, a new possibility of a different kind of life. John wrote about the final glory of Jesus: 'He who was seated on the throne said, "I am making everything new!"' (Revelation 21:5), and he is preoccupied with making us into new creations.

- *Build up the areas in which you are even mildly gifted and pay some attention also to the weaker areas.* You will be surprised what God can do for you. Never would I have imagined I could do statistics, but something came up in my work last year that meant I had to master one or two simple ones. I might even understand standard deviations next year, who knows.

- *Learn a few very important scriptures and think about them daily.*

  Do you not know that your body is a temple of the Holy Spirit, who is in you, whom you have received from God? You are not your own, you were bought with a price, therefore honour God with your body. (1 Corinthians 6:19–20)

  Yet to all who received him, to those who believed in his name, he gave the right to become children of God — children born not of natural descent, nor of human decision or a husband's will, but born of God. (John 1:12–13)

  How great is the love the father has lavished on us, that we should be called children of God! (1 John 3:1)

  If anyone is in Christ, there is a new creation; the old has gone, the new has come! (2 Corinthians 5:17)

Post-Traumatic Stress Disorder (PTSD)

Introduction

The Bible has said there will be wars and rumours of wars until the Lord comes again. There have certainly been recent wars in every continent except Antarctica, and even there we hear of a developing economic struggle as major powers look for minerals and oil. In addition, there is a world climate of violence, although I read last night that a few countries are managing to get their violent crime rates down a little. It is no wonder therefore that missionaries get caught up not only in wars, but also in things like armed robbery, rape, and similar threats against person and property. This is now such a common part of the missionary scene that some larger sending agencies are conducting special pre-departure courses to prepare overseas workers for the possibility.

Not everyone who experiences a severely threatening event will develop PTSD. In my thesis, about 10% of 150 serving missionaries had suffered violence, armed robbery (often in the presence of children) being the commonest, two had been raped at knife point, and four had been evacuated urgently because of local instability. Of these 150, only four mentioned PTSD, which they quite rightly included as a form of stress different from the other kinds of stress the questionnaire had examined. These figures do not, of course, give the whole picture; they are only a sample, but are enough to make us realise the importance of advance preparation so that people know what to do (Foyle, 1999). In the business world a sample of 209 business expatriates were asked to name the most stressful thing in their assignment, and threat to personal safety was highest on the list, with a mean score of 52.9 (University College London and CBI Employee Relocation Council, 1991).

The responsibilities of the sending agencies

A survey of the best way to prepare candidates for possible trauma of this kind is currently under way (Lovell, personal communication), but at present two major sending agencies in the UK utilise frank discussion of the possibility and classes to help improve coping strategy techniques. One interesting bit of advice called 'defusing techniques' comes from the business world. In a nutshell, if friends are made as widely as possible on location overseas, and should the population then split into two camps to fight each other, having friends in both camps may make personal safety and subsequent exit somewhat easier (Van Brabant, 1998).

In a wise paper on meeting the challenge of possible threat to missionaries, Quarles (1988) wrote 'rarely is the issue of crime, guerrilla warfare or terrorism discussed in policy manuals.... Instead of being reactive we need to be proactive... there must be a plan, and the better your crisis management plan is the better your tools enabling you to solve the crisis.' He quotes Cole (1980): 'Any measure that plans in advance for a crisis ... any measure that removes risk and uncertainty from a given situation and thereby allows one to be more in control of one's destiny is indeed a form of crisis management.' Goode (1995) describes forms of disaster that can affect missionaries, and gives very good practical advice for advance planning. He covers things like the need to have adequate finance immediately available in case of evacuation, and how to shelter safely in your house if war begins where you live. He emphasises the need to try to notify authorities about your predicament, and to live circumspectly till it is safe to leave. If living in a high-risk area for kidnapping he advises missionaries to watch for people following them, to refuse unexpected packages, and to let others know their travel plans. Townsend and Laughlin summed all this up in 1998 when they wrote 'Critical incident debriefing should only be a part of more thorough preparation and responses of any organisation to traumatic situations. It cannot replace adequate personnel policies and support structures.' In the context of this chapter, therefore, the maxim is that more and better preparation may reduce the risk of serious post-traumatic consequences, particularly when it includes clear guide-lines about what to do when the local situation becomes dangerous.

The idea that PTSD can be avoided if traumatised people are seen within a certain period of time after the event is currently under discussion, but experience shows that the sooner they can be helped the better. The usual pattern of assistance to missionary personnel is based on a three-tiered approach. The first is the initial help and support given by team leaders within the area, whether or not they have any training in counselling. I once saw this in action, a group of people affected by a bomb being beautifully cared for by their usual leaders and the close fellowship and support of their colleagues. This initial aid formed a marvellous basis for the subsequent work done by trained people who had to travel to reach the disaster area.

The next stage of care requires help from mental health personnel living reasonably near the disaster location, 'reasonable' indicating something like one day's air journey away, or the land transport equivalent. These workers can either go to the disaster area, or stay where they are located and see people as soon as they get out. Basing mental health trained personnel reasonably near serving missionaries is currently high on the agendas of mission agencies world wide.

The third tier is crisis intervention teams, people with adequate training living in their own home countries or in central places overseas who are on call to go to areas where missionaries have been involved in major trauma. They continue the care already given by the first two tiers of workers, using their own preferred methods. These usually involve, among other things, private interviews to assess the need for treatment or evacuation, and group meetings for support and mutual sharing.

It is essential that personnel involved in care obtain written permission from their client to discuss future care requirements with the local doctor and/or mission administration if it proves necessary. This policy reassures the sufferer that nothing will be disclosed without them knowing about it and giving permission. The only exception is where there is a suicidal risk, in which case confidentiality must give way to the responsibility to inform someone in authority.

Symptoms and signs of PTSD

Initial reactions to violent trauma are a mixture of fear, anxiety, a period of hyperactivity if responsible for others followed by total loss of energy, insomnia with repeated images of the trauma scene, guilt at not doing what you felt you should have done even though you had to choose between the best of two bad alternatives, and a sense of total shock. Where a death of an important person has occurred, there is also the beginning of bereavement reactions, so the whole picture is really mixed up.

PTSD is the prolongation of some of the initial symptoms and the development of new ones. The full picture of the disorder may emerge immediately, within a few days, or, rarely, after some months (Gelder et al, 1996). For a more detailed description see Carr (1994), but in brief the following are the major features of the developed case:

- *Startle reactions*. Any noise that resembles the original one makes them jump. I saw this in action when conducting a group meeting after a bombing event. Someone dropped a metal pipe outside the door and about 50% of the group nearly jumped out of their skins. Related to this may be irritability and anxiety, poor concentration and sometimes depression.
- *Flashbacks*. When something reminds them of the event, or they are trying to go to sleep, vivid pictures of the terrifying sight they saw come into their minds. This may recur for some years. I only once saw a major horrifying sight, the unburied remains of a terrible atrocity. That night I went home on a BA flight, and every time I closed my eyes I saw again that terrible scene. When I reached home I had a phone conversation and later a supportive interview with a psychiatrist friend, and began to settle down. It is easy to understand the flashbacks people who were actually present at an atrocity may have to endure any time of day or night.

In addition they may also have terrifying dreams if they do finally manage to get to sleep.

- *Avoidance.* This is the result of the other two symptoms. They are both so unpleasant that the long-term sufferer will go to any lengths to avoid being reminded of the original event. This means limiting what they read or watch on TV, and if persistent may lead to their becoming almost a recluse for fear someone begins to talk about something that will remind them again of the past.

Treatment usually consists of much time to talk as a group or alone with an experienced person, using temporary medication to get them over the hump into calmer waters, and having a permanent carer for a time, someone kind and friendly who will comfort, reassure, pray with them and be generally helpful. There are other techniques such as using cassettes to 'decondition' the event, but the person in charge will choose the right one. It is important to remember that in our current cross-cultural team pattern the way people cope is often related to their individual cultures, which should be incorporated in the treatment pattern. It is a tragic fact that sometimes the culture may prove a barrier to good care. As Carr points out (1997), 'for in-house reasons of their own the mission agency may ask a missionary to reveal some parts of the trauma but not others. It is more difficult to process and resolve a trauma when restrictions are placed on what can be discussed.'

The major thing is not to feel you are weaker than others because you have got this prolonged reaction. Everyone is different, some are susceptible to flu or diarrhoea, and you happen to be susceptible to PTSD. It is very important that you get proper professional help, for good diagnosis is vital to good treatment, and in this connection please remember that not all psychiatrists have two horns and a tail! One place I worked in I spent ten days after arrival sitting in the garden watching the birds while the local missionary community covertly watched me, finally deciding that I was OK and not from the pit!

There are good things that emerge from the experience of PTSD. One is that you have opportunity not only to look the current episode in the face but also to deal with older problems that may be making the PTSD more severe. Never forget that people may emerge stronger the other side of the illness, despite the possibility of certain aspects of their health being a little damaged. If we end up like weakened Jacob leaning on his staff, we will be enabled to continue to worship God, for our illness makes no difference to our relationship with God. He never lets us go, however awful we feel, and will actually use the weakness we experience to enhance our relationship with him and to increase enormously the help we can give other people.

12

Re-entry Stress

Missionaries returning home after a period overseas are often surprised by their own reactions. They may feel confused, unusually fatigued, and uncertain of things like behaviour and dress. The day I managed to modernise myself and go to the beach in T-shirt and shorts my sister let out a cheer! The commonest reactions however are insecurity and loneliness. In reality, at re-entry missionaries experience a reverse bereavement, with the same reactions as those discussed in Chapter 3. National and expatriate friends, home, job, church, educational system, food and climate have again been lost, so a mourning period preceding final readjustment is very common. It is interesting that mental health workers have noted bereavement reactions occurring when people have only been overseas for a few weeks on a very short assignment.

Part of the problem is that on return, things have **changed**. The mind thinks of 'home' as it was when they left, not realising that in their absence much may have changed. Hence the old 'host' country now feels like 'home', and the old home feels remarkably like a host country. This is a particular problem for children, who may have been born overseas and never seen what their parents still call 'home'. In addition, the home-based family has changed. Missionaries may have occupied a particular niche in a family, but after leaving the gap is closed, the family moving on without them. So family jokes and words that convey particular meanings are sometimes incomprehensible, and may have to be explained. Social and local conditions have also changed, so we need to ask what they mean, and that makes us feel stupid. After four years in a small town area in Nepal where there were no wheeled vehicles, I returned to London and went out on a public bus. I noted all along the roads big orange globes flashing, and finally turned to a lady beside me and asked what they meant. She looked at me in absolute astonishment and said in the local slang, 'Where you been living ducks, on the moon?' They apparently marked zebra crossings, places for pedestrians to cross the road safely. The important thing is to keep on laughing rather than getting upset. The key expression to use is 'silly old me, but I'm learning!' Then everyone laughs with you and not at you.

Some struggle with **professional changes** which make them feel definitely inferior. They may take a course on some topic related to their profession, and if there has been a few years gap since they worked at home whole sections of it may be almost incomprehensible. Initials are a major problem. Once when I was on leave I sat through a clinical meeting in the US where initials were used for everything, and they might have been speaking ancient Greek for all I could understand. I also got a professorial frown in the UK when I did not understand GHQ — if he had said 'General Health Questionnaire' I would have known where I was.

Missionaries do not expect these reactions. They do not realise the extent to which they have integrated with the culture overseas, nor the rapidity with which things change in the home country. As Africa Inland Mission wrote in its book on re-entry, 'missionaries find themselves out of phase with their own culture' (AIM). This chapter will aim at discussing the most traumatic aspects of re-entry, looking at what mission agencies are doing to help, and giving some practical advice.

As a preliminary, mention must be made of the difficulties surrounding the word **debriefing**, one of the central parts of re-entry care. Personnel understand this to mean interviews with management or counsellors before going home, after arrival home, and after special periods of trauma. However, complications have arisen. A recent literature review by Rose and Bisson (1998) concluded that there was no evidence to show that debriefing for those who had been traumatised was useful in the prevention of mental health problems. (See also Wessley et al, 2000). The media became interested, for they had given widespread publicity to the specialised debriefing utilised for hostages after their release and after other major tragedies such as the Locherbie aircrash. The tone of their comments was that since the results of debriefing were not all that positive, why bother? The extension of this for missionaries is that routine forms of debriefing as well as the specialised trauma work may all come under the same cloud, and personnel will begin to wonder whether it is required at all. Lovell, in an excellent chapter on debriefing (manuscript in preparation 2000), has clarified this. She has shown that unsatisfactory technical aspects of the research utilised cast doubt on the conclusion that debriefing was not helpful, and that much more research is required before we can be sure of the truth.

I intend therefore to continue to use the word 'debriefing' to indicate three of the many types of re-entry care: routine interviews at the end of each term of service, pre-retirement interviews, and the specialised type of debriefing used after severe traumatic events overseas, defining the context each time. Basically I believe all three to be useful, and was encouraged by the findings of a research questionnaire on re-entry which showed 'surprisingly few problem areas, temporary re-entry appearing to be more stressful than permanent. This would indicate that the current re-entry programmes are working successfully' (Foyle, 1999).

The technique of debriefing has been admirably described by Lovell (2000) to whom I am indebted for permission to give a brief outline of her material. She feels no hesitation in using traumatic stress principles for most forms of re-entry care, since she regards the whole overseas experience as 'a critical incident'. She has therefore modified the critical incident technique to suit the routine interviews, using introductions, identification of the most troubling thing, discussion of day-to-day difficulties as well as traumatic experiences, presence of psychological symptoms, and explanation of the normality of many of their reactions. Both Dr Lovell and I are in agreement that it is most important to include the positives during debriefing sessions. We do experience trauma overseas, none of us doubt that, but there are also major positives which must be expressed if any form of debriefing is to be complete.

Temporary re-entry

This is called furlough, home assignment, or leave. In this chapter the term 'leave' will be used.

Adult problems

Three particular areas of leave were found very stressful: deputation work, loss of role and general resettlement problems. All these were significantly related to the development of psychological symptoms, but housing and finance were not (Foyle, 1999). Most of the deputation stress was due to fund-raising (see Chapter 5), although as indicated there a recent correspondent told me she had lived with fund-raising all her career and had found it a valuable way of continuing personal contact with supporters. This has not been the experience of the majority I questioned through personal conversation and a postal questionnaire. Coote, in a study of North American missionaries on leave (1991), found the same as I did, that deputation work and fund-raising were very stressful, and in his work housing also emerged as a leading stressor.

Periods of service are now so short that many do not experience leave at all, but for those who do there are certain things that help ease re-entry. Generally speaking, **advance planning** for leave is the norm in most missions. This should begin a long time before leave is due, with the individual being consulted about how they want to spend their time at home. Obviously not all the time should be spent on deputation. There may be a need for professional development, or for coping with special family problems, and time for renewing contact with the home church, a holiday, and physical and spiritual refreshment. As part of this planning there should first be an overseas debriefing interview with the expatriate and/or national leader, or other appointed person. The purpose is to hear about the past term, to discuss good and bad things, to ease emotional upsets, and to think about the future.

One essential of good care before going on leave is **documentation**, and I personally believe that the overseas leader should discuss with the worker how much of the content of their interview should be reported to the home office. Staff at home need to know what they can do to make leave helpful and to make future terms of service more meaningful, which is difficult to do without some feedback from overseas. Therefore, a signature should be taken at the debriefing interview allowing the field leader to send a report, a copy of which should be given to the person concerned and discussed. Where personnel disagree strongly with what the field leader thinks, this should be included in the report so that the home staff can start from the beginning and try to sort it all out. I realise how difficult this may be in practice, but it seems to be the only way of maintaining personnel confidence in leadership as well as providing necessary information to the home staff.

Similarly, adequate medical documentation should be sent. Nowadays more and more expatriates hold their own records containing basic details of their health overseas. There are, however, occasions when further documentation may be needed, so the usual consent signature should be taken and information sent direct to the doctor employed by the agency at home. E-mail and fax make this so much easier, and enable confidentiality to be protected. This is one of the reasons why I feel all missionaries should have access to lap-top computers in their area. This enables communications to be sent to private confidential numbers in the home and overseas offices, but personnel can write more freely and safely than ordinary mail allows. However, Roy and Jan Stafford in the UK have reminded us that there is growing unease about missionaries owning lap-tops, which have been described as a modern form of colonialism: whoever has the e-mail has the power. Ownership also indicates untold wealth to the local people, and may make personnel likely targets for theft with violence. They plan to publish an article on this topic (personal communication). However, I feel that in these difficult days in many overseas countries when evacuation may be required, someone in the area should have one.

An additional medical comment concerns returning overseas from home leave when personnel have been sent home ill. When they go home they should take with them adequate medical documentation from the treating doctors overseas, and when ready to return they should not do so until documentation has been sent from the treating staff at home to the overseas medical officer, and return agreed between them. Too much trouble has resulted from failure to adopt this policy.

Missionaries themselves are sometimes remarkably uncooperative on this issue. They may have been told they need physical or mental health care, and have refused any help. The power to do this is part of individual human rights, but agencies who realise a return overseas could have disastrous consequences for the individual and others also have the right to say 'no treatment no return'. This is not a popular policy and may involve confrontation, but a lady I heard about exemplifies its importance. Her story has been heavily disguised and mixed with a little of someone else's story, but the principle is true. This lady worked overseas in a very isolated area, with little medical care. Her husband was a very gifted man with a type A personality and of course was longing to go back to a new and challenging location. The lady herself was anaemic, and had a medical condition that could be managed in the home country but possibly might be adversely affected by a poor climate and isolated location. Objectively the doctors had to give a negative decision, which led to great heart searching by the couple as to whether to disobey the doctors' advice and return to the overseas location without the consent or support of their mission agency, or to accept it and seek new work in the home country.

I heard later they had wisely decided to stay in UK and take up a ministry which would satisfy her husband and would not involve her leaving the country.

Arrival home

Obviously the advance planning has ensured that people will be met and that they have somewhere to go on arrival. Remembering the usual mental confusion, it is wise to let people hibernate for a day or two, apart from a welcome home card from the home office and a phone call to indicate concern and readiness to help. When personnel finally go to the office for their debriefing they are usually bursting to talk, and adequate time should be given. For married people it is better if these interviews are one-to-one plus a joint one. To re-emphasise what has already been said, it is important that positives be discussed as well as negatives, since the danger of much of the work currently being done to care for missionaries is the major concern with negatives. Positives need as much documentation as negatives, for we learn from both

May I suggest that interview rooms in agency headquarters be made as comfortable as possible? Chairs should be of equal height, and sideways to the light source. That way no one dominates and there is no third-degree spotlight effect shining on anyone. I have always remembered an interview I had where the person meeting me was rather large (I am a small person). He sat on a high armchair and I was given a lower one so that he towered over me. I felt doomed before I began! Do please switch off the mobile and ask for phone calls to be diverted while you are interviewing. People may be on the edge of telling you something really personal when the phone goes, and those moments never come again. If interviewing one person alone the sex of the interviewer and personnel member are important, for these days accusations of sexual harassment can be made against anyone. Hence it is good either to have a glass window in the office so you are visible but not audible, or else to have the door open onto a quiet corridor with another staff member reasonably near. Following the interview the missionary needs to feel free to come again, unless their needs can be adequately handled by a periodic small conference of returnees with few or no prepared talks, and a lot of time for discussion, exchange of views and joint relaxation.

The important thing about leave is the need for balance. Rest and holiday, friends and family, church and home time, professional development, spiritual refreshment and deputation are all involved in the balance, and those who have to organise personnel on leave have my deepest sympathy. One thing that helps is remembering the differing personalities of those on leave. Some love deputation, others really dislike it, and a few have even had to have treatment for anxiety because of it. Hence there is a need for individualisation of leave, deputation, for example, being maximised for some and minimised as far as possible for others. For professional people, national regulations as well as their own wishes may demand time being spent in their profession if they are to maintain accreditation.

Housing

This of great importance during leave, although in my survey it did not prove to be as stressful as it was on permanent re-entry. It is customary nowadays for the sending church to be asked to arrange accommodation, but people still experience difficulties. They should be asked what they want to do about housing, since if they own a home it may be let out to good tenants whom they do not want to lose. Some want to go to relatives' homes, others definitely do not. Many churches and agencies still have the idea that single people automatically go back to the parental home, feeling the family will be hurt if they do not. However kind the family is this does not always work, for single people need freedom and privacy to do their own thing, and space to get themselves together and to adjust to being back home again. The solution is to have housing on leave as a part of the job contract, and then people understand. Living with families rarely works for married people either, especially if they have children, for it is almost impossible to bring up your children under the watchful eye of your in-laws. It does work if there is a private apartment attached to the parental home, thus ensuring both privacy and permanent baby-sitters.

Role problems

Missionaries often hold positions of some responsibility overseas, and may even be holding more senior positions than they would in their home countries at their age. Home leave may therefore be something of a shock for them. For example, if they do a short professional appointment they know little of recent changes beyond what they have read, and their past experience is not valued. This is beginning to change in that some people have made a valued contribution to their profession based on overseas experience. A good example is a recent book on 'Gentle Surgery' by Dr Perrill (2000), who learnt how to operate gently in India, where infection was common and blood transfusions rare. Usually however, the return to professional work even for a short time makes missionaries feel behind the times, and therefore somewhat inferior. This is the same in the business world where returned expatriates find everything has moved on and people are not the slightest bit interested in what they have been doing overseas.

Deputation work may also increase role problems in that they are longing to do their own job but instead have to spend time speaking at meetings. This is not done grudgingly, it is recognised as a part of the job, but there is often a sense of longing for their proper work to the point of mild mourning.

The basic need is to keep your sense of humour. People find us funny in a nice way, and may laugh at our mistakes, but this can be fun for us too. My family never stopped reminding me of the day I was alarmed when we put the turkey outside the window in the snow, because there was no room in the refrigerator. 'What about the rats?' I said. 'Rats, what rats?' they said. 'We don't have rats in this part of London.' I shook my head to wake up my brains, and remembered I was not coping with

India but was back in London which was a bit safer in terms of verminous pests. Then we all laughed our heads off.

Children's problems

As indicated above, when children go home with their parents they are really leaving their home (overseas) country and going to a host country, the parents' home country, and this is very confusing for everybody. In a discussion group several missionary children said to me, 'Furlough was the worst part of it. We vaguely remembered the place, and it took us a long time to understand how it worked. By the time we had adjusted we had to go back again.' For some of them over-exposure to the public was the worst part. One family used to dress the children up in national dress and get them to sing a song in the national language. It was all right when they were little but as they grew older they began to dislike it so much they refused to do it. Agreement was finally reached when the parents agreed to pay them for each appearance, a great offer which the kids could not resist. However, exposure of this kind has had a profound influence on some missionary children, and nowadays is very rare. The whole family may stand at the front of the church once, then the work is done by the parents with no further involvement of the children.

A major point of resentment among the children I talked to was the pressure put on parents to raise funds by their mission agencies, and it made the kids feel pressurised too. 'We did not see why we should be dragged into it, after all it was not our job, it was their job' was the comment of one stressed-out child. I also found that some children, to use modern speech, felt their parents were being professionally abused by the small allowance levels on which they operated. By contrast however, many children accepted the financial structure as a way of life, and later on came to respect their parents for the financial sacrifice they had made, and to rejoice in the way God had provided for them all.

Sometimes leave is so long that children have to attend local schools for a short period and this can be traumatic. 'Why are you white if you are an Indian' was the comment one of my small friends received, and no amount of explanation could help the other children understand that although she lived in India she was not Indian. Sometimes the teacher gives facts about the country the child lives in which are not exactly correct, and if he stands up and says so then the teacher may be annoyed and the other kids think him a show-off. It sometimes feels to the missionary child like a 'no win' situation, which has been further discussed in Chapter 10.

Difficulty arises over the amount of time one or both parents are away. If possible the whole family should stay together for a month after arrival. Thereafter, I discovered it is easier if one parent goes away for short periods of time rather than a long stretch. The basic need is for the presence of at least one parent during special periods of stress, such as starting school, or taking an exam. Of equal importance is the presence of at least one parent at special events at school, especially if the child is participating.

Despite the difficulties, many children enjoy home leave and have mixed feelings about going back again. Sometimes adjustment is so satisfactory that they feel they have two home countries, one overseas and one at home, and they simply commute between them.

Prevention of children's re-entry stress

Certain things can help. One is to keep the parents' home country alive in the children's minds. This is now comparatively easy with videos, TV spreading all over the world, the Internet, e-mail, transmission of photos by scanner, telephones and personal conversation. It helps to practise shopping in the mall or supermarket, cooking what they will eat at home, and discussing for months what treats they will have when they get home. If the overseas location is with a group of expatriates, then it is good to discuss with the older children the fact that everybody at home is not as good or kind as they are, and gently to prepare them for the dangers without scaring them.

Many parents feel guilty when their children suffer re-entry stress. They are aware that if they had not gone overseas and so set up a migrant life-style, the children would not be having their current difficulties, and this is dealt with in detail in Chapter 10. When children are stressed they may reproach their parents for causing their troubles. 'If only we had stayed at home this wouldn't have happened.' Naturally the parents feel hurt, but they need to remember that such complaints are common to all growing children. When things go wrong it's usually the parents, or siblings, or even the cat that's to blame, not the child. So they should just wait patiently, be supportive, not make a big issue of it, and see what the child says once the current crisis is over. They also need to remember that when God calls them he will also be involved in their children's lives, offering them his loving concern, care and protection.

Permanent re-entry

Adult problems

Several different categories are included in the words permanent re-entry, such as those who go for one short period and return at a comparatively young age, those who have completed their working years overseas and go home to retire, those who return aged around 50 and need to find a job, and children who return to finish their education, sometimes without their parents.

Re-entry for **young missionaries** after a short contract is perhaps the easiest, since such people have usually kept roots at home, may have their own housing, and are young enough to be able, hopefully, to get a job and go on with their lives. However, as previously mentioned these people may also experience bereavement reactions. Many have felt very fulfilled in their work overseas, and have had the experience of a lifetime.

They feel they have really accomplished something, a basic need for the young of gen X. As so many have said to me, 'I just loved it and wanted to stay.' They need time to talk, to meet the agency staff and some of their old mission friends, and the opportunity for ongoing care should they fail to readjust. Most agencies stay in touch with short-termers for as long as they wish, and in some groups there is an association of returned missionaries which stays together by letter, has periodic meetings, and so maintains the feeling of belonging. This type of support may well be useful to short-termers, although they probably prefer to do it by e-mail and Internet chat, with an occasional get together in various local areas. They tend to drop out of the group quite quickly, so leaders have to be prepared for constant change.

Things are more difficult for the **middle-aged person** who has to return prematurely due to family or health problems. We all know how hard it is to get a job when you are over 50, yet there are years to go before becoming pensionable and they have families to support. There are few re-entry situations that demand more faith, and I remain amazed at the provision of God for his children, as person after person in this category demonstrates God's care by finding the right job. The agency support services should be available to them for as long as they need, although obviously the financial policies of the agency must also be adhered to. Some of the caring agencies such as Interhealth in London have a careers counsellor attached whose role is to stand by such people, give informed advice and help, and ongoing support.

For those who have a professional job offer another dilemma arises. They fear they may not be up to date and at that point cannot afford an upgrading course. Their only alternative seems to be to take the job and hope for the best, although revalidation requirements will soon preclude this. Indian missions appear to have addressed this by the creation of a special fund for professional courses (Rajendran, 1998), and it would be good to have such funds universally available in other countries, not only for those retiring early but also for those on leave who want to upgrade.

For those returning early who have **children of school age**, educational problems loom large, and in fact is one of the major causes of severe stress for parents at this time (Foyle, 1999). Many children have had excellent education overseas and loved their schools, but a similar type of education in the home country is usually very expensive indeed. Parents therefore need much advice and help on return so that they can get their children into good schools, this of course being further complicated by lack of permanent housing. All that can be done is to walk with them as they sort this out, be practical, and encourage and support them.

When people have to return early because of **health problems** in the family there is often much guilt floating around. It is not so bad for singles where only one person is involved, but a sick family member impacts on the whole group. For example, a sick eldest son may lead to a father and mother losing a loved job, younger siblings having to leave a good school, and the return of the whole group to massive insecurity. No wonder the boy tends to feel guilty, and the other family members feel equally guilty, because they are upset at having to leave rather than giving the patient unquestioning support. Psalm 91 helps here, although it is rather a mysterious passage. Despite what it says, there are times when God has not protected us. He did not protect the sick boy from 'pestilence' in terms of illness, and the arrows have got through and pierced the work the parents were doing for God. As a result they feel they have fallen by the wayside as a wounded family. Possibly they had interpreted Psalm 91 as indicating this would never happen. I think the Psalm indicates something else. What God is saying to us is that we may experience these things, but if we make him our refuge and dwelling the damage will never defeat our inner being. True there may be residual damage to things like health, and we may never recover our old life-style, but by giving ourselves back to him at this time rather than resenting it and feeling bitter, our inner turmoil will be defeated, we shall learn to cope, and there will be progress in our relationship with God. However long it takes to sort out, he will give us courage, wisdom, fortitude and increased personal and spiritual development as we walk through it with him.

Dr Jock Anderson's recent book *In the Stillness* (1999) demonstrates God's care of his children in difficult circumstances, as does a story I was told of someone who because of a chronic illness was in a wheelchair, and felt very frustrated. She was encouraged to learn computing, and now has more work to do from her own home than she can cope with, and feels so much better mentally that she is studying for another degree. So we need to hang on and to cling to God in blind faith, for the time will come when the felt love of God will once more shine on us and we shall move on with him. Psalm 91 quotes the Lord as saying to those who love him, even when it is very hard to do so, 'I will rescue you; I will protect you for you acknowledge my name; you will call upon me and I will answer you, I will be with you in trouble, I will deliver you and honour you' (vs. 14–15). Bitter resentment and anger against God could kill the honourable deliverance he wants to give us. In reality the trouble may never be fully resolved, but the spirit is freed to continue to love and rejoice in God and to serve him to the best of our ability.

The third category of re-entry concerns those who **retire** after many years of overseas service. Being of pensionable age work is no problem, but money and housing may certainly be major ones. Reactions to retirement range from painless re-entry and relief that the work is done, to genuine mourning reactions which may be prolonged. Once again the grief is related to what has been lost, such as role, friends, home, church, work, national food and climate, and all the other things that have become familiar overseas. Add onto this the loneliness that may follow retirement, the unfamiliar culture of what used to be home, and uncertainty about any future role, and there is a scenario for plenty of emotional trouble. It is amazing that people survive it so well, indicating their resilience and trust in God for this next stage of their lives.

Several things can make this mourning period worse. One is inadequate closure, people being prevented for various reasons from saying proper goodbyes. This leaves them feeling in a vacuum. I was fortunate at this point since my farewells went on for three days, but by the end I was beginning to wonder if they were not so much saying 'goodbye' as 'thank goodness she's going'! Some people however have to leave their locations quickly and never return to them, which leaves them emotionally up in the air. This is especially true for children. Under these circumstances I have long advised that finances be made available to send them back to their old location on holiday when it is safe enough to do so, thus enabling them to make a proper closure and so recover their emotional health more quickly.

Another area that causes trouble is loss of role, although this was not reported as a serious stressor in my survey (Foyle, 1999). Overseas missionaries may have held senior positions, but whatever they did they were usually widely known in the community, and often loved and respected. Returning home involves loss of both status and role, for they become just another old person walking round the shops, few people know them or speak to them in the street, and if they go to a professional meeting they usually do not know anyone at all! It is an experience hard to describe and hard to go through, but is a reality to many who do not settle back into a community where they were known before going overseas. They have to make a new niche. It does help to join a church immediately, and to take up some interests locally, but most important of all is to make a mental adjustment to being 'nobody' compared to being 'somebody' overseas. Ways can be devised to help you feel useful again, for there are many opportunities if you look for them. As mentioned earlier, at professional meetings speaking to delegates from the countries you have worked in is a wonderful experience. They are always delighted and an immediate rapport is established. Some are very lonely and value a chance to talk with someone who knows and understands their backgrounds. The same applies in shops. Locally I have three Urdu-speaking shop assistants and one Nepali, all of whom are delighted with my stumbling efforts at remembering a bit of my old languages. In fact, once you get over the adjustment period there is an awful lot of fun to be had as well as serious opportunities for ministry, which should be sought out as a replacement for loss of an active working life.

Housing may be a problem at permanent re-entry and a few more comments are required. Many years ago if you owned a house or apartment, it was the custom to sell it when you went overseas as a missionary, the major reason for this being the very long terms served overseas due to lack of air travel. As a result, when you came home on leave or retirement you had nowhere to go. Things have changed, and since periods of service overseas are usually much shorter than before, those with flats or houses tend to rent them out, the rent paying the mortgage. This is a great help at final re-entry.

Those with no provision at all experience a major problem, for which there are several different solutions. In the UK a charitable trust has been established to help provide housing for retired missionaries and I have met similar schemes in the US. There are snags in that the housing is not always where you want to live, but that is a minor disadvantage compared to being homeless. Churches are increasingly being made responsible to meet this need for the long-term worker, even though it is not always easy for them to accomplish. I have long wondered if it would be a good idea to create a centralised missionary housing advisory panel to advise about the best way of starting to search, although this should begin long before actual retirement. It is interesting that retirement housing has proved just as much of a problem in India, a new sending country, as it has been in the old sending countries. Dr Rajendran (1998) wrote in his fine book on Indian Missions: 'Missions can recognise the worth of their missionaries by planning for their housing and pension after retirement.' He comments that in 1984 Indians formed a Missionary Upholders Trust to provide, among other things, retirement accommodation.

Financial problems at permanent re-entry have not proved as significantly stressful in my research as I expected, but nevertheless they are a very great problem for many people. They have been discussed in the Indian context by Dr Rajendran (1998), the Indian agencies feeling that an early solution to the problem must be found as their missionary movement develops. He points out that Muslims and Hindus expect to care for all the retirement needs of their priests and have already taken steps to organise it, while Christians appear to lag behind in care.

Part of the world-wide problem relates to increased costs of living, higher social standards and general expectations of the countries from which missionaries come, for to slot back into these on a very limited income is not easy. In countries where there is no health service or social security the situation is worse. It would, therefore, seem right to spend time preparing to meet re-entry needs through increased strategic mission and church planning, rather than expecting individual missionaries to work it out alone.

None of this is intended to negate the primary responsibility of God to provide for his children. That he will do so is stated frequently in promises such as 'My God will meet all your needs according to his glorious riches in Christ Jesus' (Philippians 4:19), which can be added onto 'everyone who has left houses or brothers or sisters or father or mother or children or fields for my sake will receive a hundred times as much and will inherit eternal life' (Matthew 19:29). I remember sitting in church one day after my own re-entry when I was in despair about housing. I said to God, 'I don't want 100 houses, I just want one and you can give the 99 to someone else.' Incidentally I was housed within a week after that despairing wail! However, the fact that practical re-entry problems are strongly related to God's promises makes it all the more important that churches and mission agencies co-operate with him by setting up some workable advisory pattern.

Ignorance needs to be considered. While overseas missionaries know how to cope. They know how to travel, shop, keep house, manage different work patterns, and many other things. However, even if they have only been overseas a few years much may have changed by the time they come home. It is hard to itemise these since many seem so petty, but as an example at the supermarket you may be asked if you want 'cashback'. Missionaries may have no idea what this is and have to ask, which makes them look and feel stupid. Groceries can be ordered by the Internet which you may not know how to use, goods in the supermarket may be priced in kilograms, but you still think in pounds and ounces, and you are swimming in a sea of unfamiliar things like DVD and Digital. It is vital to keep a sense of humour, and to turn all these minor changes into a game, seeing how much you can learn in any one day. Perhaps one of the biggest problems is language. The TV has had a profound influence, conversation often revolving round what happened on a soap opera last week. Children who want to describe something they like simply say 'wicked', a word which re-entered missionaries interpret as something unpleasant. For a long time after I came home people kept saying 'let's face it', the *in* expression of the time, but because it had not just grown up with me, I had to learn to use it! So one can end up feeling really ignorant, but it passes with a bit of time, patience and humour.

In conclusion, despite the possibility of re-entry being related to bereavement reactions and a great deal of uncertainty, it can be a good experience. There is so much to learn and to enjoy, it is wonderful to be with the family again, to be able to rely on safe milk and water, to enjoy church fellowship unhampered by language, and to set up again a full life on a new pattern. Thus it becomes no more than the next event in our lives, a new page in our service for God which becomes very exciting as we see what he chooses to write on it.

Children's problems

These are much the same as already discussed under temporary re-entry, but there is one other to be considered. That is re-entry into the academic world, whether they are entering school or going to university. One very sensible young man told me that as soon as he got back to the parents' home country he had to enter the first year of his university studies. He felt totally out of place socially, although he was well ahead academically, this being a known pattern in the MK community (personal notes from Manila Conference on MKs 1984). In order to enter the main stream of university students he teamed up with the 'odd-ball' group, those who for various reasons did not quite fit into the mould. He learned from them a great deal about living in his new home country, and was rapidly able to 'graduate' to the ordinary life of the other students. This is an important principle. So often returned MKs resent being different, but instead of that they can use it, as the young man in my example did, with the result that being a temporary odd-ball becomes very useful rather than a source of unpleasant resentment.

During the process of final re-entry, children may overcompensate and refuse to talk about the country they have left, this being the way they try to speed up their integration with their new peers. Once they feel comfortable in the new home country, then it normalises and they will incorporate their experiences as a part of their history and feel free to talk about them. One other reaction that concerns parents is that the children may lash out at them in anger, and blame them for their present troubles. In reality this is only an expression of their inner anxieties, and does not represent the real feelings they have for their parents. It is best to comfort them and wait patiently, for as they settle down so their emotions will normalise.

Making children's re-entry easier
- Adequate **preparation** is as important as the preparation to leave and go to a new country, and much the same methods

can be used, TV and videos, photos, general instruction on how things work, and a lot of reassurance.
- Adequate **closure** has the same beneficial effect on children as on adults (q.v.).
- **Support** conferences for re-entered children, and the creation of a society or association which is given a name and which keeps ex-MKs together. Very few formal talks should be given, most of the time being spent in recreation and talking together informally and in groups, with staff at hand to give guidance and counselling. Regular newsletters are usually sent out. In large countries this needs to be done on a state basis, smaller ones can usually do it nation-wide.
- **Parental patience and support** until they are strong enough to cope with their new country on their own.

CHAPTER
13

Caring for Missionaries

This chapter will deal with the important topic of looking after missionary health and well-being. In recent years various aid and missionary agencies have joined together to prepare Codes of Best Practice for looking after employees, and these all emphasise the importance of care from 'cradle to grave', i.e. from the time of selection and orientation, through service years to the end of re-entry. The major UK document comes from People in Aid. In a nutshell they have a seven-point code which says that the work depends on people who should be cared for as well as possible, who should be consulted when policies concerning them are developed, whose needs are recognised in budgeting, who receive adequate training and support, and whose security and well-being are a vital part of agency care. Global Connections UK has devised a code for short-term workers

At the end of the twentieth century, the topic of caring for missionaries was deemed important enough to warrant a separate clause in the Declaration issued after a World Evangelical Fellowship conference on Missiology in Iguazzu, Brazil (Taylor, ed., 2000):

Clause 14. Member Care. Service of the Lord in cross-cultural environments exposes missionaries to many stresses and criticisms. While acknowledging that missionaries also share the limitations of common humanity, and have made errors, we affirm that they deserve love, respect and gratitude. Too often agencies, churches and fellowships have not followed biblical guidelines in dealing with cross cultural workers, We commit ourselves to support and nurture our missionary workers for their own sakes and for the gospel witness.

Introduction to missionary care

During the past 50 years taking good care of missionaries has become increasingly important to the agencies concerned, although for over a hundred years the need for this had been recognised and documented. For example, as early as 1904 a committee of very eminent doctors used to meet regularly in London to discuss missionary health and welfare, and they appointed a special doctor to the largest missionary society to care for missionary health (Foyle, 1999). Literature on the topic remained sparse for the first half of the twentieth century. It has only been in the last half of the century that the importance of holistic care for missionaries has taken off in a big way, resulting in a marked increase in literature, regular world and national conferences, and the appointment of personnel dedicated to missionary care. To name only a few, in the US the World Evangelical Fellowship appointed two workers specifically to look into missionary health and welfare needs, which resulted in the formation of 'Member Care' world-wide, (Memca). In Canada the Missionary Health Institute was opened many years ago in Toronto, as was the Link Care Centre in Pasadena, USA. Scotland created Care for Mission, and in London a similar clinic called Interhealth was opened in 1986 which offers a full range of physical and psychological care for missionaries as well as travel clinic facilities. UK interest in missionary welfare is being widely stimulated by Global Connections. In France Le Rucher has been established to care for missionary well-being, and there are many other caring units around the world (O'Donnell, 1997). Recent books include *Missionary Care* (O'Donnell, ed., 1992), and *Too Valuable to Lose* (Taylor, ed., 1997) which contains an extensive list of member-care centres, and much detailed information about missionary care.

This chapter will discuss three aspects of member care; care at selection, at orientation, and during the service years. Re-entry has been dealt with in Chapter 12 with additional material about children in Chapter 10.

Missionary selection

This is a most difficult topic to write about, since there is little prospective research, and in any case nationality impacts on the best pattern to use. It is therefore almost impossible to devise a universally applicable system. Additionally, almost every missionary, agency and church has different opinions about how selection should be done, so nothing one writes can please everyone. Interestingly enough the business world has the same problem, a plethora of papers coming out with different ideas and opinions (Foyle, 1999). It would seem wise therefore to try to look at the principles, and to avoid comment on how people work these out in their own culture.

By way of introduction, the importance of fitting the selection process to the current world social climate, and of asking the right questions should be underlined. Schubert has pointed out that in the US candidates come from 'an enlarging pool of bruised individuals' (1991), relating these, among other things, to dysfunctional families, being adult children of alcoholics or survivors of sexual abuse, and individually unresolved emotional problems (1992). A survey by Jones of a British Bible college where missionary candidates also trained, found similar problems (1989). The figures make rather startling reading:

- 16% of students came from families where the parents had separated, 9% of these being divorced. 10% had been sexually abused, and the same percentage physically abused.
- 8% of the total had used drugs.
- 8% of the women had had a termination of pregnancy.

Not all these were missionary candidates, but the seriousness of these figures provides the strongest possible evidence that selection processes are needed, for as Larcombe stated, 'Problems encountered at home are likely to be exacerbated abroad' (1994). My own candidate figures between 1986–1991 did not reveal problems of this magnitude, probably due to preliminary screening out of the most damaged people in the agency offices, but the data from serving missionaries who consulted me between 1972–1991 did reveal a very large amount of early trauma that had not been fully investigated during the selection period (see p. 134).

General principles of selection

Candidates should understand the purpose of the selection procedure

No one should feel that selectors are doubting God's call to Christian service. There are those who dispute the reality of a call, but in my experience this is such a personal matter that only the individual can decide if God has or has not called them, although it should be carefully discussed. For some agencies, the call is enough and selection procedures are irrelevant. For the majority, however, the view is held that the selectors' duty is to try and discern the best location in which the individual's call can be fulfilled. In other words, the call should be respected and nurtured, selection procedures being used to clarify and direct it.

For this reason I always introduce a selection session by saying, 'No one is doubting that God has called you to serve in his kingdom, that is between you and him. What we are trying to do is to help you work out just where he wants you to do it.' Not accepting an application is capable of arousing anger and serious disappointment if it is interpreted as a rejection, but I have found that by using the above careful introduction to the selection process, those who are unsuitable for service in the particular location or mission envisaged can accept it more as an indication that their search for the right location is not yet over rather than a personal rejection. As an added bonus, not being accepted may lead on to a real resolution of the reasons behind it, hence at the time the candidate is told they have not been accepted, these should be explained, and the candidate offered help and advice about what they need to do.

As an example (remembering that all examples explain a principle but are disguised so that they do not represent any one individual), there was a man who had many long-term problems which emerged during psychological selection. These were discussed with him, he was advised to withdraw his application for the time being, to get trained help and see how things went for a year or two. He decided to act on the advice, and as he came to terms with his problems realised he had been using the hope of overseas service as a way of escaping from them, which of course never works. Having got things sorted out he entered a very worthwhile ministry in the home country and remained grateful that he had been advised not to go overseas which could have had devastating effects on his mental health.

Selection procedures should have a recognised goal and suitable methods

The goal is to produce an overall profile of the candidate, using data collection methods commonly employed by selection agencies such as forms, interviews, and physical and psychological examinations. From the results a decision can be made as to whether the candidate is a 'good fit', as the business world says. The fit includes agreement with the spiritual policy and ethos of the mission agency, and suitability for the proposed overseas location, this including professional and spiritual suitability, personality, mental and physical health, ability to fit into a team, and general evidence of cope-ability during stressful situations. As a large voluntary organisation in the UK has said, 'Selectors must ensure that candidates have the qualities needed to survive the problems they will undoubtedly face' (Anon., 1986).

The basic structural method of using forms, interviews and examinations needs a different approach for short and longer-term applications. Generally speaking, applications for **3-6 months' service** are screened through forms, personal interviews and references. Increasing numbers of agencies are asking for both physical and psychological assessments, although some use only the physical check during which mental health questions are asked. Although there is no definitive research, experience shows this is often adequate, although I would personally like to see psychological assessments used for all in this category, as is common practice in one very large Christian developmental agency. This group also utilises another interesting method. They have created a register of persons willing to go overseas for a short period of time should need arise. Before they are registered they have all the preliminary screening mentioned above except for the psychological assessment, which is not done unless they are actually required for service. They are currently in the process of discussing this, for it seems to me wiser to do everything before the people are registered, which gives opportunity for any psychological problems to be dealt with well before they are actually needed overseas. Presumably there is another quick check if a person who has been registered for a long time is finally called upon.

The biggest problem arises for agencies who send large numbers of people overseas **for a few weeks**. In general, it is usually enough to ascertain through interview that they are in sympathy with the Christian work they will be sharing, and to have a reference from their church pastor. Health is more difficult. In my experience short-termers going overseas for only a few weeks may develop serious physical or mental health problems, and in some cases the trouble could have been avoided. For example, people may be taking medicines when they go out, and either did not tell the examining doctor or had no medical examination at all. Overseas, something in the location, or perhaps taking additional preventive medicine such as antimalarials, causes them to have severe physical or mental reactions. I am fully aware of the difficulties, yet I continue to believe that all persons being sent overseas by missions should have at least a physical check-up during which mental health questions are asked, and it is helpful to use a standardised form which makes it easier for a busy doctor to know what the agencies are looking for. Another way round the problem is to give short termers a health questionnaire, and have the forms looked over by a doctor or nurse experienced in overseas health situations, but this is not as good as the hands-on approach.

Long-term applications. The developmental agency mentioned before calls anything over six months long term, although most others would use this term for service of more than twelve months. The average period of long-term service seems to be one to four years, although some do serve for twelve years or more. The following procedures are adopted:

- General forms including the whole life story are useful, each agency having its own style, and regularly modernising the forms.
- Interviews remain the core of selection procedures, on a one-to-one basis as a rule.
- Physical and psychological examinations are common practice, although there are still those who do not wish their candidates to have psychological assessment by professionally trained people, preferring to rely on their experienced interviewing staff. When I was in South Africa it was interesting to note that nobody I spoke to questioned the need for psychological assessment, it was part of normal procedure.
- References, for what they are worth, are usually obtained from the church, occupation if relevant, and one or two friends. Unfortunately church references may suffer from what is called 'the halo effect'. A dedicated church is delighted when a member decides to be a missionary, and this delight may cloud judgement, leading to an over-glowing reference. Despite this I feel references are worth while, but referees should be given the opportunity to telephone the agency if they prefer to give important information verbally.

It is important to remind ourselves again that we are not trying to keep people from going overseas. What we are trying to do is to select carefully and thus to help people get the best out of their overseas experience, as well as to prevent the vulnerable from breaking down during cross-cultural ministry for which they are not really suitable.

Three important areas in selection

Occupational history

Fifty-seven per cent of 147 missionaries serving overseas complained of severe occupational stress (Foyle, 1999), which requires further comment in the selection context. Two problems are important. The first is candidates who have never worked, and this requires careful consideration during selection. It is all right for students — they are not expected to have had work experience, but an older person who has never worked cannot really be expected to learn working skills overseas. If a medium length overseas assignment is being considered, a good plan for such people is to give them work experience in the agency office or some other area such as their church where feedback could be obtained. This may help in discerning the reason for their permanent unemployment, and the likelihood of them being able to work full-time overseas.

The other problem concerns repeated jobs changes in excess of the current mobile employment style of generation X. This should be discussed at selection. Does it indicate a personality problem, or is there a simple answer such as the social circumstances within the family, or redundancy, or current national working customs for their age-group? Work references help, especially a talk on the telephone if preferred. The problem of dual-career families are important here, as has been discussed in Chapter 9.

Physical examination

This is common practice which everyone offering for long-term service expects. The important thing is that the doctor conducting it has some knowledge of overseas health problems. It is interesting to note that in the old sending countries health problems were one of the big four reasons for attrition (Davies, 1997). A good preliminary health check is doubly important for Koreans whose cultural belief may be that health should not be a problem if called by God. Since physical health problems proved to be the second commonest cause of missionary attrition in Korea (Moon, 1997), it is possible that fears of getting ill, and so shamed before their community, puts additional stress on personnel who have to survive in foreign environments with multiple possibilities of catching strange illnesses. Having seen a little of the loving attitude of the Korean church I am sure their fears are relieved by the caring concern they receive on return home.

In both old and new sending countries, to start a missionary career with a health problem that is inadequately assessed at the time of selection can do nothing but harm. This is supported by Dipple (1997) who says that 'some of the problems could have been avoided if more adequate and appropriate preparation had been given in the area of health care.' Lindquist, using asthma as an example, states, 'I often marvel at people with pulmonary problems who reach the final candidacy stage of psychological assessment without having had anyone ask them how they expect to function in an extremely polluted environment overseas when they have not been able to function well in a cleaner environment in their home country. Such problems should have been addressed early in the screening process' (1997).

Psychological assessment
By 1905 the group of doctors meeting regularly in London to discuss missionary care were commenting on mental health problems. They were concerned at the 'frequency with which neurotic individuals came to grief on returning overseas after home leave to the same co-workers and circumstances', and felt this was a reflection on the poor care offered to missionaries with nervous problems. They also realised the importance of

psychological selection, a very famous member of the group called Dr Mary Scharleib saying, 'Please do not send out people with nerves, they do not do well' (personal copy of Minutes book). By 1913 candidates were being rejected for nervous trouble (Price, 1913), (Foyle, 1999).

Throughout the 1960s attention was concentrated on the high rate of missionary wastage, now called attrition. Williams wrote in 1973 that mental health problems and failure to adjust accounted for over 30% of missionary resignations in one large mission. Much effort has gone into reducing wastage, and the Southern Baptist group was able to reduce a return rate of 23.5% in 1965 to only 3.7% in 1981 (Bridges, 1982). The latest figure on attrition is that 5.1% of the missionary work force return prematurely every year, health problems being fourth in rank order (Brierley, 1997).

With this as a background, efforts have been made to find out whether attrition could be preventable. Are there factors present at the time of selection that could indicate possible trouble during overseas service? The need to find such factors was supported by my own findings that of all the 497 missionaries with mental health problems that I interviewed overseas and in their home countries, 45% were complaining of the same problems as were present at the time of selection (Foyle, 1999). These had either been ignored, over-spiritualised, or under-valued as possible predictors of poor mental health during service.

Unfortunately there are still very few reliable psychological predictors of doing well overseas, and the modern consensus of opinion is that it is the overall picture that matters. In my own research, however, cases of overseas missionaries with depression were studied, and the findings indicate a few pointers that will help us give wiser advice during candidates' psychological selection.

As a preliminary to outlining the predictive factors, we need to remind ourselves that there are two kinds of depression (see Chapter 2). One kind is *not* significantly related to a stress-overload, these being called mood disorders, and the other kind *is* significantly related to stress-overload and is called adjustment disorders. The former often have personal and family histories of psychological problems, the latter do not. These differences are shown in a table, importance being indicated by use of the word 'significant'.

For those like me who usually find tables incomprehensible, herewith a few words of explanation. There are two major vertical columns: 'Findings', indicating what the patient told me, and 'Diagnosis overseas', indicating my own diagnosis of which type of depression the person had.

Findings from patient's history:	Diagnosis overseas	
	Mood disorder	Adjustment (stress-related) disorder
1. Past personal history of mental health problems at home	Significant	Non-significant
2. Family history of mental health problems	Significant	Non-significant
3. History of stress-overload overseas	Non -significant	Significant

These findings in missionaries with depression indicate pointers that may help us during candidates' selection:

• If a candidate has a past personal history and/or a family history of mental health problems, they are more likely than others to develop a mood disorder overseas. As was indicated in Chapter 2, this is *not* inevitable. Most with these histories have learnt a great deal and are often strong survivors, but at the candidates stage they do need to be examined by competent mental health personnel so that the impact on them of their personal and family histories can be assessed. I have met candidates who have survived a huge load of family mental illness and emerged unscathed, and after careful assessment it was decided to send them overseas, where they did very well. I have also known people who broke down within two days to eight weeks after arrival overseas, and on enquiry their personal and family histories were loaded with serious mental health abnormalities to which they had not adjusted satisfactorily. Because their selection process was confined to their spiritual state, physical and mental health examinations were either not done or were inadequate.

• Since there is no significant relationship between those who developed adjustment disorders overseas and their family and personal histories, these provide no pointers to help us discern which candidates may prove vulnerable to a stress overload. However, if candidates have a history of psychological reactions to stress in the home country, it is obviously important to help them learn better coping strategies, and probably to locate them initially to a low stress area.

• The great unknown remains assessment of the type of personality that will survive and flourish overseas. We need to continue our research efforts in both personality structure and personality disorders in the overseas context. Dr Evelyn Sharpe has written a very useful paper on the implications of personality problems for personnel during screening and care (Sharpe, 1995), and agrees with me on the importance of the longitudinal view of the candidate gained by a psychiatric interview. Schubert has also produced helpful material on this which will provide a basis for further work (1991, 1992, 1993). She finds the MMPI a useful tool, but obviously, as she says, care must be taken to use a version standardised for the national population, and proper training is required for its interpretation. Other workers use Myers-Briggs, but here the problem is that it is possibly being utilised in excess of what it was designed to do and this has led to its abandonment by some business companies (personal communication, Dr E.V. Fraser). Missionary personnel, however, find it very helpful in learning more about themselves. In fact I have been at social gatherings where new people are present and they introduce themselves by name and then during conversation announce their four Myers-Briggs letters as a sort of pathway to others knowing something about them, although I am sure the designers did not foresee this!

The need for psychological assessment is accepted by most mission agencies, but the form of assessment varies enormously. Some rely on interview techniques, others on psychological tests, and others on a mixture of both. Whatever the form, I feel there are certain broad principles that may be helpful:

- Assessments must be done by persons trained in mental health. If they also have overseas experience that is an absolute bonus (see also Lindquist, 1983).
- Signatures giving consent to write to the agency should be taken.
- Assessments must include the candidate's whole life history in its broadest sense.
- Candidates must be interviewed and tested individually, marital partners counting as two candidates, and ending up with a joint interview. Children should be involved (see Chapter 10).
- Candidates should be told the results of the session by the psychological assessor, so that relevant findings can be discussed, recommendations made, and agreement reached on what the assessor plans to tell the mission agency.
- Physical and psychological assessment should be done early in the selection procedure. There is no point in a candidate having formal interviews with the agency, proceeding to orientation which may involve giving up a job and possibly a home, and after all that having physical and psychological checks done and being found unsuitable. In addition, candidates should never be accepted 'provided the physical and

mental health check-ups are satisfactory'. Or even worse, as has happened to me, 'provided Marjory agrees'. This starts the interviews off with a minus, and if the unfortunate mental health worker finds glaring obstacles to then being accepted, the mission agency then has to un-select people, and all the wrath and disappointment falls on the head of the health worker who said no.

- Selection should include **positives**. We pay so much attention to the negatives that this may be forgotten. Do selectors ever begin their letters 'This nice young man has much to offer the missionary cause'? We are looking for reasonable adaptability, a certain degree of knowledge of personal strengths and weaknesses, and a humble learning attitude that does not see the self as God's answer to the needs of a foreign country, but as a humble servant, wanting to learn a lot and to give a bit. Most important of all may be insight capacity, people who can assess the needs of others, and understand the good and weak points of their own contribution to the work without getting unduly introspective or disheartened. Realism is an important part of such insight, the wonderful gift of being able to sit back and say, 'Well, that bit I did was OK, but I could have improved on the other.' This is not painful, it is reality, and contributes to a more phlegmatic approach to our lives of service — you win some, you lose some.

Sensitive areas need to be addressed during selection. These are often culturally related, areas sensitive in one culture being the norm in others. If possible therefore assessors should know something of the candidate's cultural background. It is important that the whole panel of interviewers agrees who will ask the sensitive questions. I once raised one of these with a candidate who blew right up and said, 'I have been asked this question six times by different people.' I apologised hastily and dropped it. This repeated invasion of privacy must be avoided. Personally I feel that questions on sexuality, for example, should be handled by the psychological assessor or the agency personnel officer, unless it comes up spontaneously with someone else.

Sensitive issues include both past history and current issues involving sexuality, drugs, alcohol, abortion and occult involvement. They are more complicated for missions these days because of 'political incorrectness' and this is dealt with in the section on the legal aspects of selection.

It is impossible to make comments on certain sensitive areas such as sexuality without displeasing someone, since mission policies world-wide are so different. Each mission must define its own policies on homosexuality, homosexual partnership (or marriage in some countries), single sexuality and unmarried people living together as partners. What is even more important is that the church in the location to which the candidate will go will find them acceptable. This came up some years ago when church leaders overseas were asked whether they would accept a homosexual couple, and the answer was 100% no. Hence there is no point accepting those whose current practice in any of the sensitive areas is unacceptable to the Christian community overseas.

Assessors need to use a little common sense, tinged with humour. I once interviewed a very nice young man who finally told me he was on cannabis and wanted to go overseas so that he could more easily get supplies, at which we both laughed, making him relaxed enough to see immediately that this was an inadequate motivation! Incidentally, any cases of old drug dependency require a medical opinion, for LSD-users may have flashbacks for years, and for old injectors multiple physical health problems must be considered. The same applies to a history of sexual promiscuity, and it is important that agencies have proper medical clearance for candidates in these categories.

In conclusion, it does appear that the form of psychological assessment is related more to the individual experience and preference of the assessor than to anything else, and constant follow-up research needs to be done. Torleif Ruud (1999) has done fine work in his prospective study of stress in missionaries followed from selection throughout their overseas service, and similar prospective studies may perhaps enable us in about fifty years time to find some universal formula for improving missionary fitness overseas. In the meantime, let every nation use methods with which the professionals of that country are familiar and which are relevant to expatriate status, and ensure that any psychological tests used have been standardised for the national population concerned.

Despite all the difficulties we have discussed, it is encouraging that of respondents to a general question on selection in a recent questionnaire, 40% made the spontaneous comment that psychological assessment had been very helpful and should be mandatory (Foyle, 1999). By experience, however, I know that the one thing that arouses anger and distress worldwide is the now rare practice of doing a lot of 'paper tests' with candidates and never discussing the results with them. Such ignorance of test results is not only highly stressful to the person concerned, but also denies the individual of the right to know the results so that they can benefit by their assessment and take steps to rectify any problem areas.

The final comment must come from Britt who wrote a most pertinent statement in 1983:

> The history of one's behaviour, past responses and experiences tends to be the best predictor of the future. God's call and motivation are important, but in the ambiguity and stress of another culture, past experience and events tend to shape how the individual will respond. Consequently a combination of God's call, motivation and past experiences must be used in selection.

Legal problems in selection
In some countries of the world employers are not allowed to ask questions about personal and family issues such as health, sexuality, drug use and reasons for previous job losses, and this

is creating problems for mission agencies. The situation is further confused by uncertainty as to whether or not one can call volunteers 'employees', and if so who is their employer — the church, the agency or their financial supporters? Talking with a senior leader in occupational health yesterday I discovered that missions in the UK are legally allowed to ask the questions required to ascertain whether or not there is a mission 'fit'. Just as a soccer football club needs to enquire whether their candidate plays soccer not rugby, thereby ensuring he will be a good 'fit' for the job, so mission agencies are free to do the same. The idea is that if the fit is not right for the agency then there is no legal contraindication to refusing the candidate. This would cover the sensitive issues mentioned, many of which are not in accord with basic doctrinal principles of many missions. It is interesting that a recent legal case in the UK has cleared the way for extensive enquiries into a candidate's past to ensure there is no contradiction to appointment to the job proposed. It is therefore important that in each nation missions discover whether or not they are classed as employers, and if so what the legal requirements are as regards selection.

In conclusion, it is interesting that some personnel officers in the business world have recognised the value of the kind of selection process outlined above:

> In one organisation in the oil sector, the Human Resources adviser expressed concern that expatriates were still selected, by personal recommendation, on the basis of their technical skills and not on the basis of other increasingly important factors such as adaptability, cultural sensitivity and family circumstances. She would like to see the introduction of a more systematic process. (UMIST, 1995)

Missionary orientation

There are two kinds of orientation, pre-departure and post-arrival. Most colleges and mission agencies are now so skilled at **pre-departure orientation** that I intend to do no more than outline the basic principles involved, and give some helpful 'client comments' on the experience.

It is axiomatic that orientation should be about the place to which the candidates are going as well as including general lectures on missiology, spiritual life, relationships with each other and the national hosts, culture, language, health, stress management, much practical advice, and any other topic that by experience has been found helpful.

The largest numbers of missionaries I surveyed gave an enthusiastic response to their **pre-field orientation**. One college was so satisfactory that many who had been there wrote variations on the following quote: 'It was all so good I feel I was well prepared, and everyone should go there or somewhere just like it.' Both marital partners usually attend the courses, and increasingly children are also being oriented.

Twenty-six per cent did experience severe stress during orientation, their criticisms relating to old-fashioned methods like too many lectures and too little discussion, too much centralisation with too little specific information about their area, and too few individual tailor-made courses. Several people would have preferred an individually designed course of reading and study on the tutorial system, with only a few joint lectures. Most missionaries underlined that those teaching orientation classes should have knowledge of expatriate life, and interestingly enough business companies consider this so important that employees are brought home on temporary leave specially to teach in courses for employees going overseas for the first time (Foyle, 1999). I can hear some missionaries saying lead me to it!

Post-arrival orientation is a different matter. This appears highly unsatisfactory to too many missionaries. Thirty-two per cent of 143 missionaries were highly stressed by this topic, some saying there was none (WHAT orientation? was the common response to the question), and others saying it was totally inadequate. This is disappointing, for much hard work has been put into post-arrival orientation by expatriate leadership.

The complaints reveal that newcomers expect it, and want it to be modern in its approach, relevant and flexible. They want time to ask questions and discuss, rather than formal lectures. They want to be informed about current affairs and politics, as well as the necessary mission and church information. It is obvious that a lot more research is required if we are to satisfy their expectations.

Selection and orientation problems of independent missionaries

What I have written is not relevant to the increasing numbers of missionaries being sent out as individuals by their own churches. Many feel that in the modern era this is the best way to fulfil the Lord's commission to go into all the world, and by sending direct from church to the overseas work the church remains responsible for them in a highly individualised way. This is a matter of personal choice, and must be respected, but I feel it is important that some specific pre-departure orientation is given and arrangements made for adequate post-arrival orientation. I am always impressed by the story of the sending out of the disciples by the Lord. He sent them off in twos, and gave them careful instructions beforehand, this being a sort of pre-departure orientation period (Luke 10). We know nothing about who cared for them on their mission, but probably the close companionship was the key point of their survival plus their strong sense of direct commissioning for the task by the Lord. However, when they came back they all had an interview with him where they could unload what they had done and tell him of their experiences. Later on, they became responsible to the church which sent them out under the guidance of the Holy Spirit, but we know little about their preparation or in-service care.

I do not think there is any problem in having different routes to fulfilling God's commission to go into all the world. Some may choose to go out as missionaries directly from their church, and others choose to go via a mission agency with the church giving them its blessing to do so. Where problems may arise is if either route involves inadequate selection, orientation and care. The first groups the Lord sent out were the hand-picked. He spent time instructing them about what to do and how to do it, and what is more important he knew what he was talking about. He knew the world, he knew people, and he knew the problems that might face them. What we need to remember is that he had foreknowledge and powers of perception that we do not have, and because of this he knew what people were like inside when he talked with them. Despite the gifts of the Spirit we do not have the same depths of understanding that Jesus had, so we need to be extra careful of our selection and orientation processes, and look after those we send overseas properly. I believe this involves all the care processes we have discussed, whatever route we are using to send people to fulfil the Lord's command.

In-service missionary care

There are now many books and publications about member care and it is not my intention to duplicate material. I intend therefore to aim at a summary of principles not previously covered in this book, illustrated by practical examples of the problems missionaries face during their service, and good methods of meeting their needs.

Pre-departure information

Missionaries are concerned about several important things and want plenty of information about them, such as who will meet them on arrival and help them find where they are to go. Tragically there are still missionaries arriving whom nobody meets, and very terrifying it is too. Before departure they also want to know if housing will be arranged, and if they have to find their own who will help them? What kind of health care is available, how do they obtain it, and how good is it? How do they pay for it? There are certain home-based companies that arrange health insurance at a price missionaries can afford and they need to know about this. A very big question concerns children's education, an anxiety-provoking topic which was discussed in Chapter 10. Although GenX does not like personnel policies handbooks there is no doubt they are a great means of reducing arrival anxiety, and these books plus additional informative handouts should be made available to personnel before they leave home.

Mentoring

This has been mentioned under orientation but a little more needs to be added. Mentoring is carried out by various levels of personnel carers. The first is **management**. It is still common practice for the national host and the local expatriate representative to work together to mentor and care for missionaries. The groups I have surveyed say that initially they need an expatriate, but as they settle in a national is more useful. Be that as it may, it is essential that if there is an expatriate representative involved he/she should visit regularly, and much time should be allocated to the missionary 'flock' instead of spending the whole time with national leadership on administrative business. However, adequate time should also be given to the national representative, for much depends on the relationship between the two leaders. Where there is no expatriate representative, it is important that one be nominated from within the country, even if missions have to share one. There are a few problems that expatriates need to discuss with expatriates, since they are home-country related matters about which the national may have no background knowledge. I am treading on delicate ground here, and I know my national readers will understand my love and respect for them, but by talking with people I have realised that a national leader alone cannot always meet their need. This is not due to any failing on their part but to a lack of experience of the country from which the expatriate comes. I was truly blessed by God when I was almost the last expatriate in the area, with no expatriate leader. The national bishop was my good friend, and having travelled widely in the West he knew the problems of both continents. Nowadays this is not always the case, for although the national leaders often have an encyclopaedic knowledge of their own countries and continents, they may not know so much about the countries from which their expatriate workers come. Under these circumstances I believe expatriates should use every opportunity to seek support from the national leader, but also to have available some experienced expatriate to whom they can occasionally turn for advice, even if it involves travelling. Despite my marvellous national support I very occasionally went a night's journey on the train to see an experienced English clergyman who was able to understand my personal background and encourage me.

The second level of mentoring is **non-management expatriate personnel** specially appointed for the task. In my own mission we had a splendid system of group leaders. They were not management, they were often wives without a visa post, and were made responsible for the welfare of the missionaries in their own catchment area. They arranged to visit their flock, called an occasional day meeting, wrote letters, and were available to see people whenever there was need. They acted as a liaison between the individual member and the management, and were usually wonderfully supportive to personnel.

The third level of care, and these are not arranged in order of importance, is provided by **local nationals**, usually church members with whom firm friendships are forged and who became wonderfully supportive. Associated with this is the friendship of one's own colleagues, both national and expatriate, the whole forming a close network of mutual support and friendship.

Health care
The importance of physical health overseas was revealed in my study of 397 missionaries with depression. Physical health

problems were significantly related to both mood and adjustment disorders (see page 255), and the patients said to me that they felt these had a definite effect in precipitating or prolonging their depression (Foyle, 1999). Kisley and Goldberg (1997) wrote that 'physical ill health made an independent contribution to the outcome of depression one year later', i.e. it increased the time needed to recover. Hence both physical and mental health should be taken seriously.

Information is vital. As well as the initial information about local health care services as described above, there is need for regular bulletins on health matters and changes in preventive medication to be sent to all personnel, written in non-technical language! I think this could be part of the function of home agency medical staff who would of course ensure that the right information went to the right country.

In addition, isolated personnel may feel relieved if they had e-mail or Internet access to medical personnel in their home countries or in a major medical centre in their host country. Some centres, like Interhealth in London, are willing to answer e-mail questions from those they have previously screened, and probably this service is available in many other countries although I have no firm information.

Location may be anxiety provoking. Recently an isolated couple, who had been able to cope with medical matters because one of them had some medical knowledge, had their first child. This added a new dimension of stress. They managed to cope until the wife got pregnant again, and then it became too much for them. They discussed it with their very wise management, and finally they all agreed it would be better for them to move to a less isolated location while they had their next child, even though there was no satisfactory substitute available to care for their old work. This indicates the advantage of having trustworthy leadership, of a good communications system, and of the flexibility that may be required from leadership in individual cases.

Preventive care works well, for generally speaking missionaries are very reliable in taking the recommended injections and pills on their location. Little more needs to be said except to remind personnel that things can change. For example, if any-one develops a depressive illness they should not continue to take Mefloquine without further medical advice. The other comment I have to make concerns being sure to take supplies of your antimalarial with you if you cross a national boundary. I was recently at a conference where several members from another continent complained of symptoms resembling malaria, from which they had suffered several times in their own countries. They had not brought any of their usual medi-cation with them, and as we were in a country where this was not readily available it was very difficult to help them. Therefore, if you are going out of your location, pack your malaria pills first, both preventive and curative, and take enough to see you through till you can renew your supply.

Related to this is the vexed question of annual medical examinations. These have gone out of fashion in some mis-sions, partly because it is a lot of work for already over-stretched doctors. I remain unrepentant in feeling that they are one of the keys to successful longer-term service. They give doctors the opportunity to talk with missionaries as well as doing the usual 'stethoscope and knee-jerk' work. They do vital preven-tive work by checking for anaemia and intestinal parasites, but predominantly they are enormously comforting, unless of course the doctor hates doing them so much they are simply rushed through, which I am sure is not the case with your doc-tor! Records are kept by the doctor as a rule but in addition a report card carried by the missionary is of great benefit in such a mobile population of people.

A study of missionary health by Peppiatt and Bypass (1991) found intestinal problems and malaria to be the two common-est health problems. In my experience neither of these are due to carelessness, but due to some nasty bug just slipping through the net. However, also within my experience, are some, usually the young alas, who just do not bother to follow local advice about water, milk and fresh fruit and vegetables. Despite the risk of annoying all my experienced readers, I wish to quote the last sentence of the safe food section of Dr Ted Lankester's excellent book *The Travellers' Good Health Guide* (1999): 'Cook it, peel it, clean it or leave it'.

Availability of satisfactory care is important. This is a very delicate matter. Some expatriates feel it is wrong that they should seek more sophisticated medical care when the people they live among do not have access to it. One of these told me he was admitted to a simple national hospital for a rather complicated physical matter, and confessed that the stress of his illness plus the overwhelming culture-shock of the basic hospital care he received proved far too much to bear, and was one of the precipitants of a post-illness depression.

I do not wish to bend the scriptures but I think the story of Barnabas and John Mark is relevant here. Obviously there were interpersonal problems between Paul and John Mark, and I am making a guess that John Mark was pretty stressed out. So Barnabas took him out of the culture and took him home to Cyprus for care. The benefit of taking him out of the local scene is shown by his full recovery and later usefulness to Paul. When we are expatriated, we have a lot to cope with, and I doubt if one should push this still further by attempting to integrate fully with the local form of health care in isolated areas. Taken to its full extent, this would mean allowing your wife to have her baby alone in a mud hut with a very dirty local woman repeatedly examining her intimately with no sterile precautions of any kind. It is encouraging that questionnaire response from 150 serving missionaries showed that there was a high rate of satisfaction with outpatient treatment from local doctors and specialists, and only a few needed further treatment in the home country (Foyle, 1999). However, inpatient care in a small isolated village hospital rings nothing in my mind but alarm bells.

In recent years making physical and mental health care available to all personnel has become a matter of primary importance. Kelly O'Donnell and Dave Pollock from the US, and many other mental health workers have gone all over the world to give lectures to missionaries on psychological well-being, and to have private consultations, and the member care movement is expanding. In future it should not be so difficult for serving missionaries to find adequate mental health care when they need it.

Spiritual care

This was one area in which 25% of questionnaire respondents were dissatisfied, although this was not to a significant level in relation to psychological symptoms (Foyle, 1999). Because they could understand very little of the local church language they felt spiritually dry. This underlines the need for training personnel to be able to draw directly from God, plus periodic visits to personnel by people with ability to provide spiritual food, annual conferences with good Bible readings, and a good supply of tapes and spiritual reading from the home country.

A personal relationship with God is the basis of drawing spiritual strength directly from him, and means different things to different generations. The first thing I was taught when I was converted was to begin a daily Quiet Time, called 'QT' by most of us. We read a bit of the Bible, usually following helpful notes, and prayed along the pattern someone had told us, and then added on intercession for various things. Of course as time went by we modified this to suit personal choice, but the principle remained firm. The QT had its good and bad points. The good was the regularity of meeting with God. The bad was that it could become stereotyped and communion with God lost its spontaneity. Most people however just let their prayer life develop, and I certainly learnt that there was value and strength in combining the QT system with learning to talk to God at any time and in any place. Another thing that helped me was to sit down to read the Bible with a pen in my hand, which I have done for over 50 years now. It indicates to God that I have come to learn something, and it is a habit I value deeply, plus singing a daily hymn!

The culture of the new generations makes the development of a personal devotional life more difficult, for daily contact with God is usually done in small groups or pairs, and little is learned of being alone with God. This of course is related to the need for community referred to in Chapter 1, and may have a profound impact on modern short-term missionaries in lonely situations. Without a previous experience of a private prayer time alone with God they may find it very difficult to maintain their spiritual lives. Part of orientation classes therefore should include some teaching on drawing spiritual strength from God. Roy and Jan Stafford reminded me that these days the word of God tends to be dissociated from prayer and worship whereas in earlier generations they were all one, so teaching people to keep a small Scripture booklet in their pockets and to use words from it as a form of prayer might reunify them. Reading a few verses of Scripture and praying short prayers at any time in any place is remarkably strengthening. The other thing we need to get over to candidates during spiritual orientation is that God is longing to meet them, which stops the daily prayer time becoming dreary. In human terms, and writing with deepest reverence and awe, understanding this longing means prayer becomes a time when two who want to meet each other get together.

Different people find various aspects of spiritual life more important to them than others, and because of the way they live overseas may be deprived. One example is the communion service, which may have to be missed due to living in an isolated community where there is no national church, or else being frequently on call for emergencies. Amy Carmichael, a famous missionary in southern India, was bed-bound for years, and developed the practice of turning her breakfast into a communion service, using tea and toast. In Nepal where we lived as a small community of expatriates with no national church, we took it in turns to lead a communion service using tea and home-made bread or cake, which was all we had. Some people from more liturgical backgrounds may not feel free to do this, but I have certainly taken communion alone if I was detained in the hospital, using bread and water, and repeating some of the lovely prayers from the service we use at church. Some might like to use one of these if it suits their pattern of worship, and I include a modern paraphrase of one of the prayers from the *Book of Common Prayer* that I use:

> I do not presume to come to your table, merciful Lord, trusting in my own righteousness but in your great mercy. I am not worthy to gather up the crumbs from under your table, but you are a God whose nature is to be merciful. Gracious Lord, I eat this bread and drink this wine in remembrance and gratitude that you died for me — so that I might be cleansed from my sin, and dwell in you, as you dwell in me.

Even though local church services may be incomprehensible, there is a certain strength in attending, singing words of familiar hymns in your own language, getting help to find the sermon text and meditating on it while the sermon goes on. It is amazing how quickly you can pick up a local tune and join in with your stumbling language. You are always so welcomed that it is positively heart warming, but be prepared for surprises. In some countries, sitting on a floor is decidedly uncomfortable, and forgetting to take your shoes off indicates gross disrespect to God and the rest of the congregation. The most annoying thing may be the music. Most new churches have retained some of the old style Western hymns, using their own language but the same tune. Unfortunately the tune is often slightly altered so that you may suddenly find you are happily singing your own version but everyone else is singing in a different key or musical time, and you are out on your own! Very disconcerting till you get used to it.

Most missionaries have united prayer meetings at intervals, and in some places daily prayers may be possible. It sometimes takes discipline to attend at the end of a long day but it is really worth while. One reason is that it is hard to remain furious with someone if you sit together praying! Another is that prayer works, and problems concerning the work and individuals may well be resolved after persistent believing prayer.

Communications

Good communication systems are one of the most important parts of missionary care. Usually they are outlined in the mission handbook, but their implementation depends on the skill of those responsible. The biggest thing to remember is that accidents happen, people are not informed of something important that concerns them and so get very upset. Usually it is due entirely to a managerial oversight and is not meant to convey that personnel are just being pushed around. I have heard someone in this position complain bitterly of being 'cannon fodder', an unpleasant old term used in wartime to indicate sending people off into a bad situation with no consultation or thought for their welfare. In my experience moving people around without consulting them did happen in the older generations, it was just the way things worked, but it rarely happens nowadays. Personnel should, however, be ready to at least consider an urgent appeal to move to a new location if some emergency has arisen, but they should expect to make the final decision themselves unless a clause in their original contract has said they could be moved at any time, and they had agreed to this.

Management-personnel relationships are usually based on a vast amount of loving good will, but this does not mean contracts are unimportant. I am no lawyer, hence I know nothing of the technicalities of contracts, but their big advantage is that both sides sign a paper of agreement to the terms and conditions of service, and everybody knows where they are. This usually applies equally to very short-term workers, but their contract letter is much less detailed. A contract agreement really helps to keep you going when all you want to do is go home, for it is something that you personally signed, and is legally binding unless all agree that it can be broken.

Conclusion

Most mission leaders are in agreement that we need to care for our personnel in every aspect of their cross-cultural ministry, and it is right to do so, but it is also necessary to put in a word of warning. We need to be careful that we do not create a generation of dependent missionaries, who look first to their counsellor or caring services, and only second to the help God wants to give them. We need to raise resilient, independent missionaries, capable of both decision making and discipline, humble yet proud of their task, and prepared to make sacrifices for the work God has given them to do. This requires a careful balance between preserving the attitude that is willing to give to God, to sacrifice and to suffer, and yet to provide these same people with the caring services they may require at some time in their lives of cross-cultural service.

14

God's Model of Missionary Care

The story of Elijah is one of the best models of the care that
God takes of his servants. The story begins in 1 Kings 17 and
continues through to 2 Kings 2.

Elijah was personally selected and trained by God and after
a long period of experience was given a major task. The task
was twofold, the restoration of Israel to God through confrontation with the prophets of Baal, and the battle to win the soul
of Ahab, the evil king who had wandered far from God. Elijah
did exactly what God told him to do. He first confronted Ahab
in 1 Kings 18:1 after a long period of drought and famine, presumably related to Ahab's evil rule. He got to see him with
some difficulty and found Ahab already knew about him and
called him a trouble-maker.

Elijah decided the time had come to make the people choose
between the Lord and the god Baal, so he asked Ahab to sum-
mon all the priests of Baal to Mount Carmel. There the famous
confrontation occurred, the prophets of Baal working themselves into a frenzy in their efforts to make fire fall on the altar
they had built. When nothing happened for hours Elijah said
quietly to the people, 'Come here to me.' He set about making
things very difficult for himself by pouring water all over the
altar, and then in the quietness that had fallen made a simple
prayer to God to prove himself and to prove that Elijah was his
servant. Then the fire fell, the people dropped to the ground
and worshipped God, and the prophets of Baal were seized and
executed.

Elijah then told Ahab the rain was coming, although there
was as yet no sign of it, and in typical fashion the king sat
down to have his dinner. Elijah meanwhile went to the top of

the mountain and engaged in a real prayer battle until a small cloud appeared and he knew the answer was on the way. Interestingly he sent word at once to Ahab to go home quickly, for he did not want him to be drowned while the battle for his soul was still going on. As the rain began to fall, Elijah was anointed with strength by God to run to Jezreel and arrive there before Ahab turned up in his chariot. When Ahab arrived he told his wife Jezebel what had happened to all the prophets she had supported, and she was furious and threatened to kill Elijah by the next day.

This is the turning point of the story, for we read that Elijah was afraid and fled for his life, going first to Beersheba and then alone into the desert. There he sat down under a tree and said to God, 'I have had enough, Lord. Take my life, I am no better than my ancestors.' Quite obviously human exhaustion had taken over, and he felt worn out and depressed. Surprisingly he was able to sleep, for often in this state sleep is very difficult. Then an angel woke him and gave him food and sympathy, what we would call today TLC, tender loving care. He said to him, 'Get up and eat,' the meal of bread and water being an easily digestible menu suitable for such a tired man. Then Elijah slept again until the angel woke him. This time he gave him supernatural food and more TLC as he said, 'Get up and eat for the journey is too much for you.' Elijah then began to walk, and went on walking for 40 days to the holy mountain of Horeb. It is likely that he did not go there directly for it is not as long a journey as that. Probably he spent the time wandering round getting healthy exercise, and praying and thinking as he went.

On arrival he went into a cave intending to sleep, but suddenly God spoke to him and said, 'Elijah what are you doing here?' Then Elijah poured out all he had been thinking during his wanderings. He reminded God he had always been careful to serve him to the best of his ability, and had now begun to feel as if he was the only one left in the whole land who was committed to serving God, and yet his own life was in danger.

The tone of the passage is somewhat resentful as if God was being unfair to him (after all I've done for you God).

Then God asked him to come out onto the mountain top, and stand there alone as a furious wind, an earthquake and a fire passed by him. God was in none of them, as if to indicate that the time for huge demonstrations of his power through Elijah had gone, and something new was to happen. So after all the power and might of the elements there came a 'gentle whisper', God speaking directly in the stillness to troubled Elijah. The same question was asked as before, 'What are you doing here?' and again Elijah made the same complaint to God: 'I have always served you, and I am the only one left who worships you, and now they are all trying to kill me.'

We do not know what God said to Elijah but I feel sure he showed him that there was too much me... me... me on the scene. God had used Elijah in a terrific way, but his complaint shows that he had begun to feel he was indispensable to God. This is always dangerous, so God had to lead him onto a new stage of his religious experience by reminding him that God was sovereign and would use people for a time to do a job in the public eye, and then transfer them to another which might be a completely hidden ministry. No one person was indispensable to any role in God's service.

Then God gave Elijah his new job. He told Elijah to go back and anoint two new kings, and then to anoint Elisha to take over his own old role. The time for fireworks through Elijah had gone, and a new approach was required such as Elisha could give. But as God took away the old role he comforted Elijah by promising there would remain 7,000 people faithful to the true God.

The turning point for Elijah came when he accepted and obeyed what God had said, going off to find Elisha on whom he cast his cloak as a sign of anointing as his successor. Incidentally Elisha did not take up the full role immediately but stayed and worked with Elijah until he died, after which he took on the anointed role.

I think Elijah expected to have a completely hidden ministry for the rest of his life, but as it happened he was prominent twice more. After his meeting with God he could obviously be trusted with prominence without again thinking he was indispensable. God sent him back for one more meeting with Ahab, one last attempt to win his soul back to God. When Elijah went to see him, the effect was so profound that Ahab repented and humbled himself before God. It did not last, but at least was a sign that he was starting to think seriously about God's claims on his life, and we do not know his spiritual condition when he died. Finally Elijah had a problem with the new king, and once again the old public ministry was used for a short time as fire fell on the king's officers. The end of the story is that Elijah was considered by God as too important just to die a human death, so he sent chariots of fire to take him to heaven. Elisha saw it happen, this being the final confirmation that he was anointed to replace Elijah, which was immediately obvious to all Elijah's old disciples as he used Elijah's cloak to divide the waters.

What does this mean for missionaries? Like Elijah they are called by God to do a job for him. This they do in his power and strength, and there are often visible signs of a successful ministry. Sometimes, however, they can begin to think they are indispensable to the work, and wonder what will happen to it when they are no longer there. Because there is always such a lot to do and they feel personally responsible, they overwork and use up a vast amount of physical and mental energy with inadequate recharging of the batteries. In these circumstances, like Elijah, it all catches up with them. Some develop multiple physical illnesses, others feel exhausted or depressed, and then they begin to wonder if they will ever be any use again.

It is at this point that God's pattern of caring for Elijah teaches us so much. First of all we need to stop work, to see a good doctor (the angel in Elijah's case), and to rest, sleep as much as we can, receive loving care, food and fluids, and do a little gentle exercise. As health improves and people start to feel they can concentrate a little better, God begins spiritual restoration. He gives them the opportunity to think about their pattern of life, which often includes the feeling of being indispensable, and to discuss it with trained helpers. As health and understanding improve, people often have a new meeting with God, their own personal Horeb, during which they recognise the reality value of the work they have done, but also understand the mistakes they have made and accept the forgiveness God so readily gives. Then like Elijah they move on to the next stage of their Christian service, either going back to the old role a wiser person, or else being moved on to the next job God has prepared for them.

This sort of pathway is not what everyone experiences, many learn what God wants to teach them in other ways, but for those who have experienced feeling really broken up by their missionary service I would say, 'Take heart, do not despair. You are the honourably wounded, mistakes and all. Through this experience God will take you to Horeb where you will learn something new from him, grow a little more, and return to his service a stronger person.'

References

Adler P S, 1975, The transitional experience, an alternative view of culture shock, *Journal of Humanistic Psychology* 15, pp.13-23.

Adolph H, 2000, 'Trends in Medical Missions Today', *Echoes Missionary Magazine*, August 2000, pp.341-343.

Ahmed S H, Arif M, 1982, 'Culture and Symptomatology in Depression', *Pakistan Journal of Medical Research*, Vol. 21.2, April-June 1982.

Ahmad S H, Zuberi H, 1981, 'Depression, Anxiety and Headache', *Journal of Pakistan Medical Association*, Vol. 31, December 1981.

Anderson J, 1999, *In the Stillness*, Alpha.

Anon., 1986, 'Selecting Volunteers for Work Overseas', *Personnel Management*, March 1986, p.71.

Anon., 1996, Relocation Guidelines C.B.I. People Issues, p.3.

Baker J C, 1984, Foreign language and departure training in US multinational firms, *Personnel Administrator*, July.

Bowers J M, 1984, 'Roles of married women missionaries, a case study', *International Bulletin of Missionary Research*, January 1984, pp.4-7.

Bowers J M, 1998, *Raising Resilient MKs* (Association of Christian Schools: Colorado Springs, USA), p.3.

Brewster E T, Brewster E S, 1976, *Language acquisition made practical* (Lingua House, Colorado Springs, USA).

Bridges E, 1982, 'Missionary resignations down, but reasons still complex', *Foreign Mission News* (Richmond Southern Baptist Convention), p.1.

Brierley P, in Taylor, ed., 1997, *Too Valuable to Lose*, p.86.

Britt G W, 1983, 'Pretraining variables in prediction of missionary success overseas', *Journal of Psychology and Theology*, Vol. 11, No. 3, pp.203-211.

Bull G, 1955, *When Iron Gates Yield* (Hodder and Stoughton), pp.188, 241-242.

Carlson D, 1981, *Overcoming Hurts and Anger* (Harvest House: Eugene, Oregon), p.35.

Carr K, 1994, 'Trauma and post-traumatic stress disorder among missionaries', *Evangelical Missions Quarterly*, July 1994, pp.246-255.

Carr K, 1997, 'Crisis intervention for missionaries', *Evangelical Missions Quarterly*, October 1997, pp.450-458.

Carter J, 1999, 'Missionary Stressors and Implications for Care', *Journal of Psychology and Theology*, Vol. 27, No. 2, pp.171-180.

Chalmers S, 1994, *Research in Christian Mission* (Glasgow Bible College, BA(Hons)), 1994.

Cho Y J, Greenlee D, 1995, 'Avoiding Pitfalls on Multinational Frontier Teams', *International Journal of Frontier Missions*, Vol. 12.4, October-December 1995, pp.179-183.

Cole R, 1980, 'Executive security: A corporate response to abduction and terrorism', *Wily Interscience* (New York), p.75.

Collins Concise English Dictionary, 1992, Third Edition (Harper Collins).

Coote R T, 1991, 'A boon or a drag', *International Bulletin of Missionary Research*, January 1991, pp.17-23.

Davies S, 1997, *Too Valuable to Lose*, p.156.

Dipple B, 1997, *Too Valuable to Lose*, p.223.

Dobson C B, 1983, *Stress, The hidden Adversary* (MTP Press Ltd.: Lancaster, England), p.293.

Dodds et al, 1995, *Stressed from Core to Cosmos* (Unpublished conference paper).

Donovan K, 1991, *Growing through Stress* (Aquila Press, Australia), p.44.

Donovan K, Myors R, 1997, *Too Valuable to Lose*, pp.41-73.

Dye T W, 1974, 'Stress-producing factors in cultural adjustment, *Missiology* 2, pp.61-77.

Erikson E, 1950, 1965, *Childhood and Society* (Penguin Books).

Fletcher M, 1993, *Dual career couples* (Employment Conditions Abroad Ltd.: London).

Foyle M, 1999, *Expatriate Mental Health* (University of London thesis for postgraduate degree of Doctor of Medicine).

Foyle, 1992, 'When does suffering become unethical for our children?' *Interact*, May 1992, pp.13-15.

Foyle, 1994, 'Problems of Expatriate Children', Behrens R H, Wiley W, eds. *Caring for expatriates and workers abroad* (British Postgraduate Medical Federation international meeting).

Freudenberger H J, Richelson Q, 1974, *Journal of Social Issues*, pp.30,159.

Gelder M, Gath D, Mayou R, Cowen P, 1996, *Oxford Textbook of Psychiatry*.

Gish D, 1983, 'Sources of Missionary Stress', *Journal of Psychology and Theology*, Vol. 3, pp.236-242.

Goode G S, 1995, 'Guidelines for Crisis and Contingency Management', *International Journal of Frontiers Missions*, Vol 12, October – December, pp.211-216.

Harrison M S, 1984, *Developing Multinational Teams* (OMF: Singapore).

Hayes N, Orrell S, 1987, *Psychology, an Introduction* (Longman: London and New York), pp.312-314.

Hilton J, 1987, *Goodbye Mr Chips* (MacMillan).

Holy Bible New Revised Standard Version, Oxford University Press, 1995.

Jones M, 1994, quoted in Chalmers, *op. cit.*

Kang Sung-Sam, 1997, *Too Valuable to Lose*, p.263.

Kisley S R, Goldberg D P, 1997, 'The effect of physical ill-health on the course of psychiatric disorder in general practice', *British Journal of Psychiatry*, 160, pp.536-540.

Lankester T, 1999, *The Travellers' Guide to Good Health* (Sheldon Press).

Larcombe G D, 1993, *Care for Mission Conference*, quoted in Chalmers, *op. cit.*

Lazarus, 1993, 'Coping theory and research, past, present and future', *Psychosomatic Medicine Journal*, 55, pp.234-247.

Limpic Ted, 1997, *Too Valuable to Lose*, p.149.

Lindquist, 1983, 'Is the psychological test worth it?' *Evangelical Missions Quarterly*, April 1983, pp.114-119.

Lindquist, 1997, 'Mission agency screening and orientation' in *Too Valuable to Lose*, p. 245.

Lovell D, 2000, manuscript in preparation, *Caring for Missionaries*, O'Donnell, ed., 2000.

Lysgaard W, 1955, 'Adjustment in a foreign society', *International Social Sciences Bulletin* 7, pp.45-51.

Mayou R, 1987, 'Burnout', *British Medical Journal*, 295, 1 August 1987, pp.284-285.

McNair R, 1995, 'Room for Improvement, management and support of relief and development workers', *Network Paper 10* (Overseas Development Institute, and Red Cross et al).

Moon S S-C, 1997, *Too Valuable to Lose*, p.195.

Mumford D B, 1998, 'The measurement of culture shock', *Social Psychiatry and Psychiatric Epidemiology* 33, pp.149-154.

Mutchler K, 1997, 'Keys to the effective home schooling of MKs', *Evangelical Missions Quarterly*, April 1997, pp.168-174.

Ng B, 1997, *Too Valuable to Lose*, p.279.

Neale R, Mindel R, 1992, 'Rigging up Multicultural Teamworking', *Personnel Management*, January 1992.

O'Donnell K, 1992, *Missionary Care* (William Carey Library: Pasadena, CA).

O'Donnell K, 1997, 'An international guide for member care resources' in *Too Valuable to Lose*, pp.325-338.

Peppiatt R, Bypass P, 1991, Survey of the health of British missionaries, *British Journal of General Practice*, 41: 159-162.

Pollock D, 1998, 'Developing a flow of care' in *Raising Resilient MKs*, Bowers, ed., pp.36-40.

Pollock D, Van Reken R, 1999, *The Third Culture Kid Experience* (Intercultural Press: Yarmouth, Maine, USA).

People in Aid, 1998, *Code of Best Practice* (International Personnel, BRCS, 9 Grosvenor Crescent, London SW1X 7EJ).

Perrill C V, 2000, *Gentle Surgery* (Storter Childs Printing Company: Gainesville, USA).

Price G B, 1913, 'The causes of invaliding from the Tropics', *British Medical Journal* 2, pp.1290-1293.

Quarles, 1988, 'The threat of terrorism to missionaries', *International Bulletin of Missiological Research*, October 1988, pp.161-164.

Rajendran K, 1998, Which way forward, *Indian Missions* (SAIACS Press, Bangalore), p.120.

Rajendran, 1999, Conference paper, Iguassu Missionary Consultation, H-14.

Rees D, Cooper C L, 1992, 'Occupational stress in health service workers in UK', *Stress Medicine*, 8, pp.79-90.

Roembke L, 1998, 'Building Credible Multicultural Teams', *Verlag für Kultur und Wissenschaft Culture and Science publication* (Dr Thomas Schirrmacher: Bonn), p.174.

Rose S, Bisson J, 1998, 'Brief early psychological interventions following trauma: a systematic review of the literature', *Journal of Traumatic Stress*, 11 (4), pp.697-710.

Ruud T, 1999, 'Distress and mental health during cross-cultural adjustment' (doctoral thesis, University of Oslo).

Scharleib M, 1905, Unpublished Minute Book of Medical Officers in Charge of Missions.

Schubert E, 1991, 'Personality disorders and the selection process for overseas missionaries', *International Bulletin of Missiological Research*, Vol. 15.1, January 1991, pp.33-36.

Schubert, 1992, 'Current issues in screening and selection' in O'Donnell K, 1992, *op. cit.*, pp.74-88.

Schubert E, 1993, 'Personality disorders and overseas missions: guidelines for the mental health professional', *Journal of Psychology and Theology*, Vol. 21, 1, pp.18-25.

Scullion H, 1992, 'Recruiting and developing international managers', *Multinational Employer*, April 1992, pp.14-18.

Seyle H, 1974, *Stress Without Distress* (New America Library).

Sharp L, 1988, 'Toward a greater understanding of the real MK' in *Helping Missionaries Grow*, O'Donnell, ed.

Sharp L, 1990, 'Boarding schools; What difference do they make?' *Evangelical Missions Quarterly*, January 1990, pp.26-35.

Sharpe E, 1995, 'Personality problems — Implications for personnel screening and care', VAMA meeting, December 1995. Copies from CMF office, 157 Waterloo Road, London SE1 8US.

Simpson M, 1993, 'Love me love my spouse', *Human Resources*, 44, Summer 1993, pp.44-48.

Sine T, 1991, *Wild Hope* (Word: Dallas, TX).

Stephenson, 1981, *Enjoying Being Single* (Lion: Oxford), p.55.

Storr A, 1963, *The Integrity of Personality* (Penguin), p.37.

Stott J, 1999, *New Issues Facing Christians Today* (Marshall Pickering), pp.382-410.

Taylor W D, 1997, ed., *Too Valuable to Lose* (William Carey Library).

Taylor W D, 2000, *Global Missiology for the 21st Century* (Baker Books, Paternoster).

Tiplady R, 2000, 'Let X=X: Generation X and World Mission', *Global Missiology for the 21st Century*, William D Taylor, ed. (Baker Books/ Paternoster).

Torbion I, 1982, *Living Abroad* (Wiley: Chichester), pp.98,102.

Townsend and Laughlin, 1998, 'Preventing Post Traumatic Stress Disorder among International Aid Workers', VAMA newsletter (see Sharpe).

UMIST, 1995, University of Manchester Institute of Science and Technology, et al. Assessment, selection and preparation for expatriate assignments.

University College and CBI Employee Relocation Council 1991, Survey on stress and mobility.

Van Brabant, 1998, Verbal information. See also *Cool Ground for Aid Providers*, Disasters 1998, 22(2): 109-125.

Werner D, 1992, *Where There is No Doctor* (Macmillan Press, London).

Wessely S, et al., 2000, 'Brief psychological interventions for trauma-related symptoms and the prevention of post-traumatic stress disorder', *Cochrane Review* (Cochrane Library), Issue 3, 2000, Oxford Update software.

Wickstrom D, Fleck J, 1988, 'Missionary children, correlates of self-esteem and dependency' in *Helping Missionaries Grow*, O'Donnell, ed.

Williams K, 1973, 'Characteristics of more successful and less successful missionaries', doctoral dissertation (US International University).

Wrobbel K, Pluedemann J, 1990, 'Psychosocial development in adult missionary kids', *Journal of Psychology and Theology*, Vol. 18, No. 4, pp.363-374.

Useful additional books

Echerd P, Arathoon A, eds., 1987, *Planning for MK Nurture* and *Understanding and Nurturing the Missionary Family* (Compendium of ICMK conference, Quito. William Carey Library).

Fail, Helen, Some of the outcomes of international schooling. Dissertation for MA in Education Degree, June 1995, Oxford Brookes University, England.

Fawcett G, 1999, *Ad-Mission: The briefing and debriefing of teams of missionaries and aid workers* (Youth with a Mission).

Knell M, 2001, *Families on the Move: Growing up overseas – and loving it!* (Monarch: London).